THE NATIONAL
GEOGRAPHIC TRAVELER
PARIS

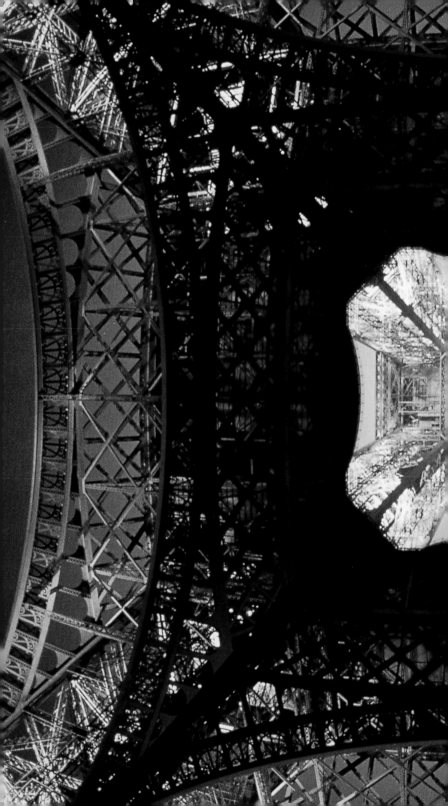

THE NATIONAL
GEOGRAPHIC TRAVELER

PARIS

Lisa Davidson & Elizabeth Ayre

Contents

How to use this guide 6–7 About the authors 8
Paris areas 45–210 Excursions 211–32 Travelwise 233–64
Index 265–69 Credits 270–71

Page 1: Café life,
Place des Vosges
Pages 2–3: Beneath
the Eiffel Tower
Left: I.M. Pei's
pyramid at
the Louvre

How to use this guide

See back flap for keys to text and map symbols

The National Geographic Traveler brings you the best of Paris in text, pictures, and maps. Divided into three sections, the guide begins with an overview of history and culture. Following are 13 area chapters with featured sites chosen by the authors for their particular interest and treated in depth. Each chapter opens with its own contents list for easy reference. A final chapter suggests possible excursions from Paris.

A map introduces each area of the city, highlighting the featured sites and locating other places of interest. Walks, plotted on their own maps, suggest routes for discovering the most about an area. Features and sidebars offer intriguing detail on history, culture, or contemporary life.

The final section, Travelwise, lists essential information for the traveler—pre-trip planning, getting around, communications, money matters, and emergencies—plus a selection of hotels and restaurants arranged by area, shops, and entertainment possibilities.

To the best of our knowledge, site information is accurate as of the press date. However, it's always advisable to call ahead whenever possible.

Color coding

66

Each area of the city is color coded for easy reference. Find the area you want on the map on the front flap, and look for the color flash at the top of the pages of the relevant chapter. Hotel and restaurant listings in **Travelwise** are also color coded to each area.

Musée de Cluny

▲ Map p. 62

✉ 6 place Paul-Painlevé

☎ 01 53 73 78 00

🕐 Closed Tues.

💲 $$

🚇 Métro: St.-Michel, Odéon

Visitor information

Practical information is given in the side column next to each major site (see key to symbols on back flap). The map reference gives the page number where the site is shown on a map. Further details include the site's address, telephone number, days closed, entrance fee ranging from $ (under $4) to $$$$$ (over $25), and the nearest Métro stop. Visitor information for smaller sites is listed in parentheses within the text.

TRAVELWISE

Color-coded area name

Category name

Hotel name & price range

Address, telephone & fax numbers

Brief description of hotel

Hotel facilities & credit card details

Category name

Restaurant name & price range

Address & telephone number

Brief description of restaurant

Restaurant facilities & credit card details

Hotel & restaurant prices

An explanation of the price ranges used in entries is given in the Hotels & Restaurants section beginning on p. 240.

AREA MAPS

Important featured sites

Points of interest

- A locator map accompanies each area map and shows the location of that area in the city.

WALKING TOURS

Start point

Featured site (in bold) on walk route

Walk route

Red numbered bullets link sites on map to descriptions in the text

Point of interest not on walk route

Building outline

Direction of route

- An information box gives the starting and ending points, time and length of walk, and places not to miss along the route.

EXCURSION MAPS

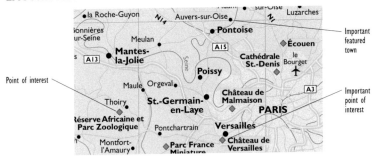

Point of interest

Important featured town

Important point of interest

- Towns and cities described in the Excursions chapter (pp. 211–32) are high-lighted in yellow on the map. Other suggested places to visit are also high-lighted and are shown with a red diamond symbol.

THE NATIONAL GEOGRAPHIC TRAVELER

PARIS

About the authors

Lisa Davidson is a writer and editor living in Paris. She has written for *Village France*, *France par Excellence,* and *World Media Network,* an international press agency based in Paris; and has published *Baboushka and Dedoushka,* a memoir of the Russian Revolution. She is currently working with *Beaux-Arts Magazine* and Paris-based publisher Gallimard.

Elizabeth Ayre is also a writer and editor living in Paris. She has written for the *International Herald Tribune, The Independent,* and *Village France* and *France par Excellence* guidebooks. She is the author of *They Don't Take No for an Answer* and editor of the journal *Variations.* She is currently working with Paris-based publisher Gallimard.

With contributions by:
Heidi Ellison, who wrote the Travelwise chapter, pp. 233–64.

The authors would also like to thank the following people for their collaboration in this book:
David Applefield (Bridges), John Calder (Literature), Tina Isaac (Fashion), Lisa Nesselson (Cinema), Julian Nundy (Paris today), A.J. Paterson (Paris today and research on the History section), Robert Such (Dance, Theater, and Opera), and Karen Werlander (Fashion).

History & culture

**Detail of figure from the
Basilica of St.-Denis**

Paris today

"PARIS VAUT BIEN UNE MESSE" (PARIS IS WELL WORTH A MASS), SAID HENRI IV, perhaps France's greatest king, on converting to Catholicism in 1593. Then as now it would have been hard to disagree. Paris was the political heart of France, and since then has more often than not been the political as well as the geographical heart of Europe.

Known as the City of Light, Paris is considered by many people the world's most beautiful city. Its monuments and treasures are better preserved than those of any rival city. But Paris is much more than that. It is an international city that controls the larger part of France's economy, an economy second only to Germany's in Europe, and one that reaches far beyond Europe.

The French capital for over a thousand years, Paris was central to the establishment of the modern French state, which developed out of the initial domain of the Capetian kings (roughly Paris to Orléans) over some six centuries. The city is the governmental, economic, and cultural axis around which French society has revolved, a trend that has grown since the French Revolution. This historic trend has been diluted by recent economic decentralization measures. Whatever their success, France remains the creation of a capital of which it has often been a mere extension—in other words, as the saying goes, when Paris sneezes, France catches cold.

THE PARIS REGION & ITS ECONOMY

Paris is blessed with great natural assets: Straddling the middle reaches of the Seine, the city lies at the center of Europe's greatest sedimentary basin (the Bassin Parisien). The basin's agricultural resources, which exploit the rich alluvial soils of its plains and low plateaus, have traditionally been the backbone of the French economy. The Paris region dominates a wide area extending from Normandy in the west, around Picardy and Champagne to the north and east, and through the Beauce country of Chartres between the Seine and the Loire to the south. Within this broad geo-

The popular Bateaux-Mouches and Bateaux Parisiens tour boats ply the Seine day and evening.

graphic area, today's Région d'Île-de-France (one of 22 French metropolitan regions) covers a little over 4,500 square miles (12,000 sq km), forming a threefold concentric ring of eight départements around the capital, which, since 1976, has resumed its status of

commune (one of some 36,000 in France) with its own mayor.

One of the great victories of Paris has been to contain the city proper within the Périphérique ring road, keeping the city a manageable size. With a clean, extensive, efficient, and constantly modernized transport system, this means that few journeys across town take more than 40 minutes.

With some 11 million inhabitants (just under a fifth of the French total) concentrated onto little more than 2 percent of the territory of France, the Île de France region is not only a national economic powerhouse, it is also a fully international metropolis, one of the dozen most important in the world. Its demographic impact on the greater Paris basin has therefore been tremendous: Within a radius of some 150 miles (250 km) around Paris, the population of such ancient cities as Reims, Dijon, and Orléans has stagnated at between 200,000 and 250,000 inhabitants.

The Île de France's gross domestic product is now around 250 billion dollars (nearly 30 percent of the French total), generating 50 billion dollars worth of imports against 32 billion dollars in exports. Agriculture, accounting for 60 percent of the region's land use but

employing only one percent of its workforce, remains intensive and competitive (7.5 percent of French wheat production in 1990), while the automobile industry (17.5 percent of the region's exports abroad) and the electrical, electronic, and computing sectors (a fifth of those exports) are driving forces in the national economy. Indeed, no fewer than 65 percent of French companies have their head office in the Île de France, clearly marking it as France's dominant region, economically as well as politically.

PARISIAN POPULATION

The city's population began to stabilize during the 1920s, at about 2.5 million inhabitants, while the suburbs began their rapid expansion from just over 2 million people to the 7 million today. The "Franciliens," as the inhabitants of the Parisian region are now called, are a reflection of Paris's leading role in the profound transformation of French society over the last two centuries, and the strains and stresses this has produced. Paris is a microcosm, reflecting the nation's political tensions. Immigration has also influenced the city's demographics. From the mid-1950s to the 1970s, labor shortages led to massive recruitment campaigns in North Africa and poorer European countries like southern Italy, Spain, and Greece. Today, the Parisian upper and middle classes are more likely to reside in the western urban area, while the immigrant working classes live in the east.

Paris is also divided into 20 districts called arrondissements, which spiral out in circles from the center (Châtelet) like a snail shell. Parisians tend to identify strongly with their own "quartier" (neighborhood), whether it be the stodgier 16th arrondissement or one of the lively multiethnic areas of Belleville, Chinatown, or Ménilmontant to the east.

Industrial decentralization—clearing industries out of the city to concentrate on the capital's role as a leading European business center—has taken hold. Construction has shifted from residential to office building, bringing a dramatic rise in housing costs. This has driven a large number of less well-off Parisians into the suburbs (as well as young families looking for more space for less money), whose population has doubled since

the 1960s. The working-class suburbs of Paris, hardest hit by recession, unemployment, and immigration, present one of the great social challenges of the next century.

PARISIAN LIFE

In the last decade of the 20th century, Parisian life has reflected the uncertainties of European integration and the global economy. The monumental *grands travaux* so characteristic

Where the chic and famous come to party—the exclusive Les Bains nightclub

of French presidents from Pompidou to Mitterrand are winding down. Some of the projects—such as the bold plans for a whole new district around the four huge towers of the François Mitterrand Library near the Gare d'Austerlitz—have been scaled down. The emphasis is on restoration, on removing garish neon, and on installing Third Republic-style street accessories. Promised bicycle tracks have appeared, with their own handlebar-level traffic lights to remind cyclists—who are as anarchic as all other Parisian road users— that they too must respect some rules. At the same time, the grands travaux have aged embarrassingly quickly, revealing too much corner-cutting. Funds are now being redirected

toward the economic and social rehabilitation of deprived areas. Insecurity has increased—as in many large cities of the developed world and despite an overall drop in the crime rate—as a result of a rise in acts of random violence and vandalism, often committed by teenagers too young to be prosecuted, many of whom also live in recession-hit areas.

At the dawn of the third millennium, Paris is still looking for its socioeconomic equilibri-um. Great hopes are placed in the *technopole sud*, extending from La Défense to Orly, as a European center for business. Serious attempts have also been made to counter industrial decline in the east by developing international transport and logistical facilities from Roissy to Marne-la-Vallée, the latter also home to the vast Disneyland Paris theme park.

Two thousand years of Parisian history have demonstrated the aptness of the city's

The panoramic view from the Eiffel Tower, with the Dôme Church at Les Invalides prominent in the center

motto, "*Fluctuat nec mergitur*—Battered by the waves, but not sunk." The city has repeatedly shown its capacity to bounce back from such crises as its destruction during the barbarian raids of the third century, its sufferings during the wars and pestilence of the 14th and 15th centuries, its civil strife during the religious wars of the 16th century, its ordeal during the Prussian siege and the days of the Commune (1870-71), and its Occupation during World War II. And whatever challenges await in the future, Paris will undoubtedly remain an architectural showcase proudly projecting France's image to the world. ∎

History of Paris

THE HISTORY OF PARIS IS VERY MUCH PRESENT THROUGHOUT THE CITY today. Various quarters—the Napoleonic Opéra area or the 17th-century Marais, for example—bear the mark of the rulers governing at the time.

THE CELTS

The site of Lutetia was occupied from as early as the fifth or fourth millennium B.C. until the early Iron Age (circa 800–700 B.C.). Neolithic man inhabited the island that would become Île de la Cité, as well as a rocky spur on the left bank that served as an observation point. The island subsequently was abandoned, probably due to climactic changes, until around 250–225 B.C., when a Celtic tribe called the Parisii settled there. The Parisii lived mainly from river trade until approximately 90 B.C., when they began to strike high-quality gold staters. This continued until the Romans arrived in the middle of the first century B.C.

In 53 B.C., seizing upon Lutetia's strategic geographical position, Julius Caesar used the island as his base during his campaign to quell the insurrection of the neighboring Senones. By 52 B.C., the Celt Vercingétorix had convinced the Parisii to revolt against the Romans. Caesar dispatched his lieutenant Labienus and four legions to crush them, but the Celtic general Camulogenus held the left bank of the Seine against him. When Labienus crossed the Seine and moved down toward the right bank plateau (where Les Halles would later stand), the Gauls (Gaul was the Roman name for France) set fire to the Cité and destroyed its bridges. Labienus then surrounded the Gallic positions, killing Camulogenus and routing the other Gauls. Historians are divided over where the battle actually took place, Caesar's *Gallic War* being the only account; it was possibly the plain of Grenelle.

Lutetia flourished under the Romans. The settlement was reconstructed and a wall built round it in the early second century A.D. Rustic Gallic dwellings were replaced with homes built along actual streets. A new city sprang up across the Petit Pont on the left bank, around the cardo, the main north–south street of the Roman city (the present-day Rue St.-Jacques–Rue St.-Martin). The Romans also built baths along the angle of today's Boulevard St.-Michel and St.-Germain; a theater beneath the Lycée St.-Louis; a temple to Jupiter and Tiberius (on the site of Notre-Dame); a forum on Rue Soufflot; arenas on Rue Monge; an aqueduct; and taverns serving barley beer and spiced wine.

Toward the mid-third century, Lutetia became an episcopal see through the efforts of Saint Denis, the city's first bishop. For years, the Romans tolerated Denis as he converted followers and founded churches. But eventually they clamped down on Christianity and ordered his arrest. According to legend, Denis was beaten, thrown to the lions, and crucified. Refusing to abjure his faith, he was dragged to the Mont des Martyrs (later Montmartre) and beheaded. He then rose, picked up his head, and carried it to a village north of Paris. The Basilica of St.-Denis was later built on the site of the martyr's tomb, and Denis became the patron saint of France.

CHRISTIANITY AND BARBARISM

Constantine I made Christianity the official religion of the Empire in 313. His nephew Julian the Apostate, who rose to the imperial throne in 361, would play a great role in promoting Paris as an imperial city (although a third-century decree renamed Lutetia "Paris," Julian continued to call it Lutetia). He also did

Above: A golden stater struck by the Parisii. Right: The Louvre in the early 15th century (miniature from the *Très Riches Heures du Duc de Berry*, Musée Condé, Chantilly)

a great deal to defend Gaul from barbarian invasions until he was killed in battle in 363. Over the next century, Roman power weakened, and by the early fifth century had virtually collapsed.

When word spread that Attila and his Huns were headed toward Paris in 451, the people panicked and made ready to flee. A young Gallo-Roman woman from Nanterre, named

Joan of Arc leads the storm on Paris, September 1429 (from *Les Vigiles de Charles VII*, Bibliothèque Nationale, Paris).

Geneviève, urged the inhabitants to remain and pray to God. Luckily for Geneviève, Attila's plan was not to ransack Paris, but to reach the Loire at Orléans and attack the Visigoths. She was credited with a miracle and proclaimed the savior of Paris.

MIDDLE AGES

The Merovingians

The Frankish king Merovech (*R*.447–457) and his son Childeric I (*R*.457–481) proved loyal allies of Rome against Atilla and other invaders. As the Empire disintegrated, Childeric's son Clovis (*R*.481–511) formally added the Roman provinces of western Gaul to his realm in Flanders, thus establishing the Frankish Kingdom, the forerunner of the modern French state. The educated Gallo-Romans found themselves subject to the crude culture of the bloodthirsty Merovingians—

called the "long-haired kings" because cutting their hair was seen as a disgrace that barred them from the throne.

In 486, Clovis triumphed over the Romans at Soissons. A pagan, he married a Catholic, Clothilda of Burgundy in 491 and was baptized at Reims. Clovis made Paris his capital in 508. Three years later he died, and the Merovingian kingdom was divided into four parts. One of Clovis's descendants, Dagobert (*R*.628–639), established the annual Fair of St.-Denis outside Paris in 635, and the city once again became a leading commercial and cultural center.

The Carolingians

Dagobert's descendants, nicknamed "*les rois fainéants*" or "do-nothing kings," allowed power to slip into the hands of the palace mayors, and Pepin the Short had himself elected king in 751. His bastard son Charlemagne became king of the Franks in 768 and, in 30 years reconquered a large part of the old western Roman Empire. In December 800, he was crowned emperor by the Pope, choosing Aachen (Aix-la-Chapelle) as the capital of his Holy Roman Empire.

In the ninth century, Paris became a target for Viking raiders in quest of plunder, and the city was repeatedly attacked from 845 to 885. Charlemagne's great empire had now split into three kingdoms, and was too disrupted to organize effective resistance. Disgruntled nobles and clergy, therefore, turned to the warrior Robert the Strong, Count of Anjou and Blois. He was killed by Vikings, and his son Eudes (Odo) became Count of Paris (under the Carolingians, palace mayors were replaced by hereditary counts). Parisians placed their trust in Eudes, then restored the Roman walls around the Île de la Cité and built two *châtelets*, or castles.

The Capetians

After Charles III (the Fat) was deposed in 887, the nobles set a precedent by electing Count Eudes king instead of the legitimate Carolingian heir. When the last Carolingian king—Louis V—died, Hugues Capet (Count of Paris) was elected king in 987 and crowned at Noyon. The Capetian dynasty ruled from Paris, imbuing the city with a prestige unknown since Clovis. Trade and commerce expanded on the Right Bank. The powerful abbeys and fairs at St.-Denis and St.-Germain played a key role in the development, as did Abbot Suger, a shrewd administrator who commissioned the new basilica of St.-Denis—France's first Gothic building—in 1136.

The royal domains doubled during the reign of Philippe-Auguste (1180–1223), who took a great interest in Paris. He backed a University of Paris charter and codified university studies, paved the main streets, built a market at Les Halles, and laid the Louvre's foundations. Before embarking on the Crusades, Philippe-Auguste ordered the expansion of the city's protective wall, which was to encompass areas on both banks of the Seine. Vestiges of the wall can be seen in the Latin Quarter and the Marais.

Philippe-Auguste's grandson, Louis IX (R.1226–1270), was known as Saint-Louis for his piety. He commissioned the Ste.-Chapelle to house part of the True Cross and the Crown of Thorns. By Philippe the Fair's reign (1285–1314), Paris was the site of political decision-making and the main seat of royalty. Philippe made the Parlement of Paris a legitimate court of law (not a governing body), and convoked the first French Estates-General. He also built the magnificent Salle des Gens d'Armes in the Conciergerie. His three sons ascended the throne in succession, following his death in 1314; the last, Charles IV, died in 1328 without leaving a male heir.

HOUSE OF VALOIS

Edward III of England (Philippe IV's grandson) believed he had a better right to the French throne than the late king's cousin, Philippe de Valois. This claim was denied on the grounds of a new addition to the Salic Law forbidding matrilineal inheritance. (Edward was the son of Philippe IV's daughter.) Philippe de Valois (Philippe VI, R.1328–1350) claimed the throne, launching the Valois Dynasty and precipitating the onset of the Hundred Years' War between England and France.

During this war, Parisians became instrumental in politics, as the king appealed regularly for financial support in raising war revenues. The period was marked by strife, with the Black Death plague claiming nearly a third of the French population in 1348. Étienne Marcel, who was Merchant Provost, had become a spokesman for Parisians, who were angry over government corruption and the court's lavish lifestyle. He assembled 3,000 armed men and invaded the Île de la Cité palace in 1358, slitting the throats of two advisers of the future Charles V as the boy looked on. The event was said to have traumatized Charles V (the Wise, R.1364–1380), who later moved the royal residence to the more secure Louvre. Charles V beautified Paris, with garden layouts, palaces, and private mansions. He also extended the city walls and built the Bastille in eastern Paris.

Late Middle Ages & Renaissance

France had long been at war with England. Following the Battle of Agincourt in 1415, the English, in alliance with the dukes of Burgundy, appeared victorious. From 1420 to 1436, Paris was under English rule, and Henry VI of England was anointed King of France in Paris in 1431. There was famine and rebellions, and wolves roamed the besieged city. Charles VII (R.1422–1461) finally liberated Paris and retook his capital.

France made an impressive recovery during the late 15th and early 16th centuries. The restored House of Valois regained its royal authority, and the economy began to expand. Printing was introduced, and perfumes, ladies' underwear, and forks were imported. The kings, influenced by Italian urban concepts integrating beauty with functional design, took a growing interest in their city. Gothic designs, such as the Église St.-Séverin, the Hôtel de Sens, and the Hôtel de Cluny, were added to the cityscape.

François I (R.1515–1547), an ostentatious patron of the arts who expanded royal absolutism and fostered intellectual freedom, declared Paris his residence in 1528. The city became more cosmopolitan, and artists such as Leonardo da Vinci and Benvenuto Cellini worked at his court. François renovated the Louvre, built superb castles at Chambord, Blois, and Fontainebleau, commissioned the lavish Hôtel de Ville, and drew up many of the main streets. Renaissance art found new expression in the Fontaine des Innocents, the St.-Eustache church, and the Tuileries Palace.

St. Bartholomew's Day Massacre

The Protestant Reformation began in Wittenberg in 1517, with Martin Luther's protest of the Church's sale of indulgences. In Paris, many intellectuals, princes, and wealthy merchants embraced the ideas behind the Reformation, in contrast to the capital's heavily Catholic lower classes. Catherine de Médicis, the wife of François I's successor, Henri II (R.1547–1559), wielded immense power. She played the two groups off one another, permitting an armed conflict to develop that led to the first of the Religious Wars.

Religious strife and paranoia were exacerbated by factional fighting between the Huguenot Prince de Condé and the Catholic Duc de Guise. Accused heretics were burned at the Place Maubert. The planting of a rumor that Huguenots (French Calvinist Protestants) were planning to "cut the king's throat, kill his brothers, and pillage the city of Paris" led to the St. Bartholomew's Day Massacre of August 24, 1572, during which Catholic mobs turned on Protestants. Approximately 5,000 were killed in the capital alone.

Henri III's (R.1574–1589) proposal of compromise made him hugely unpopular. His immediate heir was the Protestant Henri de Navarre, but the population backed Henri, Duc de Guise, who became leader of the Catholic League. A revolt broke out following the latter's assassination in 1588, and Henri III and Henri de Navarre besieged Paris. When a League monk assassinated Henri III in 1589, Henri de Navarre (IV) became king, founding the Bourbon dynasty.

Henri IV

Henri IV's (R.1589–1610) Protestantism remained an obstacle to his recognition by royalist Catholics who held Paris against him. In 1593 he converted to Catholicism, a step that all but completed his great task of unifying a fractious country. A year later, he was anointed at Chartres and entered the capital on March 22, 1594. He then sought to consolidate royal power. Henri completed the Pont Neuf (the first Paris bridge that was not

"Portrait of François I" by Jean Clouet, with participation of François Clouet (the Louvre, Paris)

lined with houses or shops, but sidewalks and benches); commissioned the Place Dauphine; and laid out royal squares.

But the Catholic League had not forgiven its old opponent, and—after more than 20 assassination attempts—Henri IV was stabbed to death by the fanatic François Ravaillac, in May 1610, while caught in a traffic jam on the Rue de la Ferronnerie.

ANCIEN RÉGIME

Louis XIII

Henri IV's son Louis XIII (R.1610–1643) was only eight at the time of his father's death. His domineering mother, Marie de Médicis, served as regent until Louis XIII assumed power in 1617. The real head of his government was Cardinal Richelieu (who became Chief Minister in 1624), a shrewd administrator whose centralizing policies—along with those of his successor Cardinal Mazarin—paved the way for royal absolutism. He commissioned the Palais Cardinal (later the Palais-Royal), rebuilt the Sorbonne, and founded the Académie Française. The Counter-Reformation fostered the construction of convents, chapels, and churches such as Val-de-Grâce, built in 1638 to commemorate the "miraculous" birth of Louis XIII's son, the future Louis XIV (Anne of Austria's first child at the age of 37).

Rebellious stirrings

Absolute monarchy—by divine right—reached its apogee under Louis XIV (R.1643–1715), the "Sun King," who inherited the throne at the age of five. The Parlement sought to check the young king's power by drawing up a constitution; the aristocratic opposition wanted shared power, but was fraught with dissension. Rumors that taxes were to be paid in proportion to income resulted in panic and protest. In July 1648, Chief Minister Cardinal Mazarin, co-regent for Louis with Anne of Austria, declared that the young king would not repay his debts.

The Fronde, a series of rebellions by nobles and their supporters against absolutism and tax policy, spread violence in Paris from 1648 to 1653, with troops led by the Prince de Condé besieging the city and blocking its food supply. Louis assumed full power in 1661 following Mazarin's death, and a desire for order ultimately permitted the king's absolutism to flourish.

The "Sun King"

The 23-year-old Louis embarked on a series of wars to establish France's supremacy in Europe. At first he delegated important affairs of state to Mazarin's successor, Jean-Baptiste Colbert, who sought to replenish the royal treasury and make Paris more secure. He introduced an anticorruption campaign, created the Lieutenant General of Police, and organized firefighting. He also ordered the city's reconstruction according to a classical ideal, resulting in the Place Vendôme, Place des Victoires, the Invalides, and the Observatory.

But Louis's attention was focused less on Paris than on Versailles. The Sun King poured vast amounts of money into the palace, and moved his court there in 1682. Political power was out of the reach of street movements here. He also severed the independence of high nobles, who were reduced to squabbling over who would—literally—wipe the royal behind.

But financing wars and the king's extravagance put a strain on the economy, as did the exodus of skilled artisans and merchants after the king revoked the Edict of Nantes (which granted Huguenots religious and civil liberties) in 1685. To meet rising expenses, Colbert had been forced to revert to short-term expedients to increase taxation revenue. The root of financial problems, however, was the tax collection system itself more than expenditures. Louis XIV's legacy was a modern system of government financed by a semi-medieval taxation system.

Louis XV

After Louis XIV's death in 1715, the court and young Louis XV (R.1715–1774) moved back to Paris under the regent Philippe d'Orléans, a dissipated rake who allowed the great noble families to regain their former independence. Parisians sought to forget the austerity of Louis XIV's final years, opting for bright colors and a dash of frivolity. This was the age of Watteau's lighthearted paintings and Charles Perrault's fairy tales.

A period of political stability followed under the king's chief adviser, André de Fleury, with overseas trade and improved transportation boosting commercial development. Paris grew on both banks, with the stylish new *faubourgs* (quarters outside the old walls) of St.-Germain and St.-Honoré. After de Fleury's death in 1743, Louis XV took over as head of government. He commissioned the Place Louis XV (now the Place de la Concorde), the Ste.-Geneviève Church (Panthéon), the Odéon theater, the École Militaire, and the Champ-de-Mars.

The Enlightenment

Louis XV's lack of character resulted in nearly 50 years of weak government. He sought distraction in hunting and in women, one of whom was his famous mistress, the Marquise de Pompadour. She was a friend of Denis Diderot, who recruited the major French thinkers of the Enlightenment to write the *Encyclopédie*, a remarkable compendium of ideas championing skepticism and rationalism. The first volume was published in 1751.

The 18th century brought great interest in reform, as political and financial structures were not keeping pace with social changes. Montaigne, Descartes, Newton, and others had laid the groundwork for unorthodox ideas—stifled under Louis XIV but now flourishing. By mid-century, revolutionary ideas on science and philosophy circulated through the fashionable salons held by influential women such as Madame Geoffrin.

FRENCH REVOLUTION

Louis XVI's government

The Parlements became the center of opposition to Louis XIV's weaker successors. The Parlement of Paris saw itself as the defender of constitutional liberties, and although Louis XVI (R.1774–1792) tried to enact reforms, it spread opposition and revolutionary ideas.

To gain favor with the people, the king appointed Jacques Necker as Director General of Finances in 1777. Necker was a popular figure, an ally of the commoners. The French government was on the verge of bankruptcy, due in part to expenses incurred by France during the American Revolution. In 1785, work began on the Fermiers Généraux (Tax

The upper section of the cupola of the Hôtel des Invalides (painted ca 1692 by Charles de Lafosse) shows Saint-Louis presenting his crown, sword, and coat of arms to Christ.

Collectors) wall around Paris. Heavy taxes were levied on goods entering and leaving the city, fueling popular discontent. The *vingtième*, a tax on one-twentieth of all incomes, had been introduced in 1749, but the nobility refused to pay, and the clergy led the opposition to the tax.

Third Estate

After attempts to avert bankruptcy failed, Louis XVI was forced to convene the Estates-General to try to raise new taxes. The Estates-General was composed of the clergy (First Estate); the nobility (Second Estate); and the commoners (Third Estate), each voting as a block. Its meeting in May 1789—for the first time since 1614—marked the abdication of absolute monarchy and the empowerment of the Third Estate. A new kind of revolution was to emerge, one no longer led by the Parlements, nobility, and clergy. The hidden impetus was the supply and price of food—primarily bread—following the disastrous harvest of 1788.

Representing 96 percent of the population, the Third Estate proclaimed itself the National Assembly on June 17. When their meeting hall was closed, the deputies adjourned to a nearby *jeu de paume*, or indoor tennis court, and took an oath (June 20) to meet until a constitution was drafted. Troops, largely foreign, continued to pour into Paris and Versailles, and on July 11 Necker was dismissed and replaced by Queen Marie-Antoinette's favorite, the Baron de Breteuil.

Revolt against the monarchy

On July 14, orators at the Palais-Royal incited the people to take up arms. They attacked Les Invalides to procure munitions, then stormed the Bastille's armory. Refusing to surrender, the governor was killed and his head was paraded around Paris on a pike to mark the victory. Louis XVI proceeded to the

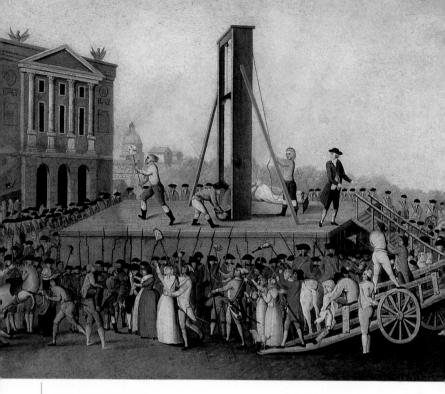

"The Execution of Marie-Antoinette on October 16, 1793," in the Musée Carnavalet, Paris. The queen was beheaded on the Place de la Révolution, now the Place de la Concorde.

Hôtel de Ville, where he accepted the tricolor cockade from the new municipal government, or commune.

In October, angry Parisians marched to Versailles to protest high bread prices—when Marie-Antoinette allegedly told them to try brioche instead. In Paris, political clubs guided the National Assembly in drafting a constitution. The king and queen fled the city on June 20, 1791, but were recognized at Varennes and brought to the Tuileries Palace in humiliation. The king accepted the constitution, thus creating a limited monarchy.

Exasperation of Parisians with the government led to the radicalization of the *sans-culottes* ("without breeches"; the lower classes wore trousers instead of aristocratic breeches) in 1792. On August 10, 1792, when a demand that Louis XVI be deposed was refused, they attacked the Tuileries, and an insurrectionary commune replaced the legally elected one.

Reign of Terror

Mobs stormed the prisons during the September massacres, killing nearly 2,000 suspected traitors. The monarchy was abolished on September 22, 1792—the first day of Year 1 of the French Republic, according to the new revolutionary calendar. The king was tried for treason and guillotined on January 21, 1793; Marie-Antoinette followed him nine months later. The Reign of Terror, ostensibly a campaign against foreign spies directed by the Committee of Public Safety—which included the revolutionary leaders Maximilien Robespierre and Louis Saint-Just—was in reality an attempt to purge "enemies from within." Thousands were guillotined, including Robespierre himself, in July 1794.

The National Convention, which had been elected to draw up a new constitution, set up a five-man Directory, fraught with internal dissension and dependent on the army to maintain control. The Directory was overthrown by a coup d'état in November 1799, and army hero Napoleon Bonaparte (*R.*1804–1814) was declared First Consul.

19TH-CENTURY PARIS

First Empire

Napoleon's popularity rose as peace returned, and he quickly shaped France into a powerful, centralized state. Although he distrusted Paris and considered shifting the imperial seat to Lyon, he understood the capital's key position. He set about marking it with his imperial stamp following his coronation on December 2, 1804—building new boulevards, palaces, and imposing Roman-style monuments, such as the Arc de Triomphe, the Madeleine, and the Bourse. He also expanded the Louvre's collections with booty from abroad.

While pursuing military campaigns, Napoleon boosted the economy and trade, established the Code Napoléon for civil law, set up the Grandes Écoles, and revamped the administrative system. But the success of his initial campaigns waned, particularly after the catastrophic invasion of Russia in 1812. In early 1814, Paris was occupied by the allied troops of Russia, Austria, Prussia, and Great Britain, and Napoleon was exiled to Elba. King Louis XVIII (Louis XVI's gout-afflicted brother; *R.*1814–1824) was restored to the throne with Talleyrand's help, but fled when Napoleon escaped from Elba a year later for his Hundred Days' Rule. Napoleon was crushed in the Waterloo Campaign (June 12–18) and was banished to the island of St. Helena by the British government.

The revolution of 1830

Louis XVIII returned to Paris on July 8. His chief ministers initially were moderates, but the ultraroyalists eventually got the upper hand. Electoral laws were revised to favor the wealthy, and civil liberties were curbed. Louis's successor, the reactionary Charles X (*R.*1824–1830), went further, dissolving the liberal Chamber of Deputies in May 1830, banning the press, and modifying electoral laws to favor property owners. On July 27, newspapers published defiantly; barricades soon went up and insurrection committees formed. A new provisional government ordered the tricolor raised, and three days of fighting ensued—the famous Trois Glorieuses (July 27–29)—forcing Charles into exile.

July monarchy & revolution

During the reign of Louis-Philippe (*R.*1830–1848), dubbed the "citizen king," class divisions became more entrenched. Those profiting from 19th-century "progress" could afford to live in spacious new districts like the 8th arrondissement, while the poor remained packed into central districts like St.-Merri.

On February 23, 1848, troops opened fire on a crowd on the Boulevard des Capucines, killing more than 40 citizens. Parisians erected barricades and tore up paving stones on the Place Vendôme and the Rue Royale. Louis-Philippe abdicated the next day.

The provisional government, presided over by Alphonse Lamartine, included "Albert the mechanic"—the people's representative. It abolished slavery in the colonies and the death penalty for political crimes, decreed freedom of expression, granted universal suffrage to men, and set up national workshops on construction sites throughout France to ease unemployment.

In April 1848, a conservative commission was voted in, and Parisian revolutionaries and socialists took to the streets. On May 21, the national workshops were suppressed. The next day, rioting broke out to shouts of *"Du pain ou du plomb!"*—"Bread or lead!"—ending in a bloodbath that killed 3,000.

Second Empire

In late 1848, elections overwhelmingly brought Louis-Napoleon Bonaparte (the emperor's nephew) to power as France's first president. He carried out a coup d'état three years later (the constitution forbade running for a second term of office), and the following year he was installed as Napoleon III (*R.*1852–1870). Paris saw it as the triumph of order.

Louis-Napoleon's plans to modernize the city reflected this sense of order. He called upon Baron Haussmann, Prefect of Paris, to oversee the major projects (see p. 160). New market halls at Les Halles were built, the Palais-Garnier commissioned, and the sewer system expanded. By the end of the Second Empire, Paris was a showcase for industrial

exhibitions, and the economy was thriving. But the euphoria was shattered when Napoleon III, recognizing that Prussia's rise posed a threat to France, declared war, precipitating the disastrous Franco-Prussian War of 1870.

Paris Commune

Following Napoleon III's military defeat at Sedan, September 2, 1870, and the fall of the imperial regime, a new Republic—proclaimed on September 4, 1870—prepared to face the advancing Prussians. By late September, the capital's troops numbered 500,000 (two-thirds of whom were grossly inexperienced). Although 30,000 cattle and 180,000 sheep were kept in the Bois de Boulogne as a back-up food supply, the besieged Parisians went hungry that winter. Horses, dogs, cats, rats—even a few beasts from the zoo at the Jardin des Plantes—were eaten in the effort to survive.

Adolphe Thiers's government negotiated a temporary armistice with Bismarck on January 28, 1871. Terms included the surrender of Alsace and much of Lorraine, and many Parisians saw the armistice as a betrayal. On March 18, Thiers sent troops to confiscate 227 guns from the National Guard in Montmartre. The people refused to give up the guns, and when the troops sent to remove them started fraternizing with the crowd, two of their gen-

"The Coronation of Emperor Napoleon on December 2, 1804," by Jacques-Louis David (1806–1807)

erals were executed. On March 28, the Commune of Paris was proclaimed, its principal demand being that Paris have a municipal government, within a French democratic republic. It laid out plans for compulsory primary education and workers' cooperatives.

Bloody Week & its aftermath

Thiers and the Versailles troops began a ferocious, five-week siege of Paris to suppress the Commune, culminating in Bloody Week (May 22–28). The greatly outnumbered Communards barricaded the streets, and shot many suspected of not resisting the troops. The government retook the city in a brutal assault, and on May 28, the Commune was defeated. Thou-

A Belle Epoque dance, by Henry Tenre

sands of Communards were shot in reprisal; 147 were executed against the Federalists' Wall of Père Lachaise cemetery, with the death toll estimated at anywhere from 17,000 to 35,000.

Despite a mutual wariness between Parisians and the French government, one long-term impact of the siege was a surge in patriotism, which found expression in such new spectacular monuments as the Grand Palais, and the Eiffel Tower—the centerpiece of the 1889 Universal exposition marking the centenary of the French Revolution.

20TH-CENTURY PARIS

Belle Epoque & World War I

During the Belle Epoque, Paris became as dynamic as it had been under Haussmann. The 1889 exposition featuring the Eiffel Tower was outdone only by the 1900 exposition, when the opening of the first Métro line launched the new century. Paris was the world's cultural capital, and artists, writers,

and musicians were laying the foundations of the modern era.

The expansion was halted by the onset of war. By September 2, 1914, the Germans were 15 miles outside Paris. Five days later, 4,000 men were shuttled to the front in taxis. Following the Battle of the Marne, a German retreat was ordered and trench warfare began. In four years, Paris was hit by 746 bombs. Big Bertha, the huge cannon in the St.-Gobain forest 88 miles (140 km) away, lobbed more than 300 shells, each weighing 400 pounds, on the city. Morale in Paris had been badly hit by the 1916 Battle of Verdun, when France suffered 163,000 dead and 320,000 wounded. Propaganda campaigns sought to boost morale, but the tide only really turned when the formidable Georges Clemenceau became prime minister in 1917 and led his country to victory.

Postwar Paris

The victory parade on Bastille Day in 1919 marked the end of a nightmare, yet the postwar years were harsh. The Depression exacerbated political crises, and on February 6, 1934, right-wing forces rallied protesters ranging from war veterans to fascists on the Place de la Concorde, ostensibly against government corruption. Riots broke out, and police killed 15 and injured 1,500, including several "war heroes." Five days later, unions organized a massive strike in support of democracy. In 1936, Léon Blum brought Radical Socialists, Socialists, and Communists together in a Popular Front government, inaugurating collective bargaining and a 40-hour work week.

France and Britain declared war on Germany in September 1939. During the subsequent "Phoney War"—with the side having declared war awaiting attack—truckloads of art left the Louvre for Chambord, the stained-glass windows of Ste.-Chapelle were removed, and gas masks were distributed. Germany attacked France on May 10, 1940, forcing many Parisians into exodus. Paris was declared an open city and the government left for Bordeaux. On June 14, Paris fell.

Marshal Pétain, who became prime minister, demanded an armistice, triggering Charles

Charles de Gaulle entering the newly liberated capital on August 25, 1944

de Gaulle's June 18 call from London to shore up "Free French" resistance. (De Gaulle, then Undersecretary of State for War, was sentenced to death in absentia by a Vichy court.) The armistice was signed, the Third Republic was dissolved, and Pétain became Head of State of the government of unoccupied France (now at Vichy), with more legal authority than any leader since Bonaparte.

The Occupation

The Germans occupied 60 percent of France, which became an ally in the Holocaust. There is no proof that Vichy acted under Nazi pressure to enact racial laws in 1940, yet it imposed a broader definition of a Jew than the Germans had. The laws also lowered the age of children subject to deportation.

During the Occupation, average Parisians were deprived of cars; bread, sugar, and other staples were rationed. Vegetable patches sprang up in parks and on rooftops. Street signs were in German, and the swastika flew over the Hôtel de Ville and the Eiffel Tower.

The Germans required the registration of all Jewish persons and launched anti-Jewish propaganda campaigns. An exhibit called "The Jew and France," designed to instruct the public on how to recognize Jews, featured a huge poster depicting a Shylock-like caricature of a Jewish man. All Jewish people over age 6 were forced to wear a yellow star in the occupied zone. They were barred from public places, many important jobs, and morning shopping hours, and had to ride in the last Métro car, dubbed "the Synagogue." Police sweeps in the Paris region began in May 1941, when Jewish men, mostly foreign, were rounded up. The first deportation train left for Germany in March 1942, half of the men being French Jews. During La Grande Rafle in July 1942, more than 8,000 people, including 4,115 children, were rounded up at the Vélodrome d'Hiver bicycle stadium in the 15th arrondissement. During the same period, the first French victims died in the gas chambers at Auschwitz.

The organized Resistance hid many Jewish people and helped them escape. Although one-third of French Jews were deported and killed, two-thirds were saved, largely through the efforts of French citizens and the Resistance.

The Liberation

The Allies landed in Normandy on June 6, 1944, and by August they were fast approaching Paris. An insurrection was launched on August 19, resulting in heavy casualties on both sides. Hitler had instructed German Commander General von Choltitz to reduce the city to ashes in case of defeat, but he did not carry out the order.

On the evening of August 24, an advance detachment from General Leclerc's Second Armored Division burst through the city to the Hôtel de Ville, and hundreds of church bells pealed above the roofs of Paris. On August 25, the main body of Leclerc's Division, in conjunction with the American 4th Infantry Division, liberated the city. The French flag was hoisted over the Eiffel Tower.

Modern France

De Gaulle emerged as the postwar leader of France, but in 1946 he brusquely withdrew during political maneuvering in forming the Fourth Republic. He was called back in 1958 during an uprising led by right-wing elements determined to keep Algeria as a French colony. De Gaulle prevailed, forming the Fifth Republic and becoming its first president. Algeria was proclaimed independent, and Paris at last began to enjoy prosperity.

This lasted until the general strikes of May 1968, which began with widespread student demonstrations against France's obsolete educational system, and more broadly against the rigidity of society itself. "It is forbidden to forbid!" students chanted as they barricaded the Latin Quarter. They were joined by workers

The 755-foot (230 m) span of the C.N.I.T. building at La Défense was a world record at the time of construction in 1958.

who, although wary of students (as their future bosses), were demanding dialogue with their own company executives. The workers called a general strike, which nearly paralyzed the country.

Ten months after this upheaval, De Gaulle resigned, and Georges Pompidou was elected president, succeeded by Valéry Giscard d'Estaing. The latter's projects for Paris included the Musée d'Orsay. In 1981, Socialist François Mitterrand came to power, instituting a series of *grands travaux*. His Bibliothèque Nationale de France was completed after his death in 1996. ∎

The arts

PARIS, THE MOST VISITED CITY IN THE WORLD, CERTAINLY OWES ITS FAME TO its monuments and its history. But above all, this vibrant city basks in a rich cultural heritage, and continues to attract leading exponents of literature, art, dance, theater, and opera.

LITERATURE

Paris has always drawn writers looking for recognition and inspiration at the center of European intellectual society.

From the 15th to the 17th centuries, the long-established University of Paris was the home of scholastic philosophy, which tried to reconcile the thinking of the old Greek philosophers—particularly Aristotle and Plato—with Christian orthodoxy. It also played a part in the French Inquisition, forcing independent thinkers like 17th-century philosopher René Descartes to choose their words carefully to avoid prosecution. But theater flourished under Louis XIV—the plays of Jean Racine and Pierre Corneille elegantly retold the ancient Greek stories using classical French verse, while the satirist Molière amused his aristocratic audiences with plays depicting the pretensions and ambitions of the growing middle classes.

18th century

Eighteenth-century literature was greatly influenced by a young aristocrat, François-Marie Arouet, who eventually went too far in his satires and was sent to the Bastille. There he changed his name to Voltaire. Upon his release, Voltaire became enormously popular, but was nonetheless forced to spend most of his life in exile. His contemporaries, Denis Diderot, Jean le Rond d'Alembert, and their circle, stayed on in Paris, producing the first French Encyclopédie. They became the center of the Enlightenment, which gradually brought intellectual tolerance to France.

Many of the next generation's circle of aristocratic and liberal French writers, whose works circulated through the famous literary salons, died while serving in Napoleon's armies. The most famous was Stendhal (Henri Marie Beyle), whose historical romances were the first important 19th-century French novels.

19th century

After 1830, the French novel progressed from Honoré de Balzac through Gustave Flaubert, Victor Hugo, Émile Zola, and Marcel Proust to achieve a new form that described everyday life, investigated character, and propagated social and political ideas, thus enabling a massive, newly literate readership to understand more about the world around it.

Artists and poets were regarded in a new light, suddenly becoming important and influential social leaders. Some 19th-century poets, such as Charles Pierre Baudelaire and Théophile Gautier, shocked society by probing the darker sides of human nature, and were even prosecuted for their work. However, as the notoriety only increased sales, they received more benefit than harm. In Paris particularly, there were strong personal links and friendships between creative artists of all kinds, so that ideas spread rapidly, encouraging the emergence of new styles in painting, literature, and music. With the rise of the comfortable middle classes, survival was no longer the only aim in life, and artists led the way in prescribing the pursuit of pleasure as a new goal.

Throughout the middle years of the 19th century, Paris became a haven for intellectual and artistic refugees from all over Europe, such as Karl Marx, Richard Wagner, and Heinrich Heine, although some, among them Victor Hugo, who angered the monarchy, were forced to flee the country. Talk of new systems in art, literature, philosophy, politics, and everyday institutions dominated the conversations at café tables from Montmartre to Montparnasse, bolstering the city's reputation as an artistic and intellectual center.

20th century

Impressionism, which started in painting, also affected literary and musical techniques. The burgeoning modernism of the first decade of

I.M. Pei's airy, geometric metal-and-glass pyramid, opened in 1989, graces the Louvre's main entrance hall.

the 20th century took many forms—symbolism, imagism, cubism, and others—which André Breton employed in his surrealist school, perhaps the most successful of the modernist art movements.

When American Sylvia Beach established her Shakespeare and Company bookshop on the Left Bank in 1919, Paris also became a haven for British and American writers.

Nin also made their mark with their explicit descriptions of love and sex, setting the groundwork for later women writers who would challenge the typically male domain of erotic literature.

Post World War I

In the 1930s, antifascists and Jews fleeing Italy and Germany joined the expatriate Americans

Influential in their time: existentialist Jean-Paul Sartre (left) and satirist Voltaire

Dubbed "the lost generation" by Gertrude Stein, the Americans included popular novelists like journalist Ernest Hemingway and F. Scott Fitzgerald; literary magazine editors like the Crosbies and the Jolases, who published in Paris and in England; and others like the Irish writer James Joyce, and Henry Miller, whose works were too outspoken and sexually frank to be published in their own, English-speaking countries. The poet T.S. Eliot collected material in Paris for his magazine *The Criterion,* and author and journalist Cyril Connolly came for the wine, food, and culture, and to get published in Jack Kahane's Obelisk Press (which was the first to publish Miller's *Tropic of Cancer* and Joyce's *Ulysses,* the most controversial books of their day).

Women writers such as Colette and Anaïs

still in Paris. These included André Gide, André Malraux, Roger Martin du Gard, Jean Cocteau, Franz Werfel, Erich Remarque, and Odön von Horvath. (Horvath, having successfully evaded Hitler's assassins for three years, was hit by a tree that was struck by lightning as he crossed the Rond-Point of the Champs-Élysées on the eve of World War II.)

During the war, a great many writers were either killed serving in the French army, the Resistance, concentration camps, or shot at borders. But throughout the war, a considerable underground press continued publishing works such as Vercors's novel *The Silence of the Sea,* about passive resistance to the Germans, and Paul Éluard's passionate poem *Liberté,* which was dropped on Paris by the Royal Air Force.

Literary café life: from postwar Paris to the present

After the war, a new generation of writers, philosophers, and intellectuals that included Jean-Paul Sartre, Albert Camus, Boris Vian, and Simone de Beauvoir came to prominence. They, in turn, were followed by what became known as the *"nouveau roman,"* a legacy from surrealism. New theater also flourished in the

today, and the city's reputation for recognizing talent sooner than elsewhere is perceptible to the interested visitor.

ART

Paris's reputation as one of the world's leading art capitals has suffered, particularly since the 1980s. The art market collapsed during the recession, with many galleries closing and

Colette was renowned in the interwar years for her intense, sensuous writing.

plays written by Samuel Beckett, Arthur Adamov, and Eugène Ionesco, who continued in the vein initiated by Antonin Artaud. These writers, some not French-born, were soon joined by other expatriates from America and Britain, who produced small magazines in English for another new movement in literature, the "Beat" writers (whose starting place was thus as much in Paris as in San Francisco).

Although there has been a decline in literary café life in the last decade, there are still cafés that recall this vibrant past, such as those circling the Place du Tertre in Montmartre—La Coupole and Le Select; the Dôme in Montparnasse; and the Deux Magots, Flore, and Brasserie Lipp in St.-Germain, where Sartre held court. The stones of Paris seem alive with a creativity that still lures artists

previously successful artists suddenly left without clients.

Parisian galleries

Yet art is alive and well in Paris, if the 500 or more galleries in the city are any indication. Most are concentrated in one of three main areas: St.-Germain-des-Prés, the Marais/Bastille, and the eighth arrondissement, just behind the Champs-Élysées, which is now filled with galleries showing traditional, recognized artists.

New artists are most likely to be found in the Bastille area, where streets such as Rue Keller (east of Bastille) and Rue Vieille du Temple (to the west) are lined with galleries. St.-Germain is no longer the epicenter of the Parisian art scene, but the dozens of galleries

clustered around the Rue de Seine and the Rue Guénégaud are a pleasant way to spend an afternoon. A group of new galleries, primarily promoting conceptual work, has banded together on Rue Louise Weiss in the 13th arrondissement, just behind the new Bibliothèque de France.

Artists' open houses

It is possible to see artwork outside the galleries: A number of artists display their work in the square at Montmartre, and there are also several artists' associations who organize *portes ouvertes*, or open houses, welcoming the public into their studios (usually in May and October). The Génie de la Bastille was the first of these, but others have sprung up in the suburbs of Ivry, Montreuil, and Montrouge, where many artists have moved to escape Paris's high rents.

Art publications

Several publications (mostly in French) provide information about current shows,

"La Gare Saint-Lazare," painted by Claude Monet in 1877

including the weekly *Pariscope,* the monthly *Beaux-Arts* magazine, and the *Guide des Galleries.* The galleries publish a map of the St.-Germain and the Bastille/Marais neighborhoods, with their locations and the dates of the *vernissages* (previews). The guidebook *Bill'Art* (by Olivier Billiard) lists more than 500 galleries, with ratings given in paintbrushes.

ARCHITECTURE

The architectural history of Paris is densely layered. Time and time again old buildings and monuments have been knocked down, or transformed or reused to make way for new ones. For example, vestiges of the Bastille prison were used to build the Concorde Bridge and the Théâtre du Marais (now no longer standing), and stones from the Roman baths and Left Bank dwellings were used in medieval times to build a medieval defensive wall on the Île de la Cité.

Paris's earliest architectural elements are over 2,000 years old, dating from the time when the original settlement of Lutetia was only a backwater at the outer reaches of the Roman Empire. The ruins of two characteristic structures remain from this period: the heavily restored 16,000-seat Arena (rediscovered in the 19th century) and the baths of Cluny, now part of the Museé de Cluny.

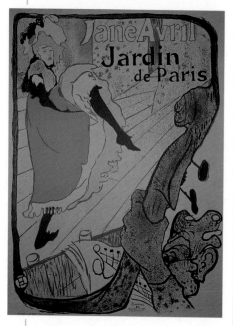

A Toulouse-Lautrec poster advertising the nightlife of the Naughty Nineties

Gothic and medieval architecture

The Île de France is the cradle of Gothic architecture, with its luminous churches heightened by their Gothic arches. In 1136, the Basilica of St.-Denis was begun, which first combined flying buttresses and ribbed vaulting; it was followed by the Cathedral of Notre-Dame in 1163, and the Flamboyant Gothic-style masterpiece, Ste.-Chapelle, built by Pierre de Montreuil in the following century. The Hôtel de Sens and the Hôtel de Cluny are the few examples of secular Gothic architecture left in Paris.

Medieval architecture persisted in Paris long after the Renaissance had replaced it else-where. Although King François I brought back Renaissance ideas in architecture from his military campaigns in Italy, he only utilized them in the Loire Valley châteaus. Meanwhile, Paris continued to build Flamboyant Gothic buildings for nearly five centuries; they include the Tour St.-Jacques (1509–1523), the St.-Merri Church (1520–1552), and the St.-Gervais Church (1494–1657). Henri IV initiated the great royal squares, the first being today's Place des Vosges.

17th, 18th, & 19th centuries

The fashionable quarter in the 17th century remained the Marais, where a number of lavish mansions—the Hôtel de Sully and the Hôtel Salé (now the Musée Picasso)—still stand. During the Ancien Régime (France's system of government before the Revolution), some of the greatest architects worked under royal patronage. Salomon de Brosse constructed the Palais de Luxembourg, François Mansart created his eponymous roofline and windows, and Louis Le Vau built Vaux-le-Vicomte. This era also saw the development of formal French landscaping, its leading proponent being André Le Nôtre.

During the 18th century, the aristocracy migrated to the Faubourg St.-Germain, where many *hôtels particuliers*, or private mansions, were built in the lighthearted rococo style; most of these now serve as embassies and government institutions.

There was little new building during the Revolution. Churches were either torn down or converted. Many of them were deconsecrated and used as warehouses or Temples of Reason. Paris was radically transformed, however, when Baron Haussmann, Prefect of Paris under Napoleon III, set about modernizing the city during the Second Empire (see p. 160). He tore down dilapidated houses, replacing them with entire blocks of apartment buildings, and sliced wide boulevards through old neighborhoods. Another legacy of 19th-century architecture were the exuberant iron structures most dramatically exemplified by the Eiffel Tower.

Modern architecture

Technical innovations and a new design aesthetic, devised by Le Corbusier, contributed to the more geometric and functional style of the modern movement after World War I. There are few of Le Corbusier's designs in Paris, although his influence was widespread.

Postwar Paris was marked by experiments in high-rise developments, where entire neighborhoods, particularly in the 19th arrondissement, were replaced by impersonal slabs of apartment buildings. President Mitterrand's *grands travaux* had a great impact on the face of the city, with some of the more admirable monuments including the Louvre Pyramid, the Grande Arche de La Défense, and the Institut du Monde Arabe; others—such as the Opéra-Bastille or the stark towers of the new Bibliothèque de France—are controversial.

CINEMA

In France, and Paris in particular, an appreciation of the cinema is regarded as an essential component of the good life. In an educational system that takes a dim view of frivolity, students may pursue a major concentration in cinema studies at the high school level, where the subject of film has the same legitimacy as French literature, or algebra-trigonometry.

History

France was the world's leading film-producing nation up until World War I. Although other inventors were perfecting motion picture devices at the same time, it is generally accepted that the movies as we know them began in Paris. On December 28, 1895, the first public screening of hand-cranked short films took place in the Salon Indien of the Grand Café on Boulevard des Capucines, courtesy of the Lumière brothers and their ingenious *cinématographe*.

The turn-of-the-century magician Georges Melies is regarded as the "father of special effects" for his hundreds of wildly inventive trick films. Max Linder, Charlie Chaplin's master and inspiration, created countless comic innovations throughout the silent era.

Development of sound & the French "New Wave"

The switch to sound at the end of the 1920s spelled doom for the silent works that had become known as the Seventh Art. However, many of these were rescued by film buff Henri Langlois, who started a collection at his house. It eventually became the Cinémathèque Française (see p. 182)—a haven for movies past, present, and future. With its movie library and cinemabilia, the Cinémathèque served as an informal training ground for the young critics and directors known as the French "New Wave": Jean-Luc Godard, François Truffaut, Jacques Rivette, Eric

Russian dancer Vaslav Nijinksy came to Paris with the Ballets Russes in 1909.

Rohmer, and Claude Chabrol. Langlois, who died in 1977 at the age of 62, received an honorary Oscar in 1974.

French moviegoing

Whereas box office statistics in the United States are less than scientific, in France the National Center for Cinema (CNC) accounts for every last ticket sold. The French government encourages its citizens to go to the movies by offering discounts to students, the elderly, members of the military, members of families with three or more children, and even the officially unemployed. The average Parisian goes to the movies 12.2 times a year.

He or she has 343 screens and 69,437 seats to choose from.

Until the 1980s, French movies attracted over half of all moviegoers, but in the past decade this has dropped to 34.5 percent, with 53.8 percent of the moviegoing public preferring American movies (the remaining 11.7 percent includes movies made worldwide). Indeed, the vast majority of viewers under the

Film director François Truffaut

age of 25 think "American" when they think "Let's go to the movies."

France has a long tradition of serious writing about cinema. The monthly journals *Positif* and *Cahiers du Cinema* have been in business for nearly half a century, each voicing occasionally sharp divisions in taste. Every major general-interest magazine includes extensive movie criticism and director profiles, often "worshiping" each new film from Woody Allen or Clint Eastwood, two critical and popular darlings, some of whose films have been released in France prior to the United States.

The sheer choice of films in Paris is spectacular—from the latest Hollywood megaproduction to first-person documentaries shot in Super-8 or video formats and blown up for commercial release. Although the art house and repertory cinemas remain far more vital in Paris than in any other city on earth, there are also major cinema chains, such as the giants Gaumont and Pathé,

which threaten independent theater owners, distributors, and exhibitors.

In addition to the small art house cinemas and state-of-the-art multiplexes, there is also Studio 28 in Montmartre, where Luis Buñuel and Salvador Dali's notorious surrealist masterpiece *An Andalusian Dog* premiered in 1928, and the huge, lavishly decorated Grand Rex cinema, which offers a backstage tour that includes an elevator ride behind the giant screen while a movie is showing. Paris also has the world's biggest IMAX-OMNIMAX, the Dôme IMAX, at La Défense.

THEATER, OPERA, & DANCE THEATER
Ever since Les Confrères de la Passion established the city's first permanent theater in

1547 at the Hôtel du Duc de Bourgogne (see the commemorative plaque at 29 Rue Étienne Marcel), the dramatic arts have diversified. They now range from street theater in summer to grandly produced plays, performed everywhere from tiny cellars to sumptuous surroundings. The 1960s counterculture and Culture Minister André Malraux's decentralization plan succeeded in broadening the appeal of theater, and plays everywhere are enjoying increased popularity.

This recent revolution, however, has not dented the deference accorded to the traditional Comédie Française (referred to as the House of Molière), created by Louis XIV in 1680, seven years after Molière's death. It is a prestigious symbol of French culture, purveying classics by Molière, Pierre Corneille, and

The Louvre's Galerie au Bord de l'Eau

Jean Racine (see p. 32), as well as plays by such modern authors and playwrights as Jean Genet, Stefan Zweig, Marguerite Duras, and Tom Stoppard.

Contemporary theater

Contemporary directors such as Ariane Mnouchkine, Peter Brook, and Robert Cordier have opted out of commercial crowd-pleasers to pursue exciting, independent theater. Mnouchkine at the Théâtre du Soleil uses this spacious venue—a transformed armaments factory—to intrigue audiences with evocative and colorful plays. Robert Cordier and partner Lesley Chatterley give plays by Shakespeare, Bernard Koltès, David Mamet,

Sam Shepard, and others a sexy, violent, humorous, and multilingual treatment in their intimate theater.

Such unconventional use of space characterizes many Parisian theaters, drawing directors from abroad, such as self-exiled Englishman Peter Brook, whose Théâtre des Bouffes du Nord is exceptional. Together with Micheline Rozan, he founded the Centre International de Recherche Théâtral (CIRT) in 1970 and Le Centre International de Créations Théâtrales in 1974. It stages Shakespearean plays, the classic Indian work, *The Mahabharata,* and vaudeville, in a historic theater deliberately kept in a state of disrepair. Some of his innovative techniques include incorporating technology in the form of television screens along with the usual staging of the play.

Cross-cultural exchange

France's commitment to continuing cross-cultural exchange is exemplified by Harold Pinter's first-time direction of *Ashes to Ashes;*

Oscar-winning French actress Juliette Binoche's off-West End appearance in London; and playwright Yasmina Reza's European-wide hit, *Art*, which has also been performed in New York. A number of resident English-language theater companies, including Dear Conjunction, the Gare Saint-Lazare Players, and the On Stage Theater Company, present bilingual productions of well-known plays, as well as their own creations. Another important theater in the artistic exchange between France and the rest of the world is the

The Eiffel Tower earned its architect— bridge engineer Gustave Eiffel—the nickname "magician of iron."

MC 93 in Bobigny, whose eclectic international program has featured American choreographer Lucinda Childs, English producer Deborah Warner, and Irish actress Fiona Shaw.

Dance

As Europe's undisputed dance capital, Paris has a rich selection of festivals, events, spectacles, and dance forms ranging from tango and ballet to hip-hop and contemporary dance.

Ballet

The Palais-Garnier, home of the Ballet de l'Opéra National de Paris, has been used almost exclusively for ballet since 1990. Generous sponsorship by the Ministry of Culture permits extravagant productions like

The lavish Théâtre des Champs-Élysées was designed by Auguste Perret between 1911 and 1913.

Rudolf Nureyev's versions of *Romeo and Juliet, Swan Lake,* and *Raymonda,* and ballets by Roland Petit and Kenneth MacMillan. Since 1973, Carolyn Carlson, Angelin Preljocaj, Jean-Claude Gallotta, and Merce Cunningham, the doyenne of modern dance, have revitalized the modern dance repertoire.

Contemporary dance

The Théâtre de la Ville, backed by the city of Paris, is a dedicated promoter of contemporary dance. It hosts Pina Bausch's Wuppertaler Tanztheater almost every year, and other regulars, including Belgian choreographer Anne Teresa De Keersmaeker and her company Rosas. The search for new artistic expression often produces aggressive, overtly sexual works accompanied by silence, grunts, screeches, and world music. Poetry, texts, and slide projections are often interwoven with contemporary dance.

The diverse program of the annual Autumn Festival is a good opportunity to view dance developments from around the globe, but dance lovers can view performances throughout the year of Indian dance with Bharatha Natyam (a school of dance that originated in Southern India) or Kathak (a classic Hindu dance from the North). Both use highly stylized hand gestures. The Maison de la Culture du Japon includes dance such as the Jiutamai-song and dance of the geishas as part of its varied program of cinema, theater, and exhibitions. The first hip-hop festival was held in 1996 at the Grande Halle de la Villette.

Opera

When the Opéra National de Paris-Bastille opened in 1990, it shifted the main opera program away from the Palais-Garnier. The Royal Academy of Music and Dance (known as l'Opéra), founded in 1669, had monopolized the theatrical and lyrical arts for decades, along with La Comédie Française.

The ingenious use of music and mime in Parisian fairground theaters laid the foundation for today's Opéra Comique, created over 200 years ago. The present building, the Salle Favart, opened on December 7, 1898. A number of operas, including Georges Bizet's *Carmen,* Claude Debussy's *Pelléas and Mélisande,* and François Boïeldieu's *La Dame Blanche,* have premiered at the Salle Favart, which, though not quite up to modern-day technical standards, is nonetheless a charming venue for lyrical theater. In contrast, the vast Opéra-Bastille has staged *Carmen* as well as weightier productions.

Another leading musical theater is the newly renovated Châtelet-Théâtre Musical de Paris, reopened in September 1999, which has built its reputation with major conductors and directors, staging operatic productions rivaling those of other, more famous, opera houses. Of the six performances per season, at least one is contemporary.

The Théâtre des Champs-Élysées provides a distinguished backdrop—worth seeing for its marble facade and beautiful interiors alone—to visiting dance companies and orchestras. It also hosts the New International Paris Dance Festival/Dance Competition. ∎

The essence of Paris is there, on the boat-shaped Île de la Cité—long the seat of royal, judiciary, and ecclesiastical power—and on the Île St.-Louis, a secluded preserve of 17th-century elegance.

The islands

Notre-Dame detail

The islands

PARIS, IN ESSENCE, WAS CREATED BY THE SEINE, WHICH WAS ONCE TWICE AS large. At one time, a string of islands stretched along the river; now, as a result of natural changes in the river's course and human intervention, there are only two—the Île de la Cité and the Île St.-Louis.

ÎLE DE LA CITÉ

"The Île de la Cité is the head, heart, and very marrow of Paris," wrote Victor Hugo in *Notre-Dame de Paris*. Indeed, the Île de la Cité—the geographical center of Paris, itself the cultural center of France, and even the world according to some—was the birthplace of the city and the site of its original settlement.

Strategic positioning played a key role in the Île de la Cité's development. Not only was it situated along a major Bronze Age trade route for English tin bound for Central Europe and the Mediterranean, but it also served as a refuge in times of war. During the prosperous time of the ancient Romans, who arrived in 53 B.C. and named the settlement Lutetia Parisiorum, the town spread onto what is now the Left Bank. This golden age lasted about 300 years, until tribes from the outer Rhine invaded in the late third century, and the inhabitants fled back to the Cité. The Romans, Franks, and

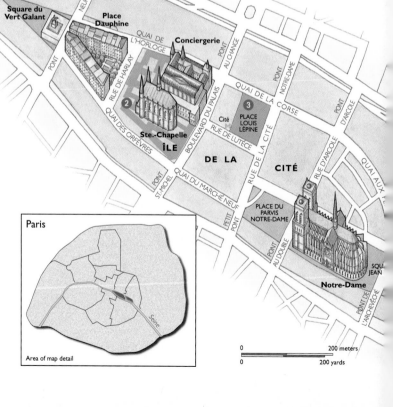

Seine

Square du Vert Galant

Place Dauphine

Conciergerie

❶

QUAI DE L'HORLOGE

PONT NEUF

RUE DE HARLAY

QUAI DES ORFÈVRES

❷

Ste.-Chapelle

ÎLE

BOULEVARD DU PALAIS

RUE DE LUTÈCE

Cité

❸

PLACE LOUIS LÉPINE

QUAI DE LA CORSE

PONT NOTRE-DAME

PONT AU CHANGE

PONT D'ARCOLE

RUE DE LA CITÉ

RUE D'ARCOLE

QUAI AUX

DE LA

CITÉ

PONT ST.-MICHEL

QUAI DU MARCHÉ NEUF

PETIT PONT

PLACE DU PARVIS NOTRE-DAME

PONT AU DOUBLE

SQU. JEAN

Notre-Dame

PONT DE L'ARCHEVÊCHÉ

Paris

Seine

Area of map detail

0   200 meters

0   200 yards

Tour boats on the Seine at night project floodlights onto the facades of the Île St.-Louis.

Capetian kings, all in their turn expanded the original settlement.

The Île de la Cité has always been an important administrative and religious center. The original seat of the Roman governor is today's Palais de Justice, where judges still dispense justice some 2,000 years later, and both the Conciergerie (the notorious revolutionary prison; see p. 60) and the glorious Ste.-Chapelle (see pp. 56–59) are to be found within its walls.

Despite the hordes of tourists and unsightly tour buses everywhere, especially around the parvis of Notre-Dame, the Île de la Cité has many charming and secluded getaways. Examples include the Marché aux Fleurs (Flower Market) on the Place Louis Lépine, the Square du Vert Galant on the far western edge of the island, and the narrow streets off the Quai aux Fleurs, such as the lovely Rue des Ursins, with its Gothic building that was once the home of the Aga Khan. Although the building is not open to the public, it has an interesting facade, and is a fascinating pastiche of architectural elements from various places and periods. Just beyond, there is a splendid perspective down the Rue des Chantres of the spire of Notre-Dame (see pp. 48–53). Walk around the back of the cathedral for a spectacular view of the flying buttresses; either illuminated at night or rising over the pale blossoms of spring, this is truly one of the city's most memorable sights.

ÎLE ST.-LOUIS

The two islands have had very different histories that have contributed to their diverse characters. The Île St.-Louis, by contrast, was a quiet, unoccupied island until 17th-century entrepreneurs came up with one of the first planned development projects, achieving a coherent architectural whole that is strikingly well preserved today. This island remains delightfully free of traffic, major shops, Métro stations, and cinemas, and a leisurely stroll around its streets will reveal many discreet vestiges of 17th-century elegance. ∎

THE ISLANDS

❶ Pont Neuf ❷ Palais de Justice
❸ Marché aux Fleurs

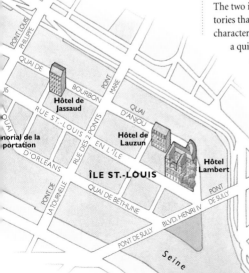

Notre-Dame

Notre-Dame

🅰 Map p. 46

✉ place du Parvis-Notre-Dame, Île de la Cité

☎ 01 42 34 56 10

Ⓜ Métro: Cité

Towers

💲 $$

Treasury

🕐 Closed Sun. and during religious holidays

💲 $

Archaeological Crypt

💲 $; free on Sun. & free daily to people aged under 27 and over 60

NOTRE-DAME STANDS OUT AS A SYMBOL OF PARIS ITSELF. Like the city, it sprang up along the banks of the Seine, its magnificent west facade rising up like "a vast symphony of stone," as Victor Hugo described it.

The cathedral's site is rich in history. It stands over the ruins of a Gallo-Roman temple to Jupiter, a fourth-century church, and a sixth-century basilica, in whose foundations were found 12 stones originally used in the construction of the Roman temple. By the 12th century, the basilica was in ruins, and Maurice de Sully (who was elected bishop of Paris in 1160) decided to replace it with a superb cathedral to rival the basilica at St.-Denis. Pope Alexander III laid the first stone in 1163, beginning what would become one of the masterpieces of French Gothic design. Work proceeded swiftly, funded by the vast sums Sully collected from the king, the clergy, the nobles, and the poor. When completed, the cathedral dominated all of religious architecture in the Île de France, as the Paris region is called, and had a sweeping impact throughout Europe.

RESTORATION

Notre-Dame's present appearance is largely the result of 19th-century restoration. In the 17th and 18th centuries, the Gothic style was no longer in vogue, and the cathedral suffered greatly as a result. Under Louis XIV (R.1643–1715), the chancel screen was partly destroyed, the 13th-century stained-glass windows were replaced with clear glass trimmed in blue and gold, and the rood screen and tombs disappeared. (A fragment of the rood screen, "La Descente aux Limbes," is in the Louvre.)

During the Revolutionary period, the church was pillaged and transformed into a Temple of Reason. Revolutionaries melted down the Treasury, burned the liberty flame on the altar, and smashed the 28 statues of the kings of Judea in the King's Gallery on the western facade—mistakenly perceived as representing the kings of France. Miraculously, 21 of the heads were subsequently found and are now preserved in the Musée de Cluny (see pp. 66–67), except for the head of King David, which is in the Metropolitan Museum of Art in New York.

By 1804, the cathedral was so dilapidated that when Napoleon I crowned himself emperor here, huge tapestries and drapings were hung to mask the damage, and plans were made to demolish it. As Victor Hugo wrote in 1831 in *Notre-Dame de Paris*, "On the face of this queen of our cathedrals, next to a wrinkle you will always find a scar. *Tempus edax, homo edacior*. Which I would freely translate: Time is blind, man is stupid." The publication of Hugo's book inspired efforts to save the cathedral and launched a movement to raise money for its restoration.

The 19th-century architect Eugène Viollet-le-Duc spent nearly 20 years restoring the statuary and glass, although his zealous efforts have been criticized. He added the 295-foot (90 m) steeple embroidered with graceful floral

Notre-Dame's South Rose Window depicts Christ surrounded by saints, the 12 Apostles, and angels.

LEGEND OF THE GREAT BELL

The great bell in the south tower (the other bells were melted down during the Revolution) only tolls on solemn occasions. Legend describes how, when the church bell was taken down and recast in the 17th century, ladies sacrificed their gold and silver jewelry by tossing it into the molten mixture—hence the purity of the F-sharp tone. ■

motifs, and replaced the sculptures on the western facade and the southern transept, reserving the most delicate work for the bays, which ultimately only succeed in approximating those of the 12th century.

PORTALS

Three portals grace the west facade of Notre-Dame, which, from left to right, represent the Virgin Mary, the Last Judgment (below), and Saint Anne. The statues decorating the portals once were brilliantly painted and stood out against a

gilt background. The Saint Anne portal contains the oldest, carved about 1170.

Framing the portals are two elegant towers (the left is slightly higher than the right), each pierced by lancets more than 50 feet (15 m) high, and decorated with gargoyles that lurk behind the large upper gallery between them.

ROSE WINDOWS

The size and brilliance of the glorious rose windows testify to the splendor of Gothic architecture. The **North Rose,** 69 feet (21 m)

West Rose Window

Portal of the Last Judgment

in diameter, with its nearly intact 13th-century glass, features Old Testament figures surrounding the Virgin.

The 43-foot-high (13 m) **South Rose,** which faces the Seine, was greatly restored in 1737; it depicts Christ surrounded by saints, apostles, and angels. The bays of the nave and the gallery rosettes were redone in 1965 by Jacques Le Chevallier, who imbued the dismal, 19th-century *grisaille* glass with the original medieval colors—rich red and blue tones—and materials.

SCULPTURES

The cathedral's sculptured works include 13th-century architect Jean Ravy's ancient choir-screen carvings; Nicolas Coustou's "Pietà"; and Antoine Coysevox's statue of Louis XIV. Against the southeast pillar of the transept stands a 14th-century statue of the Virgin and Child, known as "Notre-Dame de Paris." Religious paintings by Charles Le Brun are in the side chapels. The cathedral's treasures include the **Crown of Thorns,** a

South Rose Window

View from spire

Opposite: Notre-Dame consists of a nave with seven bays on each side, a short transept, and a round apse (pictured) with seven sections.

Below: Gargoyles, from the old French *gargouille* (throat or gullet), were originally waterspouts. Notre-Dame has both functional and decorative gargoyles, often called grotesque for their fanciful, contorted features.

Holy Nail, and a fragment of the **True Cross** from Ste.-Chapelle (see pp. 56–59). These are only on public display once a year when they are brought out and paraded before the congregation on Good Friday. Other treasures include Saint Louis's tunic, a fragment of his jaw, and a rib. The early 18th-century organ on the western wall was restored in 1868, and again in 1992, and features 6,000 pipes, 110 stops, and 5 keyboards—the largest in France. Climb up to the south tower platform for a stunning view of the spire, the flying buttresses, and the city sprawling below. The entrance is from the base of the north tower.

PARVIS OF NOTRE-DAME

The present parvis (the court in front of the church, derived from the word for paradise) is six times larger than it was in the Middle Ages. The plaques on the ground indicate the old layout of the streets and city landmarks. Where the statue of Charlemagne now stands was the site of the seventh-century Hôtel-Dieu, the oldest hospital in France. Patients weren't grouped according to sex or disease until the 18th century, and up to six people shared each bed. A new **Hôtel-Dieu**—the one now on the northern side of the parvis—was built between 1868 and 1877, after Baron Georges Eugène Haussmann (see pp. 160–61) razed the area; the old site was demolished in 1878.

Archaeological Crypt

Before leaving, don't miss a visit to the Archaeological Crypt to get a feel for the Gallo-Roman fortifications beneath the parvis. To the left are the ruins of rooms that used a heating system called hypocaust. ■

A walk around the islands

The islands are the heart of medieval Paris. The lively, bustling Île de la Cité is crammed with architectural gems, such as the magnificent Notre-Dame cathedral. In striking contrast, the smaller, quieter Île St.-Louis offers a peaceful village atmosphere, its shaded embankment lined with elegant private mansions standing as silent witnesses to a bygone era.

Begin at Point Zero on the parvis at Notre-Dame to view the cathedral in all its Gothic glory, whether wrapped in fog or washed with sun. **Notre-Dame** ❶ (see pp. 48–53) is the city's largest church. Point Zero, dating from 1769 (although the bronze star is new), is the spot from which all road distances throughout the country are gauged.

When you reach the edge of the parvis, follow the Quai du Marché Neuf, then turn right on Boulevard du Palais to see the glorious **Ste.-Chapelle** ❷ (see pp. 56–59), a fine example of high Gothic architecture.

Backtrack and turn right on Quai des Orfèvres, formerly the Île de Galilée until it was attached to the Île de la Cité in 1310. Walk along the quayside for a more scenic route, past the **Palais de Justice** on your right and on past the Pont Neuf, Paris's oldest bridge, to the beautiful **Square du Vert Galant.**

Opposite the statue of Henri IV, take Rue Henri Robert, which leads to the **Place Dauphine** ❸. One of the few areas of the islands to have escaped Haussmann's dramatic redevelopment scheme in the 19th century, the square is very central, yet intensely private. The din of cars rushing over the Pont Neuf fades as you step into the secluded Place Dauphine, where actors Yves Montand and Simone Signoret once lived. Turn left onto Rue de Harlay at the end of the square, then right on Quai de l'Horloge. Follow this past the towers of **La Conciergerie** ❹ (see p. 60), where Paris's oldest public clock (1370) still runs today.

Now follow the Quai de la Corse to the **Marché aux Fleurs** (Flower Market). Camellias, orchids, jasmine, and bamboo fill shops and stalls. (This is joined by a bird market on Sundays.) Proceed along the Quai aux Fleurs, taking a right onto Rue de la Colombe, then left on Rue des Ursins before rejoining the Quai aux Fleurs.

Go farther down the quay to the subterranean **Mémorial de la Déportation** (Deportation Memorial) ❺ (*Square de l'Île de France, Tel 01 46 33 87 56, Métro: Cité*), a stark edifice commemorating the Jewish people who were deported to concentration camps during World War II. It is faced with stone quarried from all the mountain ranges in France. Narrow staircases lead down to a high-walled platform, where the river beyond the iron bars and a portcullis evoke a powerful sense of the loss of freedom. Inside the crypt are two side galleries. Here, a series of small niches in the walls, inscribed with the names of the various concentration camps, contain urns with soil from the camps and ashes from the crematoriums.

Île de la Cité's flower market is the most famous and one of the last left in Paris.

A long, dark gallery studded with glass chips symbolizing the tens of thousands of deportees from France holds the remains of an unknown deportee taken from the necropolis of the Struthof concentration camp.

ÎLE ST.-LOUIS

Cross over the Pont St.-Louis to reach the Île St.-Louis. Originally, the two islands were one, but they were divided by a canal (Rue Poulletier) during the 14th century to reinforce the protection of the Charles V Wall. Louis XIII and his mother, Marie de Médicis, undertook the unification of the two islands—originally called Île Notre-Dame and Île aux Vaches—and the embellishment of the area in the 17th century. Reunited in 1614, the island underwent massive construction from 1620 to 1650, and was rechristened Île St.-Louis in 1726. The instability of the land hampered building: Some dwellings lean to the left or right, or have subsided, but in general they support one another.

The views from the quays are fabulous, and, if you get hungry, go to **Berthillon's** at 31 Rue St.-Louis en l'Île to sample some of their marvelous ice creams and sorbets. Other landmarks to look for include the **Hôtel de Jassaud** ❻ at 19 Quai de Bourbon, where French sculptor Camille Claudel lived in a ground-floor studio at the rear of the courtyard; and the **Hôtel de Lauzun** ❼ at 17

Quai d'Anjou, with its gilded dolphin water spouts. Poet Charles Pierre Baudelaire wrote much of *Les Fleurs du Mal (The Flowers of Evil)* here in 1857; it is now open to visitors by appointment through the National Historic Association *(Tel 01 44 61 20 89)*. The **Hôtel Lambert** ❽ at 2 Rue St.-Louis en l'Île is now a private residence. ∎

- ◭ See also area map pp. 46–47
- ▶ Notre-Dame parvis
- ⬌ 2.7 miles (4.3 km)
- ⏱ Allow 4 hours
- ▶ Hôtel Lambert

NOT TO BE MISSED

- Notre-Dame
- Ste.-Chapelle
- Square du Vert Galant
- La Conciergerie
- Marché aux Fleurs
- Mémorial de la Déportation
- Hôtel de Jassaud (Île St.-Louis)
- Hôtel de Lauzun (Île St.-Louis)

FEARSOME FLOODS

Note the plates with flood markings, circa 1910, which appear on various buildings near the Seine. These record the flood level during one of the city's most devastating floods. ∎

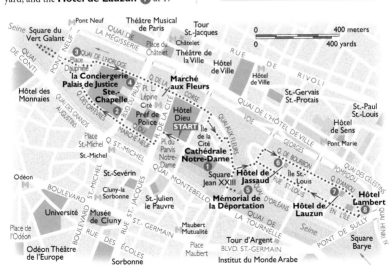

Ste.-Chapelle

A TRUE JEWEL IN THE HEART OF PARIS, STE.-CHAPELLE is a glorious example of the high Gothic style and universally recognized as a masterpiece of architecture and stained glass.

Ste.-Chapelle

- Map p. 46
- 4 boulevard du Palais, Île de la Cité
- 01 53 73 78 51
- $$
- Métro: Cité, St.-Michel, Châtelet

Saint Louis (King Louis IX) had this ephemeral chapel constructed in just six years, from 1242 to 1248, and it is generally attributed to Pierre de Montreuil (who died in 1267). It is essentially an enormous reliquary, built to house the Crown of Thorns, which Louis had purchased from the Emperor of Constantinople, Baldwin II, in 1239.

Although Louis was undoubtedly a religious man—he was canonized 27 years after his death—his motives for constructing Ste.-Chapelle were decidedly political. Louis was just 12 years old when his father, Louis VIII, died. His mother, Blanche de Castille, ruled as regent until his majority. His ascension to the throne was

The windows of the upper chapel are a pictorial Bible portraying scenes from the Old and New Testaments.

contested, and in a period when kings ruled by divine right, the Crown of Thorns—the most prized religious relic of all—represented a potent symbol for Louis's claim to the throne. Indeed, it was such an important relic (although never officially recognized by the Vatican) that it cost three times more than the construction of Ste.-Chapelle itself. The crown was brought to France and placed in the church in a magnificent reliquary, which disappeared during the Revolution; most of the relics, however, were saved, and are now held in the Treasury of Notre-Dame (see p. 51).

LOWER CHAPEL

The spectacular chapel is divided into two levels: the dark, richly decorated lower chapel, reserved for the palace servants, and the stunning upper chapel, used exclusively by the royal family, visiting dignitaries, and heads of state. The vibrant red and blue colors in the lower chapel date from the 19th century when attempts were made to reproduce the original medieval decoration. The windows are small because the lower chapel supports the upper chapel. Unfortunately, the 14th- and 15th-century tombstones on the chapel's floor have

The lower chapel suffered badly during the Revolution, but was later enthusiastically restored by Haussmann's medievalists.

been worn almost bare by nearly 900,000 annual visitors.

UPPER CHAPEL

The effect on entering the upper chapel is breathtaking. The walls are a mosaic of colored light that streams in through the 50-foot-high (15 m) windows. The 15 stained-glass windows in this chapel are the oldest in Paris, with two-thirds of them dating from the 13th century; together, they include over 1,100 scenes. With the exception of the three windows behind the altar (St. John the Evangelist, the Passion of Christ, and St. John the Baptist), and the window immediately to the right on entering the chapel (which recounts the story of the relics), all the others depict scenes from the Old Testament.

The style of the **Rose Window** is markedly different from the others; made in 1485 (200 years later than the other windows), it represents the Apocalypse. It's a good idea to bring along binoculars for viewing the upper windows.

The windows barely escaped destruction during the Revolution, when the church was deconsecrated. For 35 years, from 1802 to 1837, the chapel was converted into a warehouse for archives; the bottom 15 feet (4.5 m) of each window were removed, and filing cabinets rose 25 feet (7.5 m) up the walls. This section of the windows was eventually remade as exact copies of the originals, but mistakes were inevitably made.

SCULPTURES

The sculptures in Ste.-Chapelle depict the 12 Apostles, the spiritual pillars of the church, each placed on one of the structural pillars of the chapel. The two alcoves on either side of the chapel were reserved for King Louis (on the left) and his mother (on the right). Louis's wife, Queen Marguerite, overshadowed by her mother-in-law, presumably sat with her husband. The king entered through the main doors, which led directly to the royal apartments in the Conciergerie. ■

Stained glass

In medieval times, as in the present, the church leaders were responsible for religious education. During the golden age of stained glass—the 12th and 13th centuries—the church building itself, through its windows and statuary, transmitted this knowledge. The stained-glass windows functioned as immense picture books from which a mostly illiterate population could "read" the biblical stories. The scenes are designed to be read from left to right, and bottom to top.

Stained glass can be traced to ancient times; clear glass was used in Roman baths, and they were experts in making colored-glass vases and cups. The technique of using colored glass and lead together appeared later. Stained-glass windows were not an important element of Romanesque architecture; with the development of the Gothic rib-vaulted roof, walls no longer carried the vertical thrust of the building, allowing builders to create large openings between the pillars that could be filled with stained glass.

The basic techniques for making stained-glass windows have changed little: Colored and clear glass are cut to a pattern, then painted with *grisaille* (iron oxide) before being baked in a kiln. Then the pieces are assembled with lead strips to create mosaics. In the 12th and 13th centuries, a limited number of colors were used, and glassmakers juxtaposed the bright reds and blues to create a variety of jewel-like colors, achieving the unique style seen in many Gothic churches. By the mid-15th century, glassmakers began to imitate wall and easel painting by modeling forms, introducing a three-dimensional effect. The glass was still beautiful, but it had lost some of its essential nature; it no longer filtered a mosaic of brilliant colors, but became more like a semi-opaque reproduction of a canvas on glass. ■

Ste.-Chapelle is renowned for its exquisite stained glass.

STAINED GLASS DURING THE WARS
During both World Wars, all the stained-glass windows in Ste.-Chapelle and Notre-Dame were dismantled and stored safely out of harm's way. ■

La Conciergerie

La Conciergerie

 Map p. 46

✉ 1 quai de l'Horloge,
Île de la Cité

☎ 01 53 73 78 50

$ $

Métro: Cité, St.-
Michel, Châtelet

MEDIEVAL FIREPLACES

Each of the four huge fireplaces in the medieval kitchens had a specific function: One was for soups, another for stews, and a third for meat. No one is sure about the fourth one. ■

The 14th-century public clock on the Tour de l'Horloge (Palais de Justice) is the city's oldest.

THE CONCIERGERIE WAS PART OF THE ROYAL PALACE FROM the 10th century to 1378, before it became the center of the Paris judicial system. Philippe IV (R.1285–1314) constructed most of the medieval buildings standing today, although they were extensively renovated in the 19th century. After Charles V moved the royal residence to the Louvre Palace (see p. 124), he appointed a concierge, or keeper, to act as his steward, and the complex became a prison. The 13th-century crenelated Tour Bonbec (meaning "chatter tower") was once used as a torture chamber. Although it is no longer a prison, people are still held in custody here—away from the tourist circuit.

MEDIEVAL SECULAR ARCHITECTURE

You will enter the impressive **Salle des Gens d'Armes,** one of the largest—and finest—examples of medieval secular architecture, across the courtyard from the main entrance on Quai de l'Horloge. Its name means men at arms, and the word *gendarmes* (police) is derived from it. This hall served as the refectory for the 2,000 palace staff. Rue de Paris, at the far western end of this room, contained prison cells and is named for the executioner, who was traditionally known as

Monsieur de Paris. The royal banquet hall upstairs burned down and was reconstructed in 1622 as the **Salles des Pas Perdus.** It is now a large lobby for lawyers and clients awaiting their turn in the courts.

REVOLUTIONARY TRIBUNAL

During the Revolution, especially during the Reign of Terror, the Revolutionary Tribunal sentenced more than 2,700 people to die under the so-called democratic blade of the guillotine (previously, the nobility died by the blade of the sword; common criminals were whipped, sulfur was placed on their open wounds, then they were hanged, drawn, and quartered). Incarceration here did not follow the new democracy, however. Walk upstairs to see the three reconstructed cells, which illustrate what money could buy: The *pailleux*, or penniless prisoners, slept on straw on the floor; *à la pistole* meant real beds; while prisoners of rank had their own furniture and servants. Marie-Antoinette's cell has been reconstructed, and a chapel of atonement now stands on part of the original cell. Ironically, her accusers, Maximilien Robespierre and Georges Danton, followed her to prison and then the guillotine within a few months. ■

Medieval scholars taught in Latin—hence the name of the Latin Quarter, the seat of French university life for centuries. It still is, with the Sorbonne and the Collège de France, dozens of bookshops, libraries, cafés, and publishers.

Quartier Latin

Stained glass in St.-Étienne-du-Mont Church

Quartier Latin

SINCE THE FOUNDING OF THE SORBONNE IN THE 13TH CENTURY, THE Quartier Latin (Latin Quarter) has been synonymous with university life, and was once the greatest seat of learning in Europe. The area's very name is derived from medieval university instruction being solely in Low Latin. Although the cobblestones once lining the Boul'Mich were symbolically torn out by rebellious students during the uprisings in May 1968, the area is still in perpetual motion, with students milling about in the streets and cafés, or browsing in the Gibert Jeune bookshop.

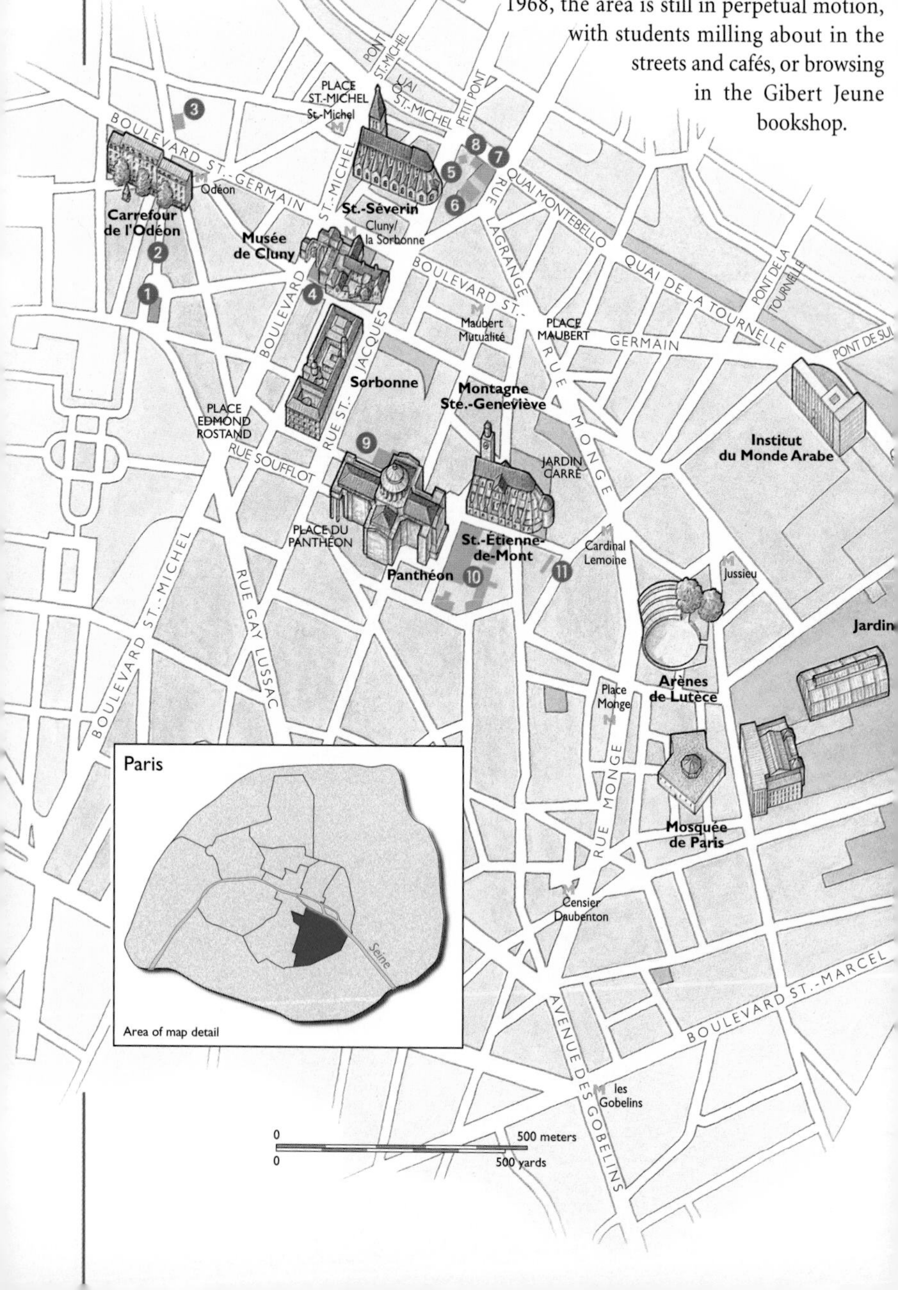

BOULEVARD ST.-GERMAIN

PLACE ST.-MICHEL
St.-Michel

Carrefour de l'Odéon

Odéon

St.-Séverin

Musée de Cluny

Cluny/ la Sorbonne

QUAI ST.-MICHEL

PETIT PONT

QUAI MONTEBELLO

RUE LAGRANGE

QUAI DE LA TOURNELLE

PONT DE LA TOURNELLE

PONT DE SUI

BOULEVARD ST.-GERMAIN

Maubert Mutualité

PLACE MAUBERT

ST.-MICHEL

RUE ST.-JACQUES

BOULEVARD ST.-GERMAIN

Sorbonne

Montagne Ste.-Geneviève

RUE MONGE

Institut du Monde Arabe

PLACE EDMOND ROSTAND

RUE SOUFFLOT

JARDIN CARRÉ

JARDIN

PLACE DU PANTHÉON

St.-Étienne-de-Mont

Cardinal Lemoine

Jussieu

Panthéon

BOULEVARD ST.-MICHEL

RUE GAY LUSSAC

Place Monge

Arènes de Lutèce

Paris

Area of map detail

Seine

RUE MONGE

Mosquée de Paris

Censier Daubenton

AVENUE DES GOBELINS

les Gobelins

BOULEVARD ST.-MARCEL

0   500 meters
0   500 yards

The Latin Quarter encompasses the neighborhoods around St.-Séverin, Montagne Ste.-Geneviève, and Place St.-Michel, with its fountain of the saint slaying a dragon. If it is your first visit to the area, try not to approach the Latin Quarter from the commercial Boulevard St.-Michel, as the fast-food restaurants and clothing outlets detract from the area's mythical status. Instead, enter across the quays from Notre-Dame, through the Square Viviani, where stone vestiges from the cathedral lie scattered through the grounds.

Next to the square is the largely touristy Shakespeare & Company, not to be confused with the former avant-garde publishing house on Rue de l'Odéon owned by Sylvia Beach (see p. 76), who first published James Joyce's *Ulysses*. In keeping with the literary tradition of the Latin Quarter, some streets—such as Rue de la Parcheminerie (originally Rue des Escrivains, or Street of Writers)—reflect this in their names, although not all do; the nearby Rue de Bièvre, for example, was named for the arm of the river that flowed through the quarter to the Seine.

The Latin Quarter—an old district with new ideas

The Latin Quarter is one of Paris's more historic areas. Here, you can wend your way past Roman vestiges, such as the Arènes de Lutèce amphitheater (see p. 76), or the third-century baths (now part of the Musée National du Moyen Âge et des Thermes de Cluny; see pp. 66–67), up to Montagne Ste.-Geneviève, named after the city's patron saint. Saint Geneviève was instrumental in unifying Paris (see p. 18), and her importance is reflected in the area, particularly around the St.-Étienne-du-Mont Church, which has the only surviving rood screen in Paris. The church stands where the basilica of St.-Pierre-St.-Paul, built to commemorate the unity of France, was once located. Next door is the Panthéon (see p. 69), originally commissioned to be a church for Saint Geneviève, but transformed during the Revolution into a temple for "great men" (and a token woman, physicist Marie Curie).

Down the other side of the hill, to the east, lies the café-lined Place de la Contrescarpe (named after the embankments of Philippe-Auguste's fortifications), and the Rue Mouffetard, one of the oldest streets, which has a great open-air market (*Closed Mon.*).

Few visitors venture farther east, where Paris's principal mosque (see p. 74) lies opposite the Jardin des Plantes (see pp. 70–71). The intriguing Institut du Monde Arabe (Arab Cultural Institute; see p. 75) overlooks the Seine, and the Tino Rossi open-air sculpture garden lines the quay (see p. 205). ■

QUARTIER LATIN

1. Odéon-Théâtre de l'Europe
2. Site of former Sylvia Beach bookstore (Shakespeare & Company), 12 Rue de l'Odéon
3. Café Procope
4. Gallo-Roman baths
5. Caveau des Oubliettes
6. St.-Julien-le-Pauvre
7. Square Viviani
8. Shakespeare & Company bookstore, Rue de la Bûcherie
9. Bibliothèque St.-Geneviève
10. Lycée Henri IV
11. Philippe-Auguste Wall

St.-Séverin & Montagne Ste.-Geneviève areas

GALLSTONE OPERATION

The first gallstone operation was performed in the burial grounds near St.-Séverin Church in 1474. Louis XI offered an archer freedom from his death sentence if he agreed to undergo an experimental operation. The operation was a success, and the archer was freed. ■

THE ST.-SÉVERIN AND STE.-GENEVIÈVE NEIGHBORHOODS are among the oldest areas in Paris, with such medieval streets as Rue du Fouarre and Rue Galande. The former was named for the *fouarre* or hay on which students would sit while listening to lectures.

ST.-SÉVERIN AREA

One of the most famous historic figures of this area was the 12th-century philosopher and theologian Pierre Abélard (1079–1142). Following his rift with the canons for challenging monastic discipline, Abélard was ousted from the Notre-Dame cloister. He moved to the Left Bank, taking 3,000 students with him. (See p. 114 for an account of his famed love affair with Héloïse.)

Rue Galande was lined with infamous cabarets during the 18th century. The **Caveau des Oubliettes** was one of the rare spots where only old French songs were featured; now jazz and country have been added to the repertoire, and La Guillotine pub on the ground floor is a far cry from the old-style cabaret. But the guillotine on which Kennedy placed his head when he visited in 1960 is still on display (a remnant of the museum of torture that was once here).

St.-Julien-le-Pauvre

Off Rue Galande is St.-Julien-le-Pauvre. One of the three oldest churches in Paris, it was built between 1165 and 1220. Originally a stopping point for travelers en route to the famous pilgrimage site of Santiago de Compostela in Spain, during the later Middle Ages rowdy student assemblies gathered here. Its simple Gothic style bears traces of the Romanesque period, and the beautiful chancel is enclosed by a wooden iconostasis (icon screen) and two beautifully carved pillars.

Square Viviani & Église St.-Séverin

Next door, the lovely Square Viviani has a superb view of Notre-Dame, a contemporary fountain inspired by Saint Julien, and a false acacia tree (circa 1601) lying against a ruined stone buttress. Don't miss the Flamboyant Gothic **St.-Séverin Church,** one of the most beautiful in Paris, with its spiraling vaults, softly lit against brilliant stained glass in the apse.

MONTAGNE STE.-GENEVIÈVE AREA

The area around Montagne Ste.-Geneviève (see p. 76), the Roman city mirroring the Gallo-Roman settlement on the Île de la Cité, is filled with winding streets and escarpments climbing up the hill.

Well-preserved vestiges of the **Gallo-Roman baths** can be found at the corner of Rue des Écoles and Boulevard St.-Michel. Circle around them to the east, up Rue de Cluny and past Square Paul-Painlevé separating the **Musée de Cluny** (see pp. 66–67) and the **Sorbonne** (see p. 68). On the corner of Rue des Écoles and Rue de la Sorbonne stood a convent, where the great poet and rogue François Villon grew up; he assassinated a priest in 1455 and was subsequently banished from Paris. The name Sorbonne is used interchangeably with the Université de Paris, but is actually the name of the most famous of its colleges. Farther up Rue St.-Jacques is the **Panthéon**

(see p. 69), dating from 1754.

On the north side of the Place du Panthéon is the **Bibliothèque Ste.-Geneviève**—the only great monastic library in Paris spared during the Revolution. It has a fine collection of medieval manuscripts. Behind the Panthéon is one of Paris's more intriguing churches,

St.-Étienne-du-Mont (see p. 74). Across the street is the prestigious **Lycée Henri IV,** the site of the sixth-century basilica built by Clovis following his victory over the Visigoths (later, the Abbey of Ste.-Geneviève). Down the street on Rue Clovis is a section of the **Philippe-Auguste Wall** (see p. 19). ∎

The intricate rood screen in St.-Étienne-du-Mont is extremely rare, since almost all others in France were destroyed in the 17th century.

The four aisles of the Panthéon radiate from the center in the form of a Greek cross.

Musée de Cluny

THE MUSÉE NATIONAL DU MOYEN ÂGE ET DES THERMES DE Cluny is actually two museums in one: the 15th-century Hôtel de Cluny, which houses the medieval collections and the world-famous "Lady with the Unicorn" tapestries; and the third-century baths, the oldest and most complete vestiges of the Roman occupation in Paris.

Musée de Cluny

- Map p. 62
- 6 place Paul-Painlevé
- 01 53 73 78 00
- Closed Tues.
- $$
- Métro: St.-Michel, Odéon

HÔTEL DE CLUNY & BATHS

The medieval building, constructed between 1480 and 1510 as a temporary residence for visiting religious dignitaries from the wealthy Abbey of Cluny, is one of the oldest surviving examples of civil architecture in Paris. The building stands around a cobblestone courtyard, and visitors used to enter through the exterior, turreted staircase—a distinguishing feature of well-to-do medieval homes.

What is unique about Cluny is that the abbots chose to build their mansion on land abutting the ruins of a Gallo-Roman bath, one of three that existed during the second and third centuries in what was then Lutetia.

The baths contained three large rooms: the *caldarium* (hot room), now in ruins; the *tepidarium* (warm room), which had bathtubs in various alcoves; and the *frigidarium* (cold room). All were once lined with magnificent mosaics. The walls and floors of the caldarium were heated by a system of lead and terra-cotta pipes that were fed from furnaces in the cellars. The 45-foot-high (13.5 m) frigidarium is intact and is now used as a venue for medieval music concerts. The room was so well designed that even in the hottest days of summer, this immense hall remains cool. The **underground vaults,** which once housed the furnaces for heating the baths, can be visited on certain days (inquire at the entrance).

MEDIEVAL COLLECTIONS

The first few rooms are devoted to tapestries, metalwork, and chests. These lead to the Roman baths via Room VIII, which houses the spectacular **King's Gallery**—21 of the 28 heads that once stood atop the figures lining the front of Notre-Dame (see pp. 48–53). Although the sculptures represent biblical figures, they were mistaken for the kings of France during the Revolution, and the heads were decapitated and left among the debris in front of the church. Historians had given up hope of finding these heads when they turned up in 1977 during excavations underneath a bank in the ninth arrondissement. This gallery is now the highlight of the room, which also displays Romanesque sculptures. The oldest sculpture in Paris, the "Pilier des Nautes" ("Boatmen's Pillar"), dating from the first century A.D., stands in a corner of the next room, near the vast frigidarium.

The upper floor contains a collection of precious metalwork, including the "Golden Rose of Basel," a delicate, wrought-iron piece made in 1330, and several exceptional altarpieces.

Room XIII, a specially designed rotunda, displays the most famous works in the museum, the "Lady with the Unicorn" tapestries (circa 15th century, southern Netherlands). Five of the pieces are allegories of the senses, while the sixth tapestry carries the mysterious motto, "To my sole desire," believed

Tapestries

In medieval Europe, tapestries developed as a way to cover cold, drafty, stone walls. They were easily transported and served to decorate and capture heat in châteaus and churches. They usually depicted moral, historical, floral, and biblical themes, and displayed a person's wealth through their sumptuous fabrics and elaborate designs.

The earliest surviving tapestry from a Paris workshop is the great set of hangings known as the "Apocalypse of Angers" (circa 1375). After the French defeat at Agincourt, Arras became the center of tapestry weaving, largely because of the extravagant patronage of the Burgundian dukes. In the 17th century, the tapestry industry developed once again in Paris with the Gobelins Manufacture, which produced panels of unprecedented technical perfection. ■

"To my sole desire" is the enigmatic inscription on one of the six unicorn tapestries in the Musée de Cluny collection. The series, depicting a maiden and a unicorn, are believed to be allegories of the senses.

to illustrate the idea of free choice. The unicorn motif, which was very popular in medieval imagery, symbolized chastity and purity; while the unicorn would fight ferociously when cornered or attacked, it could be tamed by a virgin's touch.

The museum plans to reland-scape the gardens in front and the Square Paul-Painlevé, trans-forming them into an authentic medieval garden. ■

The Sorbonne & the Collège de France

The Sorbonne

- 🗺 Map p. 62
- ✉ 47 rue des Écoles
- ☎ 01 40 46 22 11
- 🕐 By appointment only
- Ⓜ Métro: St.-Michel, Maubert Mutualité

Collège de France

- 🗺 Map p. 62
- ✉ 11 place Marcellin Berthelot
- ☎ 01 44 27 12 11
- 🕐 Courtyard open to the public
- Ⓜ Métro: St.-Michel, Maubert Mutualité

The courtyard of the Sorbonne is dominated by Lemercier's 17th-century domed chapel.

THE SORBONNE UNIVERSITY WAS LIKE A QUASI-STATE within a state for centuries, playing a major political role, while the Collège de France gave priority to educational freedom.

THE SORBONNE

The Sorbonne was founded in 1253 as a residence hall for 16 theology students, and eventually became a major center for religious education.

Strikes have been a feature of the Sorbonne since its earliest days. In 1231 the institution went on strike for two years, demanding (and winning) independence from the bishops of Paris. Some 750 years later, the violence that swept through the Latin Quarter in May 1968 was triggered by the arrest of student leaders from this same institution, protesting against a rigid, repressive, and overcrowded university system. Today, the courtyard is open to the public; the chapel, which houses the tomb of Cardinal Richelieu (see p. 21), can be visited during temporary exhibitions and on December 4, the anniversary of Richelieu's death.

COLLÈGE DE FRANCE

The Collège de France is a unique and unorthodox institution in France. In 1530 it allowed scholars to study Hebrew, Greek, and mathematics, and gave classes in the French language.

The institution's spirit of educational freedom persists to this day: An average 5,000 auditors follow the diverse lectures given by one of the 52 professors. Classes are free, there are no prerequisites, no academic credits are given, and the college awards no diplomas. Instead, anyone, from students to the merely curious, can attend lectures on topics ranging from molecular biology to Byzantine civilization. ∎

The Panthéon

THE PANTHÉON, NOW A SHRINE "TO DISTINGUISHED MEN from a grateful nation," was constructed by Louis XV. In 1744 the king fell ill and vowed to construct a new church dedicated to Sainte-Geneviève, if she would come to his aid. He recovered, and in 1754 commissioned Jacques Germain Soufflot to build a vast church that would "combine Greek beauty with Gothic space and light."

The Panthéon
- Map p. 62
- place du Panthéon
- 01 44 32 18 00
- $$
- Métro: Cardinal Lemoine

Soufflot's immense structure was an unprecedented feat of engineering. The subsoil was honeycombed with wells and quarries that required considerable shoring up. The first stone was laid in 1764 in the king's presence, although the church was only completed in 1790—an unfortunate date, as the new government abolished all monastic orders that year. It was then declared to be a "temple to the Nation," and author Voltaire, philosopher Jean-Jacques Rousseau, and politician Honoré Mirabeau were buried there. It became a church again several times during the 19th century, but was finally made into a mortuary for French heroes in 1885 during the state funeral for Victor Hugo (see sidebar below). You can see the tombs of novelist Émile Zola (1830–1902),

Resistance leader Jean Moulin (1899–1943), and physicist Marie Curie (1859–1906) within the walls of this marble-lined monument. ■

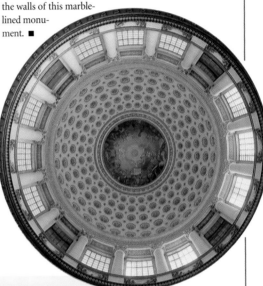

Victor Hugo

Victor Hugo was France's greatest 19th-century literary icon, becoming nearly emblematic of the century itself. He was the closest France ever came to producing a writer whose stature could be compared to that of Homer, Shakespeare, or Dante, and his works were said to have helped trigger revolutions—notably the 1830 Revolution (see p. 25). His plays revolutionized French theater, knocking it out of the fettered forms of Corneille and Racine.

He turned to politics, but politics turned on him—after trying to foil Napoleon III's coup in 1851, Hugo dodged arrest, and was subsequently exiled for 18 years, returning in 1870.

A half million people poured into the streets of Paris to mourn when he died in 1885. His body, after lying in state at the Arc de Triomphe, was taken to the Panthéon in a pauper's hearse as a sign of solidarity with the common man. Ironically, Hugo always detested the Panthéon, comparing it to sponge cake. ■

The dome of the Panthéon actually consists of three domes, one inside the other. The inner dome is decorated by Antoine Gros's painting "Apotheosis of Sainte Geneviève."

Jardin des Plantes

Jardin des Plantes

- Map p. 62
- 36 rue Geoffroy-St.-Hilaire. Main entrance: 57 rue Cuvier
- 01 40 79 30 00
- Closed Tues.
- $$
- Métro: Austerlitz, Jussieu

THE OLDEST GARDEN IN PARIS WAS NOT DESIGNED FOR the pleasure of its inhabitants, but as a botanical research garden for botanists, doctors, and pharmacists. It was created in 1635 as the royal medicinal garden for Louis XIII, but came into its own in 1739, when naturalist Georges Buffon was appointed director. His immense ambition was to gather all forms of nature together in one spot. The garden then became a huge laboratory, and all the major French naturalists worked here; many have been honored with street names nearby. The garden became the natural history museum in 1793, and over the next 30 years an assortment of animals was introduced.

The glass-roofed **Grande Galerie de l'Evolution** of the Natural History Museum recounts the story of man's role in the evolution of life.

MUSÉUM NATIONAL D'HISTOIRE NATURELLE

By 1965, the crumbling zoology gallery was closed and remained a dusty hulk until 1994, when it finally reopened after a major renovation project. The results are spectacular: Visitors enter the dramatically lit **Grande Galerie de l'Évolution,** a sort of giant Noah's Ark of mounted animals parading down the center of the building. On the lower floor, marine animals are suspended as if still swimming in the sea; the 54-foot (16.5 m) skeleton of a whale hangs in midair. Two floors of galleries upstairs explore evolution, the environment, and pollution. The museum's facelift retained some of the existing metal-frame structure, which is brilliantly incorporated into the new design. A discovery room introduces fossils and the natural sciences to children under 12, while older kids can explore displays in the science laboratory.

THE GARDENS

Nearby are two impressive hot-houses, constructed in 1834. The **Australian House** contains Mediterranean and Australian plants such as ferns, ficus, and banana trees, while the **Mexican House** includes several thousand species of cactuses and succulents, as well as tropical plants from southern Africa and Madagascar.

Three majestic avenues, lined with trees, lead elegantly away from the museum past a series of meticulously planted flower beds. Elsewhere, the geometric formality gives way to a less rigid layout. To the north lies the Ménagerie and an 18th-century labyrinth, which leads to a bronze gazebo called the

different species of plants, classified by region, flourish in this lush environment.

THE MÉNAGERIE

This is one of the oldest zoos in the world. It opened in 1794 with animals from the royal collections, and became so popular by 1827 that the arrival of a giraffe—the first ever on French soil—was a major event of the year, drawing 600,000 Parisians. Today, the rustic quarters have an undeniable charm

Ménagerie
- Map p. 62
- 57 rue Cuvier
- $$

Gloriette de Buffon, the oldest metallic structure in Paris (circa 1786). One of the oldest trees in Paris, a great cedar planted in 1734, stands on the slope of the labyrinth. Nearby is the **Alpine Garden** (*closed Oct.–Feb.*). Not easy to find, this discreet haven is buried almost 10 feet (3 m) lower than the rest of the Jardin des Plantes to provide a more varied terrain. The gardeners have some-how created a mysterious micro-climate of small valleys and hills in the garden, where the temperature can vary as much as 35°F from one spot to another. Two thousand

for visitors used to more modern facilities. Recently, the 12-acre (5 ha) zoo was saved from the claws of real estate developers by being classified a historical monument. The drawback, however, is that nothing can be changed from the original design; even renovations intended to bring in more modern zookeeping methods are ruled out. This, combined with a lack of funds, means that some of the buildings are sadly dilapidated. The curators have taken this in their stride, specializing instead on the smaller primates, reptiles, birds of prey, and a few tigers. ■

The painter Henri Rousseau (1844–1910) came to the Natural History Museum's greenhouses to sketch the lush vegetation and animals depicted in his works.

Subterranean Paris

Paris has an invisible underground life that is just as active as the visible one above ground. Although the catacombs are one of the most frequently visited underground sites (see Denfert-Rochereau, p. 201), there are lesser known crypts in unexpected places—for example, beneath the July Column at Place de la Bastille (see p. 119), where victims from the 1830 and 1840 revolutions are buried, or under the St.-Sulpice Church (see p. 83). The city also has sewer tours; a nuclear-fallout shelter underneath the Sorbonne; a French Resistance hideout underneath that; and many underground quarries, rivers, canals, and even a lake (beneath Place de l'Opéra). Lastly, there are the streamlined Métro and RER, whose rubber tires whoosh from station to station, sometimes surfacing molelike from underground tunnels into the light, but always returning to the dark recesses underground.

Quarries, sewers, pipes, & water

Paris was built with gypsum and limestone extracted from its subsoil. The Left Bank alone has 186 miles (299 km) of underground tunnels (not open to the public). However, intensive mining has caused subsidence, and although the quarries are no longer exploited and many buildings are reinforced by pilings, several houses are collapsing in areas like Montmartre. (Ironically, this has helped to spare the area from overdevelopment.) Efforts to shore up the limestone quarries are under way, and an inspection team constantly monitors the limestone for fissures and flaws.

If you take a tour of the sewers (see p. 165), you will enter the most malodorous of Paris's museums. You can learn about sewer- and water-treatment systems, Monsieur Poubelle (for whom the French garbage can is named), and purification equipment. Sewers (égouts) generally run down the middle of streets, although on broader avenues they run underneath the sidewalks. These tunnels

Opposite top: Construction of the Métro's first line began circa 1900. Now there are 14 lines crisscrossing the capital.

feature plaques corresponding to the streets above. Larger mains contain pipes for drinking and industrial-use water; pneumatic tubes once used by the post office for the delivery of letters and light packages—two are still in use today; telephone and telegraph cables; traffic-signal cables; and pipes for compressed air.

The city's first springwater-fed public fountain opened in 1184, but it was Baron Haussmann (see p. 160) who introduced the modern system. In 1852 his right-hand man, Eugène Belgrand, began diverting springs that currently supply half the city with its drinking water. Inhabitants also rely on water pumped from the Seine and Marne Rivers. The two-tiered, part subterranean, Montsouris Reservoir has a capacity of 3.25 million cubic feet (94 million liters) and supplies some of eastern Paris with water. To ensure that the reservoir supply is fresh enough for consumption, trout swim in the turquoise waters.

The Métro

The Métro is the fastest way to get around the city; its speed and design make Paris seem as if it could fit into the palm of your hand. Its stops function as reference points for the city. When construction on the Métro began during the 19th century, bones, teeth, and tusks of mammoths were found near the Montmartre cemetery and under Square Montholon. From the start, the Métro was designed for *intra muras* Paris only, and the trains deliberately traveled on the right so they could never be hooked up to trains already in existence that went outside the city.

The Métro has well over 300 stations; the busiest is St.-Lazare, the deepest is Abbesses, and the one with the most intersecting lines is République. In the late 1960s, the Louvre station was transformed with copies of works from the museum, and the vogue for theme-based stations took off.

Don't miss the replicas from the nearby Musée Rodin at the Varenne station; illustrations of the storming of the prison at the Bastille station; exhibits of engineering feats at Arts et Métiers; and the art nouveau entrances at Porte Dauphine and Abbesses. ■

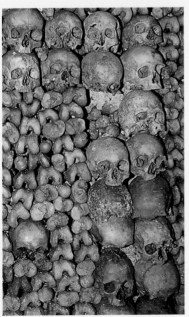

**Above: Hector Guimard's art nouveau
entrance at Porte Dauphine
Left: In the early 19th century, the bones
and skulls of the catacombs were arranged
into neat piles fit for public viewing.**

More places to visit in the Quartier Latin

ST.-ÉTIENNE-DU-MONT

St.-Étienne-du-Mont is not one of the best known churches in Paris, yet it is one of the most monumental and unusual. The church, with its highly original, three-tiered facade and asymmetrical interior, has the only remaining rood screen (a crucifix supported on a screen separating the nave from the chancel) in Paris; the tombs of Jean Racine and Blaise Pascal; an elaborate organ loft; a baroque pulpit supported by a figure of Samson; and the reliquary of Sainte Geneviève in an elaborate chapel.

According to legend, one of Geneviève's miracles included restoring her mother's sight by washing her eyes with well water; this is depicted in one of the church's stained-glass windows. Until the French Revolution (when the relics were melted down and the saint's remains burned on the Place de la Grève), the jewel-studded reliquary was a source of great veneration. In times of floods and epidemics, it was carried in a flower-strewn procession to Notre-Dame after a day of atonement.

The Renaissance rood screen, flanked by two openwork spiral staircases, is magnificent. The cloister's main gallery, the Chapelle des Catéchismes (through the sacristy), is lined with magnificent 16th- and 17th-century stained-glass windows.

🅰 Map p. 62 ✉ place Ste.-Geneviève ☎ 01 43 54 11 79 🕐 Closed Mon., Tues.–Sun. noon–4 p.m. and noon–2 p.m. Tues.–Sun. (July & Aug. only) 🚇 Métro: Cardinal Lemoine

MOSQUÉE DE PARIS

Paris's principal mosque for the Algerian-dominated Muslim community encompasses a religious center, marked by a striking green-and-white minaret jutting 85 feet (26 m) into the air; the Institut d'Études Musulmanes, where Arabo-Islamic language and culture are taught; and the beautiful Moorish tearoom, restaurant, and Turkish baths.

Inaugurated in 1926 to commemorate the Muslim war effort, the mosque was built by Charles Heubès, Robert Fournez, and Maurice Mantout. The most gifted Tunisian, Moroccan, and Algerian craftsmen were summoned

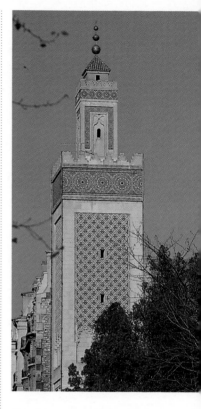

The striking square minaret of the Mosquée de Paris overlooks the handsome courtyard below.

to layer the edifice with lovely marble, tiles, mosaics, damask, cedarwood, and fountains made of porphyry. The Grand Patio inside the mosque was inspired by the Alhambra in Granada, Spain, and features woodwork in cedar and eucalyptus, a mosaic frieze bearing verses of the Koran, and a beautiful fountain. The outdoor tearoom, where you can drink mint tea, is perfect on a hot, sunny day.

🅰 Map p. 62 ✉ place du Puits-de-l'Ermite or 39 rue Geoffroy-St.-Hilaire (tearoom, Turkish baths, restaurant, boutique) ☎ 01 45 35 97 33 🕐 Closed during Muslim holidays (Ramadan varies from year to year, call for more information) 🚇 Métro: Censier Daubenton

INSTITUT DU MONDE ARABE

Inaugurated in 1987, the steel-and-glass Institut du Monde Arabe is a joint Franco-Arab project designed to encourage cultural links between the West and the Arab world. Twenty Arab states participated in this building, which includes permanent and temporary exhibition areas, a library, a bookstore, conference rooms, an auditorium, and a spectacular rooftop restaurant and café (the view alone is worth the trip).

The widely acclaimed architecture is meant to symbolize a crossroads: The northern or "Western" side facing the Seine is a sleek, transparent wall, while the inner, enclosed courtyard reflects ancient Arab influence through the innovative, high-tech reinterpretation of the traditional *moucharaby* (carved wooden screens). The 1,600 aluminum prisms open and close electronically to regulate the

Shakespeare and Company (see p. 257) bears no relation to Sylvia Beach's legendary bookstore, but still draws visitors seeking literary enlightenment.

amount of sunlight streaming into the building. The permanent collection occupies three floors and showcases the many scientific and cultural breakthroughs achieved by Arab scientists and astronomers.

🅜 Map p. 62　✉ 1 rue des Fossés St.-Bernard　☎ 01 40 51 38 38　⏀ Closed Mon.　§ $　🅜 Métro: Jussieu, Cardinal Lemoine, Sully-Morland

CARREFOUR DE L'ODÉON

Near the statue of the revolutionary leader Georges Jacques Danton (marking the site of his former home, from which he was arrested in March 1794 and later guillotined), the

Carrefour de l'Odéon is a busy crossroads that stretches south to the **Odéon-Théâtre de l'Europe,** and north to the famous **Café Procope**—the oldest café in Paris (*13 Rue de l'Ancienne-Comédie, Tel 01 40 46 79 00*). Here, Jean le Rond d'Alembert and Denis Diderot began work on their famous *Encyclopédie* in 1727, and Benjamin Franklin met with Louis XVI to draw up the agreement for the budding American Republic.

Rue de l'Ancienne-Comédie continues to the bustling Rue St.-André des Arts. The beautiful, neoclassic Odéon-Théâtre de l'Europe is best viewed from its entrance at the Place de l'Odéon. It was here that Pierre Beaumarchais's *Mariage de Figaro* was first performed in 1784; considered subversive, the play cost Beaumarchais a year's imprisonment.

Down the street, at 12 Rue de l'Odéon, was Sylvia Beach's bookstore and lending library, the famous **Shakespeare and Company,** once the home of the Left Bank expatriate American literary community after 1920. Beach was the first to publish the complete version of Irish writer James Joyce's *Ulysses* in 1922, launching the literary event of the decade and nearly making her bankrupt in the process. Despite Joyce's subsequent sale of the book to Random House for a $45,000 advance in 1932, he never offered her any of the profits. Gertrude Stein was one of the first to subscribe to Beach's lending library, but was so appalled by the publication of *Ulysses,*

The Roman arena—once a circus, now a haven of peace and quiet

which she considered obscene, that she informed Beach that she would thereafter borrow solely from the American Library on the Right Bank. (The current bookstore of the same name is at 37 Rue de la Bûcherie.)

🚇 Métro: Odéon

ARÈNES DE LUTÈCE

Hidden away behind the modern buildings of the Jussieu University are the vestiges of the Lutetia Arena, a second-century Roman amphitheater designed to seat 15,000 spectators, the second largest in Gaul. The Romans used the natural slope of what is now called Montagne Ste.-Geneviève (see pp. 64–65) for the 35 tiers of stone seats and placed the stage to the east, where performers would receive the last rays of the setting sun.

Few of the original stones remain: The theater eroded away after Parisians carted off handy building materials to build the walls of the Île de la Cité, and over the centuries the arena gradually filled in with debris. By the 19th century, most people believed that the ancient arena was more legend than reality, but Baron Haussmann uncovered the substructure of the arena when he extended Rue Monge in 1869. True to form, he dug up and destroyed about two-thirds of the arena so that a bus depot could use the grounds. In 1883, Victor Hugo led a determined campaign to save the remaining ruins, and the site was finally restored in 1917; only about one-third of today's arena, however, is original.

🗺 Map p. 62   ✉ 49 rue Monge   🚇 Métro: Cardinal Lemoine ■

St.-Germain and Montparnasse were once symbolic of the intelligentsia and artistic communities of Paris. Although these days are well and gone, you can still get a taste of what these areas once were like.

St.-Germain & Montparnasse

Rue de la Gaîté, Montparnasse

St.-Germain & Montparnasse

PARIS'S LEGENDARY ST.-GERMAIN-DES-PRÉS QUARTER SPRANG UP IN THE ninth century around one of the most famous Benedictine abbeys in all France, and is now an area of literary cafés, jazz cellars, bookstores, and bistros. Montparnasse, another literary hub, was also the turn-of-the-20th-century capital of cubism.

The Église St.-Germain-des-Prés was the heart of an abbey whose agricultural domain stretched east to the Petit Pont, encompassing today's sixth and seventh arrondissements. The Romanesque church—the oldest in Paris—holds the remains of 17th-century philosopher and mathematician René Descartes, the founder of modern philosophy. Appropriately, the 20th-century existentialist philosopher, Jean-Paul Sartre— the ubiquitous king of the "gauche caviar," or elite leftists—used to come to the nearby Café de Flore to write, vacillate, and chat with novelist Simone de Beauvoir and friends. Other intellectuals, such as Raymond Aron, drank at Les Deux Magots café or ate at the Brasserie Lipp (see p. 244), making St.-Germain-des-Prés synonymous with Parisian intellectual life. The Flore likes to see itself as the birthplace of existentialism, but it was also where the anti-Semitic daily *L'Action Française* was founded in 1908.

Montparnasse was the birthplace of what went on to become the École de Paris. Its effervescent energy lured writers, artists, and bohemians from all over the world. Ernest Hemingway, F. Scott Fitzgerald, John Rodrigo Dos Passos, and Edna St. Vincent Millay frequented the brasseries and bars; James Whistler lived nearby; Lenin played chess at the Closerie des Lilas; American poet Hart Crane was arrested for punching a waiter at Le Select; and Kiki, the exotic 1920s "Queen of Montparnasse," aroused them all with her raspy voice and seductive show.

La Ruche was a refuge for many artists, particularly those from Central Europe, including Constantin Brancusi, Ossip Zadkine, Chaim Soutine, and Marc Chagall.

Some were living in dire poverty and thus spent hours each day in cafés simply to escape the cold. Unfortunately, the advent of central heating killed off much of café life.

The famous late-night bookstore and art gallery La Hune is still open, as are dozens of bookshops scattered through the streets of St.-Germain. This area is also where France's leading publishing houses are located. But today's St.-Germain is ruled more by consumerism, with Right Bank fashion moguls encroaching on the formerly sacrosanct literary hub: Armani has bought out the legendary Drugstore Publicis; Cartier replaced a great classical music shop; Louis Vuitton is at 6 Place St.-Germain; and even the Flore has its own accessories boutique. Who could imagine the Irish playwright Samuel Beckett, who used to

---

ST.-GERMAIN & MONTPARNASSE

❶ Tour Montparnasse ❷ Closerie des Lilas ❸ Marché St.-Germain ❹ École Nationale Supérieure des Beaux-Arts

---

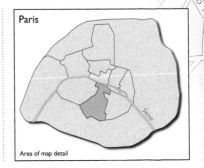

Paris

Area of map detail

drink at the Montana on Rue St.-Benoît, slipping out for a pint at what is now called the Montana Fashion Bar?

Nevertheless, St.-Germain is still a wonderful area to visit. Don't miss the art galleries that line Rue de Seine, Rue Bonaparte, and Rue des Beaux Arts, and the Musée Delacroix and the grandiose Musée de la Monnaie, where coins were struck until 1973. And be sure to sit around the octagonal basin at the Jardin du Luxembourg;

and to watch the sun slip into the Seine from the Pont des Arts as the last rays fade over the golden domes of the Institut de France.

Although Montparnasse's heyday is over, you can still get a glimmer of what the excitement was like along the strip—at La Coupole (see p. 86) and Closerie des Lilas (see p. 88). ∎

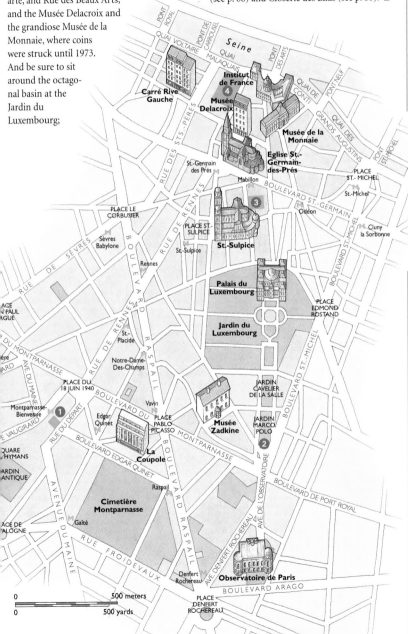

Église St.-Germain-des-Prés

Église St.-Germain-des-Prés

- Map p. 79
- place St.-Germain
- 01 43 25 41 71
- Métro: St.-Germain-des-Prés

HEEDING THE ADVICE OF SAINT GERMAIN, WHO WAS SOON to be Bishop of Paris, the Merovingian Childebert ordered a basilica and monastery to be built in 543 and dedicated to Saint Vincent (the patron saint of wine growers) and the Holy Cross. The basilica, with its magnificent mosaics and gilded-bronze roof, was nicknamed St.-Germain le Doré (St.-Germain the Gilded). One of the most prestigious constructions of the Frank realm, it was the burial site for Merovingian kings. Charlemagne (*R*.768–814) invested vast sums of money in it, and its lands extended over 74,130 acres (30,023 ha).

The Normans destroyed the abbey, but it was rebuilt as a Romanesque church around 1000; its 11th-century bell tower is the oldest in Paris. The church was consecrated in 1163 by Pope Alexander III, who laid the foundation stone of Notre-Dame a few weeks later (Maurice de Sully, the Bishop of Paris, was barred from the ceremony to assert the abbey's independence from the bishop). The church was expanded in 1245 with the Chapelle de la Vièrge and the cloister, vestiges of which can be seen in the small square outside.

The ashes of philosopher René Descartes lie in the second chapel of St.-Germain-des-Prés. His skull is buried in the Musée de l'Homme (see p. 182).

LATER HISTORY

In June 1789, revolutionaries attacked the abbey prison to free soldiers detained for refusing to fire on striking workers in the Faubourg St.-Antoine. The following year, the church was converted into a saltpeter warehouse. The former church prison, along with **St.-Joseph-des-Carmes** (*70 Rue de Vaugirard*), was where the September Massacres (see p. 24) began. It was also where Charlotte Corday, who murdered the revolutionary Jean Paul Marat, was imprisoned during the Terror. In 1794, 15 tons of gunpowder stored in the dining hall exploded, devastating nearly everything (although some of the library's 50,000 volumes and 7,000 manuscripts were salvaged).

The church was restored during the 19th century, largely due to efforts by Victor Hugo. Jean Auguste Ingres's student, Hippolyte Flandrin, completed a series of frescoes on the walls of the nave. The columns of the 12th-century chancel are from the Merovingian basilica. In a side chapel to the right of the choir is the tomb of René Descartes (who died 1650). The cloister's small garden has a bronze sculpture of a woman's head by Picasso. ■

Musée Delacroix

The entrance of the Palais de l'Abbaye, which in part now houses the Institut Catholique, opens onto the Place Furstenberg, the most romantic square in Paris—if you can't fall in love here, then it just wasn't meant to be! At No. 6 you'll find the Delacroix Museum, where the painter lived until his death in 1863. Delacroix moved here in 1857 from the ninth arrondissement while painting the murals at the St.-Sulpice Church.

The museum, created largely due to efforts by artists Paul Signac and Maurice Denis, is lined with 22 watercolor copies of the frescoes that Delacroix painted on the ceiling of the library in the Chambre des Députés of the Palais Bourbon. The collection, laid out in Delacroix's apartment and in the garden studio, includes smaller works, religious paintings such as "The Descent into the Tomb" and "The Ascent to Calvary," and the museum's most important work, the artist's second version of "The Kidnapping of Rebecca." ∎

Musée Delacroix
- Map p. 79
- 6 rue de Furstenberg
- ☎ 01 44 41 86 50
- Closed Tues.
- $
- Métro: St.-Germain-des-Prés

Delacroix was fascinated by the Orient and often painted his subjects in costume, as in this portrait of "Le Chanteur Baroilhet" (circa 1826), an opera singer who collected Delacroix's work.

Institut de France

The Collège des Quatre Nations, the predecessor of the Institut de France, was built by money that was bequeathed by Cardinal Mazarin in 1661 as a school for provincial children. Its layout—two half-moon wings designed by Louis Le Vau—reflects the influence of Italian architecture. The building, given to the Institut de France in 1806, comprises five academies.

The **Académie Française,** the oldest and the most famous, was founded by Cardinal Mazarin in 1635. Membership is limited to 40 individuals known as *les immortels.*

Orson Welles, Peter Ustinov, and Vaclav Havel have all held positions at the **Académie des Beaux-Arts.** The baroque chapel encloses Mazarin's tomb, and the east wing houses the **Bibliothèque Mazarine,** France's first public library. Nearby is the **École Nationale Supérieure des Beaux-Arts** (*14 Rue Bonaparte*), Paris's main fine arts school, housed in the vestiges of the Petits-Augustins convent, commissioned by Marguerite of Valois in 1608; its gardens are open to the public (*closed Sat. & Sun.*). ∎

Institut de France
- Map p. 79
- 23 quai de Conti
- ☎ 01 44 41 44 41
- Métro: St.-Michel

Palais du Luxembourg

Palais du Luxembourg

🅰 Map p. 79

✉ rue de Vaugirard

☎ 01 42 34 20 00

🕐 Interior visits by guided tour only; book before 1st Sun. of month through Caisse Nationale de Monuments Historiques, Tel 01 44 61 20 89 (places limited). Gardens daily, from dawn to dusk

Ⓜ Métro: St.-Sulpice, Odéon, Luxembourg

In the 19th century, people could rent newspapers and read them in the Luxembourg Gardens for two hours, and letter writers marketed their services to those of a less literary bent.

MENTION LUXEMBOURG TO MOST PARISIANS, AND THEY will probably describe this 59-acre (24 ha) elegant park, the only real green space in the entire sixth arrondissement, rather than the palace of the same name (seat of the French senate since 1799). For generations, the park has been one of the city's most popular.

ITALIAN-STYLE MANSION

Both the palace and the gardens were created in the early 17th century by the self-aggrandizing Marie de Médicis after her husband, King Henri IV, was killed. Nostalgic for the Pitti Palace, her childhood home in Florence—and especially the Boboli Gardens—she asked architect Salomon de Brosse to re-create an Italian-style mansion on the property she bought from the Duc de Luxembourg. He retained the smaller building, the Petit Luxembourg (now the official residence of the President of the Senate), and constructed an opulent dwelling for which she commissioned a series of 24 monumental paintings by Rubens depicting the major events of her life (now displayed in the Louvre). In 1630, after only five years in her lavish palace, she was forced into exile by her son, Louis XIII, on the so-called Day of Dupes.

GARDENS

Marie de Médicis' devotion to her garden is visible in the 2,000 elm trees, orchards, and formal flower beds she planted. Although the gardens were relandscaped by Chalgrin in the 19th century, they retain the formal layout; to this day, the park is impeccably maintained, and a gorgeous palette is created by rotating the flowers through the seasons.

The Médicis Fountain is one of the prettiest spots in the park, where 100-year-old plane trees shade the long pool. A number of statues dot the park including a small replica of Auguste Bartholdi's "Statue of Liberty." There's no better place to spend an afternoon with small children, as the park has a separate children's play area, with pony rides, swings, slides, and rides; a classic puppet show; and a merry-go-round constructed from plans by Charles Garnier (designer of the Opéra Garnier). ■

St.-Sulpice & Quartier

ON A SUNNY SPRING DAY, WITH THE PINK-BLOSSOMED chestnut trees in full bloom, the Place St.-Sulpice is one of Paris's loveliest squares. The best place to appreciate the monumental Fountain of Four Bishops (Joachim Visconti, 1844) and the imposing Église St.-Sulpice is from one of the tables spilling out on the sidewalk around the Café de la Mairie, where the writer Albert Camus was a regular.

Église St.-Sulpice
- Map p. 79
- place St.-Sulpice
- Métro: St.-Sulpice, Odéon

THE CHURCH

Église St.-Sulpice is a surprisingly austere yet grandiose structure, which took more than 135 years to build (which may explain the two mismatched towers flanking the colonnaded facade). The first stone was laid in 1646 to replace an earlier 13th-century building, but work was stopped 20 years later due to lack of funds. Construction started again in the 18th century and proceeded haphazardly until the north tower was completed in 1778. The highlight of St.-Sulpice is Eugène Delacroix's decoration of the **Chapelle des Sts.-Anges,** which took 10 years to finish. The tormented scenes of "Jacob's Wrestling with the Angel" and "Heliodorus Driven from the Temple" were the artist's last great masterpieces.

SURROUNDING STREETS

A famous *maison close* (brothel) at 36 Rue St.-Sulpice once catered to high-class clientele in the very shadow of the church. The brothel is gone, but the narrow, colonnaded facade with its yellow and green tiles still marks its place.

The streets all around **Place St.-Sulpice** are lined with classy clothes shops, florists, lingerie shops, and bookstores (one of the best English bookshops in Paris, the Village Voice, is at 6 Rue Princesse). The area—a shopper's paradise—stretches as far as Sèvres-Babylone, where the sturdy but sensible styles of the **Bon Marché** department store used to clothe the arrondissement's bourgeois (it was also one of Madame de Gaulle's favorite stores). A major renovation several years ago gave it a chic and expensive new look; the food display on the ground floor alone is worth the trip. Just behind the church is the **Marché St.-Germain,** its covered markets filled today with designer shops that make this a pale version of the famous medieval fair once held here. ■

In *A Moveable Feast,* Hemingway described the pigeons roosting on the four stone bishops of the fountain on Place St.-Sulpice.

Cemeteries

For centuries, Parisians buried their dead in the Cimetière des Innocents (Sts.-Innocents Cemetery) in the heart of the city, right next to the teeming marketplace of Les Halles. It was the main cemetery for over 20 parishes in Paris, particularly for those that did not have their own cemeteries, for the destitute, and for those who died in the Hôtel-Dieu hospital. Burials were in a common grave that held up to 1,500 bodies; when this was full, another was dug nearby.

By the late 18th century, the stench had become intolerable, and the grisly contents of the cemetery (the remains of nearly six million people) were transported over 15 months in convoys to the catacombs near Denfert-Rochereau (see p. 201). The cemeteries within the walls of the city were then closed, replaced by the cemeteries of Père-Lachaise, Montparnasse, and Montmartre.

Cimetière Père-Lachaise
Père-Lachaise attracts more people than any other cemetery in Paris—more than two million visitors every year. It is named after the Jesuit priest de La Chaise, Louis XIV's confessor, who owned the land here between 1665 and 1709. In 1803, architect Alexandre Brongniart redesigned the layout for a cemetery. Drawing his inspiration from English-style gardens, he integrated romantically landscaped paths and exuberant funerary statuary, which nevertheless failed to excite Parisians. The cemetery opened on May 21, 1804, but there were only 2,000 tombs by 1815, partly because it was considered too remote. Ingenious Parisian government officials figured that if they transferred the remains of a few famous people, celebrity-conscious Parisians would soon follow. In 1817 the remains of playwright Molière and poet Jean de La Fontaine, along with Héloïse and Abélard (see p. 114), were brought to the cemetery; by 1828, there were over 33,000 tombs, and several lots were purchased to expand the growing site, creating today's 109-acre (44 ha) cemetery—the largest green area in Paris, with the exception of the Bois de

Boulogne and the Bois de Vincennes.

The cemetery is laid out according to numbered divisions. The lower section is a romantic, tangled forest of tombs and sepulchers, arranged along dirt paths and cobblestone lanes. The upper section has a severe, geometric-grid layout. Maps are available at the cemetery's entrance; these indicate the most famous (though not easy to find) tombs—you may have to poke around off the main path to find what you are looking for. There are a multitude of interesting tombs, and the most intriguing are not always the graves of the really famous people. Many celebrities are buried here, including Frédéric Chopin and Oscar Wilde (originally, the figure on Wilde's tomb was anatomically perfect, but an anonymous visitor knocked off his genitals). The grave of the late Doors' singer Jim Morrison has become something of a shrine to his fans. A series of monuments near the Mur des Fédérés, or Federalists' Wall, form a moving homage to the French victims who died in Nazi concentration camps, especially the severe bronze monument representing three skeletal figures, a tribute to the dead of Buchenwald-Dora.
🗺 187 & 193 F3   ✉ 8 boulevard de Ménilmontant   ☎ 01 55 25 82 10
🚇 Métro: Père-Lachaise, Philippe-Auguste

Cimetière Montparnasse
An abbey necropolis has existed on the site of the Montparnasse Cemetery since 1654, but it became a municipal cemetery only in 1824. Divided into the Petit Cimetière and the Grand Cimetière, it is the smallest of the three, and at first sight it is less romantic than Père-Lachaise. Yet along the gridded avenues lie the remains of many of France's intellectual and artistic elite, along with a profusion of fascinating funerary art. Charles Baudelaire's tomb, for example, features the bust of the 19th-century poet perched above a gigantic bat, contemplating a stone sculpture of his own body below. The Pigeon family sepulcher is one of the more extravagant: The couple lies in a giant stone-and-bronze bed. Constantin Brancusi is also buried here:

The tomb of Oscar Wilde (above), in Père-Lachaise Cemetery (left). Below: Montmartre Cemetery, resting place of composers Jacques Offenbach and Hector Berlioz, and Russian dancer Vaslav Nijinsky.

Several of his sculptures, including "The Kiss," stand atop tombs. Serge Gainsbourg, Jean-Paul Sartre, and Simone de Beauvoir are all interred here.
🅰 79 & 196 D2 ✉ 3 boulevard Edgar Quinet ☎ 01 44 10 86 50 🚇 Métro: Edgar Quinet, Raspail

Cimetière Montmartre
Montmartre Cemetery was initially a sinister place, where the destitute were thrown into common graves. Redesigned in 1879, it now contains the remains of many celebrities.
🅰 187 & 196 D4 ✉ 20 avenue Rachel ☎ 01 43 87 64 24 🚇 Métro: place de Clichy ■

La Coupole

LA COUPOLE—ONE OF THE MOST FAMOUS, IF NOT *THE* most famous, brasseries in Paris (see p. 244)—is a *Bar Américain* par excellence, a cocktail bar that serves up odd blends like the Coffin (gin, scotch, and vodka) and the eponymous house concoction (rum, Noilly Prat, grenadine, and Grand Marnier).

La Coupole

Map p. 79

✉ 102 boulevard du Montparnasse

☎ 01 43 20 14 20

🚇 Métro: Montparnasse-Bienvenue

Tour Montparnasse

Map p. 79

✉ place Raoul-Dautry

🚇 Métro: Montparnasse-Bienvenue

F. Scott Fitzgerald and Ernest Hemingway were regular patrons of La Coupole, still as popular as ever.

Whatever you order, there are a few rules to abide by if you want to look like a regular: Never rush toward your table as if someone were going to beat you to it—this art deco brasserie seats over 400. The center section surrounding the huge gladiolas under the dome is only for snobs. Look as detached as possible, particularly if you see stars such as Catherine Deneuve or Mick Jagger. Never look directly at them—famous faces mean absolutely nothing to a regular. If you go to use the telephone, cross the room with the same look of indifference. And if you are paged—your name paraded by on the small mobile chalkboard—feign supreme nonchalance or look somewhat irritated as you walk toward the cloakroom.

La Coupole has its days, hours, and seasons, though you can eat at any time, day or night. But it is best during oyster season (all months containing the letter "r"). Try to lunch or dine as late as possible; people tend to linger at La Coupole.

You can doodle on your place-mat, too—Swiss sculptor and painter Alberto Giacometti used to draw on his, tucking it under his arm as he left (much to the chagrin of the staff). ■

Tour Montparnasse

Don't miss the 58-floor, 688-foot-high (210 m) Montparnasse Tower, the highest steel-and-glass monstrosity in Europe. It grew out of the old Montparnasse railway station, where the German army signed its surrender of Paris on August 25, 1944. The top of the tower has a panoramic restaurant and terrace, with a terrific view over Paris. ■

Although La Ruche was anything but luxurious, it provided a roof for impoverished artists, and unpaid rents were overlooked.

La Ruche

La Ruche
- Map p. 79
- 2 passage de Dantzig
- No phone
- Some studios may be visited at the discretion of their occupiers
- Métro: Convention

La Ruche, or beehive, is one of the oldest artists' colonies still operating today. The sculptor Alfred Boucher salvaged the wine pavilion built by Gustave Eiffel for the Paris Universal Exposition of 1900 and converted it into La Ruche, thus baptized because the beehive-shaped rotunda's main stairway leads to ateliers (studios) where the artists paint, sculpt, and write.

The polygonal building was divided into 24 triangular ateliers, each nicknamed *quart de brie* (slice of brie). It provided a refuge for artists like Amedeo Modigliani, Marc Chagall, and Constantin Brancusi, and writers such as Apollinaire, Max Jacob, and Blaise Cendrars, many of whom lived and worked here in dire poverty. It was also just a stone's throw from the cafés of Montparnasse. After World War I, it declined somewhat, although new artistic blood returned after 1945. The building, nearly demolished at one time, was saved by a committee headed by Chagall; it is now a classified monument and a thriving artistic hub. ■

Observatoire de Paris

Observatoire de Paris
- Map p. 79
- 61 avenue de l'Observatoire
- 01 40 51 21 70
- Guided tours first Sat. of each month (except Aug.) by written appointment
- Métro: Port-Royal

The Observatoire de Paris, founded in 1667 and completed in 1672, is the oldest observatory in the world still operating. Constructed by Claude Perrault (older brother of the fairy-tale author, Charles Perrault, who published the original *Cinderella*), the building's conception and architectural layout mirrors the cosmos: The main body of the edifice is oriented toward the four cardinal points, and the walls of the two octagonal towers on the southern facade indicate the sun's position during the summer and winter solstices.

Here the moon's surface was charted (1679), the metric weights and measures system devised (1791), Neptune discovered by Leverrier (1846), and the speed of light determined (18th century). The observatory remains a research center for astronomy and related services, but the building and its small museum can be visited. ■

A walk through Montparnasse

You can still find traces of historic Montparnasse in some of its most famous establishments, such as the Closeries des Lilas and La Coupole, although it is no longer the vivacious center of art and literature it was in the early part of the 20th century.

Begin your walk at the Raspail Métro, turning down **Rue Campagne Première ❶**. At No. 31 is Atelier 17, decorated with tall windows and ceramic tiles. American photographer Man Ray rented a studio here, then moved with his mistress "Queen" Kiki to the Istria Hotel next door. The Istria was home to numerous artists and writers, including Francis Picabia, Austrian poet Rainer Maria Rilke, Marcel Duchamp, and composer Erik Satie. Poet Paul Verlaine lived across the street at No. 14 (the house is no longer standing); when he moved out, he passed his room on to his companion, poet Arthur Rimbaud.

At No. 9, go through the door leading to another group of artists' studios at the back of a cobbled courtyard. Before World War I, many artists left Montmartre for Montparnasse, seeking lower rents and inspiration in the Boulevard du Montparnasse cafés. Italian artists Giorgio de Chirico and Amedeo Modigliani, Rainer Maria Rilke, and painter James Whistler were among those who lived in this building.

Turn right on the Boulevard du Montparnasse and head for the lavender sign of the **Closerie des Lilas ❷** (see p. 243), a favorite haunt of artists and writers such as Ernest Hemingway. Arriving in Paris in 1924, Hemingway soon settled in at the Closerie, where he wrote *Big Two-Hearted River*, part of *The Sun Also Rises*, and many of his other short stories. Its Cuban mahogany bar (where a plaque marks Hemingway's spot), red lamps, mirrored decor, and leather seats are just as inviting today as they were back then.

Outside the Closerie stands a statue of Marshal Ney, a hero of the French Revolutionary and Napoleonic Wars. Hemingway lived nearby at 113 Rue Notre-Dame des Champs (turn left from the Closerie to continue the walk) above a sawmill, which no longer exists (even the street number has disappeared; the numbers jump from 111 to 115).

Turn left off Rue Notre-Dame des Champs on Rue de Chevreuse. At the intersection with Boulevard du Montparnasse (where the Batifol restaurant is found), stood Le Jockey—the 1920s haunt presided over by the legendary singer and artist's model, "Queen" Kiki de Montparnasse.

Turn right on Boulevard du Montparnasse. At the Carrefour Vavin stands Rodin's famous statue **"Balzac"** (see p. 172).

Cross Boulevard du Montparnasse and turn down Rue Delambre. Kiki was often seen at No. 5, where Japanese painter Tsuguharu Fujita had a bathtub and hot running water—a rarity at the time—in his studio. At No. 10 is the **Auberge de Venise,** called Le Dingo in the 1920s; another expatriate hangout, it was where Hemingway first met fellow American F. Scott Fitzgerald.

Turn right on Rue du Montparnasse. The **Falstaff** (now a tacky beer bar) is on the left toward the end; it was once a favorite drinking spot for Samuel Beckett, Kiki, Man Ray, Fitzgerald, and Hemingway.

Turn right on Boulevard du Montparnasse. Ahead lies the Vavin Métro and four of the most famous cafés in the world—Le Select, La Rotonde, Le Dôme (now an upscale fish restaurant; see p. 243), and **La Coupole ❸** (see pp. 86 & 244). American critic and editor

Rodin's statue of "Balzac," exhibited at the Paris Salon in 1898, was branded by critics and caricaturists as a "riot provoking sack of plaster" and a "Colossal fetus."

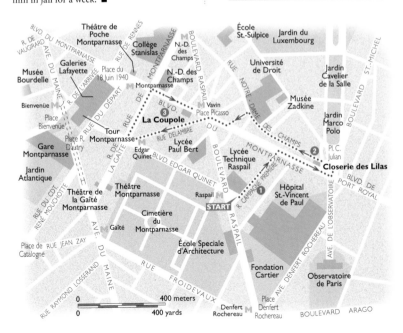

La Coupole, a Montparnasse institution, retains its 1920s decor.

Malcolm Cowley described the first three as the "heart and nervous system of the…literary colony." Russian revolutionary Leon Trotsky often met up with Mexican painter Diego Rivera at La Rotonde, and American poet Edna St. Vincent Millay ate lunch there almost every day. **Le Select,** the first café in Paris to stay open all night long, was where American poet Hart Crane picked a fight that landed him in jail for a week. ■

See also map pp. 78–79
► Raspail Métro
↔ 1.3 miles (2.1 km)
🕐 Allow 2 hours
► Vavin Métro

NOT TO BE MISSED
- Closerie des Lilas
- Rodin's "Balzac"
- La Coupole
- Le Select

More places to visit in St.-Germain & Montparnasse

CARRÉ RIVE GAUCHE

The cream of the Paris antique trade is clustered within a prestigious few blocks of the sixth arrondissement. Bordered by the Quai Voltaire, Rue des St.-Pères, Rue de l'Université, and Rue du Bac, the Carré Rive Gauche offers shops with high-quality furniture, objets d'art, and paintings. Each of the 30 or so associated shops showcases an exceptional object relating to an overall theme that is selected annually for a special one-week show in mid-May.

🅰 Map p. 79 🅿 Métro: Rue du Bac, Musée d'Orsay

MUSÉE DE LA MONNAIE

This impressive, 18th-century neoclassic mansion displays over 2,000 coins, spanning nearly 15 centuries of French history. The building, designed by architect Jacques Antoine, was originally constructed as a mint. The last coins were minted here in 1973, and the former minting halls now contain a modern, innovative museum.

A fascinating tour traces the chronology of coinage and explores how money was used to make or break kingdoms, consolidate power, and impose political ideology. Few people know that money first appeared in Gaul sometime around 300 B.C.; that Charlemagne created a monetary system in the eighth century (based on a silver standard) that lasted for nearly a thousand years of European history; or that Louis XVI's attempted escape from the Tuileries Palace would have succeeded if he hadn't been spotted by a man who recognized his image stamped on the coins in circulation at the time.

🅰 Map p. 79 ✉ 11 quai de Conti ☎ 01 40 46 55 35 🕐 Closed Mon. 💲 $ 🅿 Métro: St.-Michel, Pont-Neuf, Odéon

MUSÉE ZADKINE

This small house and flower-filled garden, just a few blocks from the Luxembourg Garden, is where the Russian-born sculptor Ossip Zadkine lived from 1928 until his death in 1967. It has remained almost unchanged since then, with sculptures spread over five rooms and scattered around the secluded garden. Several important pieces are on display, including his most famous sculpture, "Ville Détruite" ("The Destroyed City"), a tormented yet triumphant work concerning World War II, created for the city of Rotterdam.

🅰 Map p. 79 ✉ 100 bis rue d'Assas ☎ 01 43 26 91 90 🕐 Closed Mon. 💲 $ 🅿 Métro: Port-Royal, Vavin, Notre-Dame des Champs ■

Sculptures in the peaceful garden of the Musée Zadkine, the artist's former home, include "Woman With Bird" (1930) and "The Return of the Prodigal Son" (1964).

The former marketplace at Les Halles has been replaced by a giant underground shopping complex, but still is, as Émile Zola described it, the "belly of Paris."

Châtelet & Les Halles

Color-coded pipes at the Pompidou Center

Châtelet & Les Halles

THE AREA AROUND CHÂTELET AND LES HALLES, PARTICULARLY THE NARROW back alleys and roads, is reminiscent of the cobbled streets of old Paris—bustling, crime-ridden, and foul-smelling, but vibrant.

Life and death coexisted in many medieval Parisian squares, where markets and fairs often sprang up in cemeteries because of the available free space, bringing together mime artists, jugglers, musicians, the homeless, and thieves amid the mixed smells of newly slaughtered meat and the freshest farm produce.

CHÂTELET

The area around the Place du Châtelet (see p. 95) was another crime-infested neighborhood, which was associated

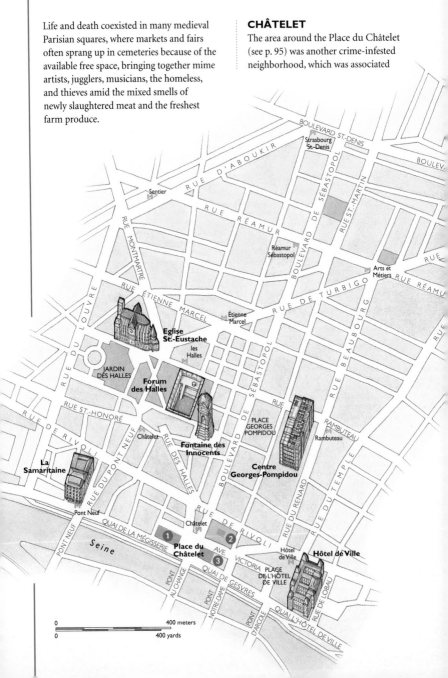

with the powerful butchers' guilds, the tanneries, and the sinister Grand Châtelet Prison (whose infamous torture methods included a funnel-shaped chamber that forced inmates to remain permanently standing). With its twin theaters and Châtelet Fountain decorated with sphinxes round the base, it is difficult to imagine the square as it once was.

The nearby Tour St.-Jacques—the Flamboyant Gothic bell tower of the church of St.-Jacques la Boucherie—was built for the powerful 16th-century butchers' guild and served as a landmark for pilgrims en route to Santiago de Compostela in Spain. The scallop shells (*coquilles*) with which the pilgrims decorated their hats

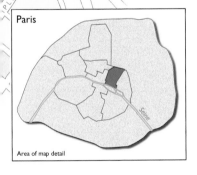

Paris

Area of map detail

and capes became a symbol of the pilgrims—hence the famous dish, Coquilles St.-Jacques. In 1648, Blaise Pascal used the tower to repeat the barometric experiments he had carried out in Puy-de-Dôme, and the tower, standing in a small park, is now a weather station *(closed to the public)*.

Until the Revolution, the Quai de la Mégisserie was the site of the public slaughterhouse; today, the attractive riverfront is lined with florists, plant shops, and shops selling caged animals, although it is not always clear whether the animals are sold as pets or for stewing.

In contrast to Châtelet's murky past, Rue St.-Denis was once a glorious pathway, whose splendor grew in proportion to that of the eponymous basilica. Once the path of the kings of France, with fountains spilling over with wine, today it is lined instead with fast-food joints, clothing outlets, and sex shops, while its northern end is now a seedy red-light district.

More upscale shopping is available at the five-store La Samaritaine shopping complex (see p. 95) on Rue de la Monnaie, where you can buy everything from hardware to toys and children's clothing. Take in the panoramic view from the rooftop café.

LES HALLES

Les Halles (see p. 98), a market for French produce for 800 years, continues to draw in the crowds—especially around the Fontaine des Innocents (where the Cimetière des Innocents was once located; see p. 102); the surrounding gardens, terraces, and sculptures; the seedy Rue St.-Denis; and the Église St.-Eustache (see p. 102)—although the actual market was transferred south of Paris to Rungis in 1969 to ease the traffic problems.

The sterile, largely subterranean modern commercial and cultural complex at Forum Les Halles that replaced the marketplace is somewhat alienating, and the area's core has shifted east, toward the modern, boldly colored Centre Georges-Pompidou (also called Beaubourg; see pp. 96–97) and the neo-Renaissance Hôtel de Ville (City Hall; see p. 94). Beaubourg, originally a 12th-century village enclosed by the Philippe-Auguste Wall, retains a touch of medieval atmosphere, particularly in its narrow side streets. The former 17th-century Cour des Miracles (see p. 99) in the red-light area of the second arrondissement was the model for Victor Hugo's description of medieval life in *Notre-Dame de Paris*: It is "a gutter of vice and beggary, of vagrancy that spills over into the streets of the capital…immense changing-room of all the actors of this comedy that robbery, prostitution, and murder play on the cobbled streets of Paris." ∎

The exterior of the Renaissance-style Hôtel de Ville features statues of the allegories, the cities of France, and 108 noted Parisians (as well as one Italian, the architect Il Boccadoro).

Hôtel de Ville

ALTHOUGH THE PRESENT BUILDING IS FAIRLY RECENT, the Hôtel de Ville's site has always played an essential role in the history of the capital.

Hôtel de Ville

▲ Map p. 92

✉ place de l'Hôtel de Ville (public entrance: 29 rue de Rivoli)

☎ 01 42 76 59 46

🕐 Guided tours for groups only. Must make an appointment 2½–3 months in advance. Tours Mon.–Fri. Possibility of tour in English.

🚇 Métro: Hôtel-de-Ville, Châtelet

Water was vital in the development of the city's municipal administration, which originated with the powerful water merchants' guild that controlled and administered trade on the Seine, Oise, Yonne, and Marne Rivers. In the mid-13th century, Saint Louis introduced a municipal government composed of leading *échevins* (guildsmen), headed by the *prévôt des marchands* (equivalent to aldermen and a mayor) who were elected by the Parisian bourgeoisie to form the *Parloir aux Bourgeois*. The seal of the water merchants (an emblem depicting a boat on the river) became the symbol of Paris.

The site of municipal administration shifted from the Place du Châtelet in 1357, when the provost Étienne Marcel bought the Maison des Piliers on the Place de la Grève (*grève* means shore), the name given to the Place de l'Hôtel de Ville until 1830. This first Hôtel de Ville (city hall) was the site of revolu-

tions, celebrations, and executions from 1310 to 1830. Louis XVI was forced to kiss the tricolor cockade here in 1789, and revolutionaries Danton, Marat, and Robespierre used the hôtel as their headquarters during the Terror (see p. 24).

Water is still present in François-Xavier Lalanne's 1980s fountains flanking the busy, bright white edifice, which is frequently the home of temporary exhibitions. A lavish nativity scene is set up outside each Christmas. The interior has a series of beautiful reception halls, glittering chandeliers, gilding, ornate woodwork (note the seven different types of wood in the Salon Bertrand), a sumptuous grand staircase with murals of "Summer" and "Winter" by Puvis de Chavannes, and triumphant Third Republic ceiling murals. Burned down in May 1871, the Hôtel de Ville was rebuilt between 1874 and 1882 by the Italian architect Il Boccadoro. ∎

Place du Châtelet

With its elegant twin theaters, monumental fountain, and great view of the river, the Place du Châtelet bears little trace of its notorious former prison and surrounding, crime-ridden streets. It does, however, retain the names of the streets where the activities of the butchers and tanneries were carried out—Rue de la Tuerie (killing) and Rue de l'Ecorcherie (skinning).

The square is named for the Grand Châtelet fortress, constructed by Louis VI le Gros (circa 1130) to defend the Île de la Cité.

It later became the seat of the courts, provostship, and prison. The area was razed in 1808 to rid it of vice, and the square was opened and replaced with Boulevard Sébastopol.

In 1862, two theaters built on either side by Davioud, the Théâtre du Châtelet (now the **Théâtre Musical de Paris**) and the **Théâtre de la Ville** (once owned by the actress Sarah Bernhardt), began to attract a more fashionable set. Today, the square is one of the busiest crossroads in Paris. ▪

Place du Châtelet
- Map p. 92
- Métro: Châtelet

BUREAU DU CHANGE
In medieval times, all foreign visitors had to change their money at the Pont au Change (Money Changing Bridge) in front of the Place du Châtelet. ▪

La Samaritaine

La Samaritaine is a series of stores that stretches over several blocks, with each building representing architectural advances from 1900 to 1930—store No. 1, Frantz Jourdain's revolutionary 1900 building, with its cast-iron frame and huge bay windows of exposed,

riveted metal (considered a vulgar material at the time); store No. 2, built from 1926 to 1928, with its art deco-style facade; and the 1930s building, with its intriguing frieze and grand staircase. The view from the rooftop terrace café-restaurant is one of the best in Paris. ▪

La Samaritaine
- Map p. 92
- 19 rue de la Monnaie
- 01 40 41 20 20
- Closed Sun.
- Métro: Pont-Neuf

At La Samaritaine

Centre Georges-Pompidou

THE NEWLY RENOVATED POMPIDOU CENTER IS ONE OF THE
city's most popular sites. Standing in the midst of Paris like a slumber-
ing giant, its blue, green, yellow, and red pipes and ducts coiled against
the gray rooftops and cityscape, Richard Rogers and Renzo Piano's arts
complex spearheaded contemporary architecture in Paris in 1977, inject-
ing an avant-garde tone into one of the city's oldest neighborhoods and
causing great controversy.

**Centre Georges-
Pompidou**

www.centrepompidou.fr

🅰 Map p. 92

✉ place Georges-
Pompidou
IRCAM: entrance on
place Igor
Stravinsky

☎ 01 44 78 12 33

🕐 Museum &
exhibitions open at
11 a.m.; Atelier
Brancusi closed a.m.

💲 $$. Call for
exhibition charges.

🚇 Métro: Hôtel-de-Ville,
Châtelet

Since the 90-million-dollar renova-
tion of the center (called Beaubourg
by Parisians), the main foyer has
been redesigned; exhibition space
nearly doubled; disabled access
improved; the library (now with its
own entrance) expanded and
equipped with 370 computers;
drama, dance, and cinema theaters
opened on the lower level; a muse-
um gallery, graphic arts gallery, and
media collection added; and a
trendy restaurant (Georges) run by
the Costes family is at the top of the
six-level center. You'll still find the
Center of Industrial Creation
(CCI), specializing in architecture,
urbanization, and visual communi-
cations; the **Institute for
Research and Acoustical/**

Musical Coordination (IRCAM)
for contemporary music; the
Cinémathèque featuring film
festivals and rare movies; the
Children's Workshop to foster
touch, color, and artistic expression
in 6-12 year olds; and conferences,
seminars, lectures, and debates. On
the other hand, the renovation was
made for a building that is less
democratic: In a plan that was high-
ly criticized by both architects, visi-
tors now have to pay to take the
escalators up for the splendid
panoramic view. But the $4.50 ticket
gives access to the Musée National
d'Art Moderne and its extraordinary
collection of 20th-century works.
Indeed, the new focus of the center is
to direct attention on the museum.

MUSÉE NATIONAL D'ART MODERNE

The MNAM's collection is second only to New York's Metropolitan Museum of Modern Art, housing some 45,000 works from the early 20th century to the present. Now there is 50 percent more exhibition space, and the contemporary display is rehung every 18 months (the modern galleries every year).

Visitors now enter through the contemporary art section on the fourth level, which has rooms devoted to pop art, Arte Povera, and other major movements, as well as to individual artists such as Yves Klein and Jean Dubuffet. They then proceed upstairs to the modern section (1905–1960), featuring movements such as fauvism and cubism and works by Picasso, Rouault, Chagall, and Matisse. New acquisitions include Francis Picabia's "Dresseur d'Animaux." In general, there is more sculpture (Giacometti, in particular) and contemporary French art, as well as furniture and design. It is easier to circulate on both levels of the museum, and the ceilings have been opened up to

reveal the pipes and ducts painted white, creating the impression of higher ceilings and brighter space. When you're tired, you can sit on the benches near the works and listen to recordings of artists, architects, and designers speaking about art. ■

Brancusi's sculpture studio

When the Romanian-born sculptor Constantin Brancusi died in 1957, he left his studio to the French government, on condition that it be fully reconstituted. Originally on the Impasse Ronsin in the 15th arrondissement, the atelier was rebuilt at the Palais de Tokyo before being moved to the Pompidou Center in 1977, where it is now located on the piazza. On view are the artist's sketches, bronze sculptures, stone and marble sculptures, original plasters, bed, wardrobe, tools, and maquettes. Temporary exhibitions are held in the studio as well. ■

The color-coded air ducts, elevators, escalators, pipes, and other logistical space constraints were placed on the exterior of the Centre Georges-Pompidou: blue for air-conditioning, green for water, yellow for electricity, and red for escalators and elevators.

Les Halles

Map p. 92

Lautréamont Terrace, Gardens, and Children's Play Area

The Forum at Les Halles, 105 rue Rambuteau (down rue Baltard)

01 45 08 07 18

No adults allowed, except on Sat. morning (10 a.m.–1 p.m.)

Métro: Les Halles

THE FORUM AT LES HALLES IS BUT A PALE SHADOW OF THE legendary "belly of Paris" described by Émile Zola, where fishwives and market porters worked through the night to load the pavilions with the gleaming heady produce of rural France by dawn.

Philippe-Auguste built Les Halles between 1181 and 1183, financing it partially by property confiscated from the Jewish residents he expelled in 1182. When the two large, 13th-century warehouses for drapers and weavers that formed the primitive market at Champeaux closed on Saturdays, the merchants and craftsmen set up their shops at Les Halles. By the mid-14th century, merchants were present three times a week. In 1851, Napoleon III instructed the architect Victor Baltard to construct

"The Carreau des Halles," by Victor Gabriel Gilbert (1880, oil on canvas)

cast-iron "umbrellas," and 10 pavilions with cast-iron frames were built in Les Halles between 1854 and 1912. In 1936 two more were added, and by 1969, the market's popularity and resultant traffic problems forced authorities to move it south of the city to Rungis. All but two of the pavilions were destroyed, and for nearly a decade a gaping hole remained where the market once stood.

In 1979, Les Halles reconstruction project took form, resulting in a widespread commercial and cultural boom. Today, the sprawling Métro-RER station at Châtelet-Les Halles acts as a high-speed crossroads for city commuters and shoppers. Crowds from all walks of life mill around in this vast, four-level, subterranean shopping complex, which also includes a photography exhibition space, gymnasium, pool, tropical greenhouse, movie complex and lounge, video library, record-lending library, center for music and dance, and billiards room.

Outside, the **Lautréamont Terrace** provides a fine view of the merry-go-round, the garden, St.-Eustache Church, and the ring-shaped Bourse du Commerce, a former grain exchange, whose strange column is said to have served as an observatory for Catherine de Médicis' astrologer, Ruggieri. The terrace leads to a conservatory of music, dance, and dramatic arts; a poetry center; an arts pavilion where temporary exhibitions are held; and a children's library.

The gardens are a great place to wind down—unless, of course, you're a hyperactive 10-year-old looking for ways to burn off energy. The elephant topiaries at the entrance lead to the open-air children's activity area. Here children can dive down underground tunnels, climb rope swings, and "swim" in a pool of green and blue balls surrounded by palm trees, bamboo, and lilacs. ■

WHERE MUD WAS FLUNG

Near the St.-Eustache crossroads stands a 14th-century market pillory where the public threw refuse and mud at exposed swindlers, thieves, and prostitutes. ■

MARKET PORTERS AT LES HALLES

To qualify as a market porter (Fort des Halles), you had to be able to carry a load of 440 pounds (200 kg) over a distance of 164 feet (50 m). ■

The mirrored facades of the Forum des Halles provide a dramatic entrance to the four-level underground cultural complex and shopping center.

Cour des Miracles

During the 15th, 16th, and 17th centuries, war and the plague spawned masses of homeless people in France. Many came to Paris, gravitating toward the side streets just inside Charles V's Wall. By day, they made a living as beggars, pretending to be crippled, maimed, blinded, and orphaned, or worked the crowds alongside the swindlers and thieves. At night, they disappeared into the alleyways, miraculously cured—hence the area's name Cour des Miracles. The Cour des Miracles was shut down by police in 1667, with the so-called cripples leading the flight from security forces. ■

Markets

For local color, nothing beats a morning at one of the many food markets scattered throughout Paris. You will be tempted by the brilliant displays of red and yellow peppers, slithering stacks of mysterious sea creatures, and countless different cheeses; extra encouragement comes from the boisterous sellers hawking their produce.

Every neighborhood has its own market. A few are still housed in old, covered buildings and, while some are permanent, others are set up for only two or three mornings a week. Although the markets are less crowded and the food is fresher early in the morning, there are good bargains at the end of the day, when vendors sell off their last few pounds of fruit cheap. Don't pick and choose, however; point out what you want and tell the vendors, and let them handle their merchandise themselves.

Permanent & temporary markets

The permanent (regular) markets are closed on Sunday afternoons and Monday, also during several hours at lunchtime. The Marché d'Aligre, on Place d'Aligre, is one of the cheapest markets in Paris. It has lots of exotic goods, like North African spices and hot peppers, as well as many secondhand clothes stalls. Inside the covered market is an excellent cheese shop, the Maison du Fromage-Radenac.

Another colorful market extends along the lower end of Rue Mouffetard; it would look like a film set if it weren't for all the tourists. Wander past St.-Médard Church and sample some of the great pastries at the Moule à Gâteaux (111 Rue Mouffetard).

For true Left Bank chic, try the Buci Market on Rue de Seine and Rue de Buci, where a quintessentially Parisian clientele crowds the busy (and expensive) stands on Sunday morning. And for organic Left Bank chic, the Marché Biologique on Boulevard Raspail offers high-priced free-range poultry, chemical-free produce, and farm-fresh cheeses. Other permanent market streets include Rue Montorgueil, a holdover from the old market at Les Halles; Rue du Poteau, a great, little known food market; and Rue Poncelet.

The largest temporary market stretches endlessly along Boulevard Richard Lenoir on Thursday and Sunday mornings. As with most

Everything from top-quality antiques to bargain-basement bric-a-brac turns up in the stalls of the city's flea markets and *brocantes*.

The stamp and postcard market, held on the corner of Avenue Marigny and Avenue Gabriel, opens on Thursdays, Saturdays, and Sundays.

neighborhood markets, locals usually return to the same vendors, but as prices and quality vary, take time to shop around. For hard-to-find, exotic products, try the Belleville Market on Tuesday and Friday mornings.

Specialty markets

Paris also has its share of specialty markets. In the shadow of the Paris law courts on the Île de la Cité is the flower market (see p. 54). On Sunday a bird market also takes place here, and the air is filled with the trilling of canaries and the squawking of myna birds. The Quai de la Mégisserie across the Seine is lined with pet and plant shops.

If you want antique or secondhand books, try the book market on Rue Brancion, near the Parc Georges Brassens, on Saturday and Sunday. The serious book collectors arrive early to browse through the weekly selection.

The area at the base of Montmartre is the place to find fabrics. There are two main stores. Marché St.-Pierre (*2 Rue Charles-Nodier*), a four-floor free-for-all, has the best prices for silks, wools, and furnishing fabrics. Across the street is the more sedate and expensive Reine (*5 Place St.-Pierre*). All around are smaller fabric outlets, selling everything from buttons and ribbons to bolts of exotic African and Middle Eastern fabrics.

MARKETS

Marché d'Aligre
 Métro: Ledru-Rollin
Rue Mouffetard market
 Métro: Censier Daubenton
Buci market
 Métro: Odéon
Marché Biologique
 Métro: Sèvres-Babyloue
Rue Montorgueil market
 Métro: Les Halles, Étienne Marcel
Rue du Poteau market
 Métro: Jules Joffrin
Rue Poncelet market
 Métro: Ternes
Boulevard Richard Lenoir market
 Métro: Bastille, Richard Lenoir
Belleville market
 Métro: Belleville
Quai de la Mégisserie
 Métro: Hôtel-de-Ville, Châtelet
Rue Brancion
 Métro: Porte de Vanves
Marché St.-Pierre and Reine
 Métro: Barbès-Rochechouart, Anvers

For information and advice about Paris's major flea markets, where you can find old books, records, clothes, and all manner of junk, see the Shopping chapter (p. 255). ■

More places to visit in Châtelet

FONTAINE DES INNOCENTS

Completed by Jean Goujon in 1549, this is Paris's only Renaissance fountain. With its delicate bas-reliefs, it's a great meeting place for lovers, skateboarders, punks, and bums alike. Although the square has suffered encroachment by McDonald's, Pizza Hut, Naf Naf, and other eyesores, it still offers proof of human creativity through performing musicians and entrancing mime artists.

Map p. 92   Square des Innocents   Châtelet

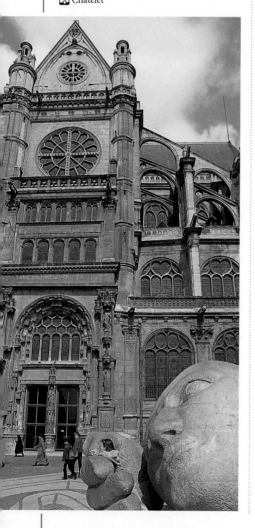

ÉGLISE ST.-EUSTACHE

Gothic and classical in plan and layout and Renaissance in decoration, this 16th-century church is second in size in Paris only to Notre-Dame. It was named for a Roman general who converted to Christianity after seeing a cross between a stag's antlers. (Note the stag's head beneath the gable point on the beautiful Renaissance transept facade.) During the Revolution, the church was converted into a Temple of Agriculture—somewhat fitting given its proximity to the market.

Many famous historical persons have made their mark on St.-Eustache. For example, it is where Louis XIV made his first Communion (1649); Molière was baptized (1622); Jean Colbert, Minister of Finance to Louis XIV, is buried (see statues of "Colbert and Abundance" by Antoine Coysevox); the funeral service for poet Jean de La Fontaine was held (1695); Hector Berlioz attended the performance by 950 musicians of his *Te Deum* (1855); Franz Liszt's *Grand Mass* premiered (1866); and Charles Gounod directed the choir. Indeed, the church's fine acoustics have ensured a long history of organ and choral music; concerts are still held regularly (check *Pariscope* for information).

Antoine Soulignac's 17th-century stained-glass windows are remarkable. There are also paintings by the school of Rubens ("Disciples at Emmaüs") and Simon Vouet ("Saint Eustache the Martyr"), and a somewhat jarringly naive sculpture by Raymond Mason.

Around the church, on Rue Montorgueil, garden stalls, butchers' shops, and boutiques give a hint of the former, bustling Les Halles market quarter. Rue du Jour has been usurped by Agnès B. and other fashionable boutiques, although the magnificent portal of the **Hôtel des Abbés de Royaumont** on this street is worth a detour. Nighthawks gather at nearby **Le Pied de Cochon** at 6 Rue Coquillère for hearty food, served until dawn.

Map p. 92   rue du Jour   01 42 36 31 05   Les Halles ■

Henri de Miller's modern head-and-hand sculpture outside the Église St.-Eustache is entitled "L'Écoute" ("Listening").

Walking through the Marais is like wandering through a vast outdoor museum, with its well-groomed squares, quiet gardens, and elaborate architectural designs.

Le Marais & Bastille

Facade, Hôtel de Rohan

Le Marais & Bastille

THE AREA FLANKING RUE ST.-ANTOINE WAS UNTIL THE 13TH CENTURY a marshy area. The name Le Marais was derived from the word for "swamp." Fed by the flooding of the Seine, it was used for market gardening. The quarter was gradually converted into a residential area; several convents were established, followed by lords' country homes, or *courtilles*, and royal residences. The religious orders, who subsisted on the market gardens in the 14th century, sold their properties to members of the nobility who were seeking land outside the city walls.

The Musée Carnavalet is devoted to the often turbulent history of Paris.

By the late 15th century, the old nobility, or *noblesse d'épée*, was firmly implanted. In the 16th century, there was an influx of newly ennobled financial and intellectual bourgeoisie—the *noblesse de robe*—which supplied the crown with much required funds by purchasing expensive titles. The royalty left after Henri II's death in 1559, but the aristocracy remained, erecting a number of superb mansions. In the late 17th century, after the court moved to Versailles, Le Marais began to fall into decline because of its remote eastern location, and by 1815, the area had become more synonymous with the *petite bourgeoisie.*

The Place des Vosges (see pp. 106–107), formerly called the Place Royale, was built by Henri IV in 1605. It spearheaded the development of the elegant Marais area, filled with sumptuous *hôtels particuliers* reminiscent of tiny, individual castles, including the Hôtel de Sully (see p. 116), the Hôtel de Rohan (now part of the Archives; see p. 117), the Hôtel de Sens (see p. 120), the Hôtel Salé (which houses the Musée Picasso; see pp. 110–11), and the Hôtel Carnavalet (see p. 113).

Unlike many other areas of Paris, Le Marais escaped the major urbanization overhaul during the 1960s, as Culture Minister André Malraux decreed that it be restored, given its great historic value. The architectural traditions were successfully preserved, and the area is dense with elaborate doorways, windows, inner courtyards, bas-reliefs (such as the "Horses of Apollo" at the Hôtel de Rohan), original street names carved in stone underneath the standard blue street sign, and historic landmarks, such as vestiges of the Philippe-Auguste Wall, the Porte de Clisson, and the nearby Place de la Bastille. Fashion designers and yuppies have moved in, and the resulting gentrification has brought kitsch and sleek lines that are glazing over much of the area's charm.

The conversion of the former *hammam* (Turkish baths) on Rue des Rosiers in the old Jewish quarter into a trendy café is a potent illustration of the changing character of the area. ■

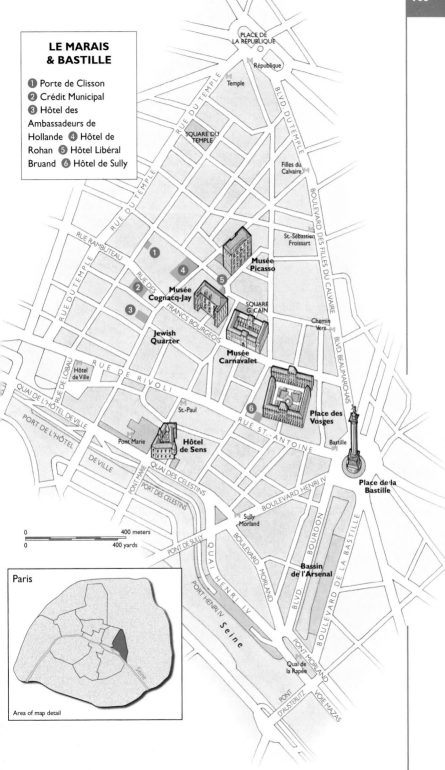

LE MARAIS & BASTILLE

1 Porte de Clisson
2 Crédit Municipal
3 Hôtel des Ambassadeurs de Hollande 4 Hôtel de Rohan 5 Hôtel Libéral Bruand 6 Hôtel de Sully

PLACE DE LA RÉPUBLIQUE

République

Temple

RUE DU TEMPLE

SQUARE DU TEMPLE

BLVD. DU TEMPLE

Filles du Calvaire

St-Sébastien Froissart

BOULEVARD DES FILLES DU CALVAIRE

RUE RAMBUTEAU

RUE DU TEMPLE

RUE DES

Musée Picasso

1

4

2

5

3

Musée Cognacq-Jay

FRANCS BOURGEOIS

SQUARE G. CAIN

Chemin Vert

BLVD BEAUMARCHAIS

Jewish Quarter

Musée Carnavalet

Hôtel de Ville

RUE DE LOBAU

RUE DE RIVOLI

Place des Vosges

St-Paul

6

RUE ST-ANTOINE

Bastille

QUAI DE L'HÔTEL DE VILLE

PORT DE L'HÔTEL

DE VILLE

Pont Marie

PONT MARIE

Hôtel de Sens

QUAI DES CELESTINS

PORT DES CELESTINS

Place de la Bastille

BOULEVARD HENRI IV

Sully Morland

BOURDON

BLVD MORLAND

BOULEVARD DE LA BASTILLE

0   400 meters
0   400 yards

PONT DE SULLY

QUAI HENRI IV

BOULEVARD MORLAND

Bassin de l'Arsenal

PORT HENRI IV

Seine

Quai de la Rapée

PONT MORLAND

VOIE MAZAS

PONT D'AUSTERLITZ

Paris

Area of map detail

Seine

Place des Vosges

Place des Vosges

Map p. 105

Métro: Bastille,
Chemin Vert, St.-Paul

THE PLACE DES VOSGES (ORIGINALLY THE PLACE ROYALE, but rebaptized in 1800) was Paris's first open-air square, with a striking, redbrick symmetry of 36 pavilions, 9 on a side, each with 4 arcades and steeply pitched slate roofs. The square replaced the Maison Royale des Tournelles, long the residence of the kings of France, encompassing a huge house and gardens surrounded by a wall and many small *tournelles*, or towers. Following Louis d'Orléans's death in 1407, it became Crown property.

**Top and above:
The Queen's
Pavilion on the
northern side of
Place des Vosges**

When Charles VI moved there from the Hôtel St.-Pol, the Place des Vosges was expanded to include several dwellings, chapels, bathhouses, cloister galleries, parks, gardens, small woods, a maze, and meadows (hence the nearby Rue du Foin, meaning "hay"). Charles VII, Louis XI, Charles VIII, Louis XII, François I, and Henri II all resided here. Four years after Henri II's death in a jousting accident on the Cours St.-Antoine (near the current Place des Vosges) in 1559, his wife, Catherine de Médicis, moved the royal residence to the Louvre, and ordered the Hôtel des Tournelles to be torn down. The square subsequently became a horse market.

Although Henri IV originally intended to convert the square into silk workshops to ease France's dependence on Italian imports, he decided instead in 1605 to build the Place Royale there, providing a square for public festivities that was otherwise lacking in Paris. The large southern pavilion, the **Pavillon du Roi,** served as a model for the others, with the **Pavillon de la Reine** opposite on the north side. Henri IV was assassinated in 1610 before the square's inauguration in 1612. The inauguration celebrated a fantastic double wedding between Louis XIII (Henri IV's successor, whose statue stands in the square) and Anne of Austria, and between Princess Elisabeth de France and the future Philippe IV. Thirteen hundred horsemen paraded to the sounds of 150 trumpets, and 80 musettes, oboes, and violins; torchbearers streamed through the streets of Paris at night, while fireworks and rockets were fired over the Bastille.

Thereafter, the square became a stopping-off spot for foreign envoys en route to the Louvre, and a hub for luminaries such as financier Maximilien Sully and the Princesses de Rohan and de Guéménée.

Each of the numbered residences has its own story. Number 1: Built with Crown money, the Pavillon du Roi was never a royal residence, but was rented out. Number 1B: The famous literary hostess Madame de Sévigné was born here in 1626. Number 4: The Marquis de Favras, who was accused of having plotted the kidnapping of Louis XVI and

the murder of Lafayette, Commander of the National Guard, lived here in 1789. Number 6: Victor Hugo lived here from 1832 to 1848, writing *Les Chants du Crépuscule* and *Ruy Blas*. In the early 20th century, the building was converted into a museum, the **Maison de Victor Hugo** (*Tel 01 42 72 10 16, closed Mon.*), containing the four-poster bed in which he died. Number 7: The entrance to the Petit Hôtel Sully, used by its owner, the Duc de Sully in the 17th century to reach the Place Royale. Number 8: The writers Théophile Gautier and Alphonse Daudet lived on the second floor in the mid-19th century. Number 9: The 19th-century tragedian Rachel (Élisa Félix) lived here in 1857; it is now the l'Ambroisie restaurant. Number 21: Cardinal Richelieu lived here from 1615 to 1623.

In 1818 the statue of Louis XIII in the square replaced a bronze one erected in 1639 by Cardinal Richelieu. Today, the square is trimmed with linden trees, and you can stretch out on grass—a rarity in Paris as this is often forbidden. Sunday afternoons are great for strolling around the arcades, listening to a variety of music, and browsing in the small stores. ■

A variety of places to eat coexist under the arcades at Place des Vosges—from the rustic Ma Bourgogne to the refined, and pricey, l'Ambroisie.

Streets of Paris

For centuries, travel was arduous through Paris's dark, muddy streets, then unmarked and unnumbered. Store signs came into use by the 15th century, and these served as addresses. At first they were unwieldy, sheet-metal plaques suspended on a long, iron arm. They were also enormous—a tooth-puller's molar was as big as an armchair, and a glove-boutique's glove could fit a small child into each finger. They made the dark streets even darker, and were noisy and dangerous on windy days. By the mid-18th century, signs were smaller and fixed above the stores. Some brilliant store signs can be seen at the Musée Carnavalet (see p. 113).

Street names

In 1728, street names were ordered to appear on corners; plaques went up all over the city, with names also carved into stone on street corner buildings. In 1844, the blue, enameled iron plaques currently in use began to bear street names. Many streets have been named and renamed—after noted merchants or residents, such as Galande; surrounding villages, like Belleville or Charonne; churches; professions (Coutellerie for the knifemaking area); landmarks like fountains or horse markets (Cul-de-sac du Ha! Ha!, now Cul-de-sac-Royale St.-Antoine); store signs (Chat qui Pêche, Pot-de-fer); historic milestones and events (Avenue Quatre-Septembre); heroes; victories; leaders; and even Métro stations. The new streets around the Bibliothèque Nationale de France in 1994 were named after writers such as François Mauriac and Raymond Aron.

In certain areas, such as Le Marais, you can still see the stone street name underneath the blue plaque. The Revolution wiped out anything religious or royal for a period; Rue de Berlin became Rue de Liège after World War I, for example. Sometimes, the names shocked residents—for example, Rue Pélican was originally a den of iniquity called Rue Poil-au-Con (a coarse reference to hairy buttocks); others merely evolved through wordplay (Rue de la Croix became Rue Eugène-Delacroix in 1868).

Lighting the City of Light

In 1318, only three public lanterns lit Paris at night, one at the Grand Châtelet fortress-prison; another at the Nesle Tower to guide sailors; and the last at the Cimetière des Innocents—the "lantern of the dead." In the first half of the 16th century, Louis XII, François I, and Henri II ordered candles to be placed in one window of each home—yet an average 15 people were murdered in the streets each night. In 1662 a mobile lighting system was adopted for those wishing to move about town at night. Porters bearing wax torches (and charging per layer of wax consumed) or oil lamps accompanied people to their doors, even if they lived several flights up.

Under Louis XIV (R.1643–1715), 3,000 lanterns were placed in the streets; these in turn were gradually replaced by oil-fueled, reflecting street lamps. There were 13,000 by 1837, and 240 lamplighters lit them as night approached, taking only three-quarters of an hour. Gas lighting spread quickly during the Restoration, with 8,000 gas lamps by 1845. Electricity first lit the Place de l'Opéra in 1878.

More recently, high-tech lighting systems using halogen lamps to bring out the sculpture and details have upgraded bridges. The Eiffel Tower, in contrast to more traditional flood-lighting, now glows from the inside.

What to look for

Paris is best seen at a slow stroll—as you go along, look up at the rooftop gardens, pilasters, caryatids, and mosaics. You'll also find a series of cityscape frescoes scattered throughout Paris. The idea for frescoes stemmed from 1930s ads painted onto walls billing the aperitif "Dubo Dubon Dubonnet"—still visible on Rue de Sèvres—or the chocolate drink Banania. In the 1970s, artists were commissioned to decorate walls with trompe l'oeil frescoes or figures. A few examples include the Egyptian ruins on Place de Torcy in the 18th arrondissement; the blue-and-purple greenhouse at 60 Rue de Reuilly in the 12th; the man on bended knee on Rue Dussoubs in the 2nd; and the giant bookshelf at 52 Rue de Belleville in the 20th. ■

Left: Detail of the Place des Victoires, inaugurated in 1686, the first royal square to be dedicated to Louis XIV

Below: Rue Norvins was once the main street of the village of Montmartre, leading to the Place du Tertre; in the background rises the white dome of the Basilica of Sacré-Coeur.
Right: Decorative lampposts grace the Place de la Concorde.

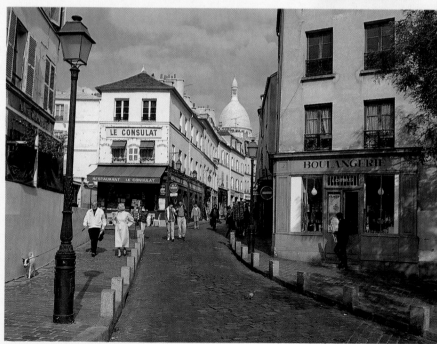

Musée Picasso

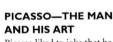
WITH ITS SPHINX-GUARDED ENTRANCE, THE MUSÉE Picasso has the largest collection of works by Picasso in the world and gives a strong sense of the freshness and inventiveness that permeated every medium he touched. It is a must for anyone interested in 20th-century art.

The Musée Picasso occupies the Hôtel Salé dating from 1656.

HÔTEL SALÉ

The Musée Picasso is located in the Hôtel Salé, built by Jean Boullier in 1656 for a salt-tax collector named Pierre Aubert de Fontenay. (*"Salé"* means "salty," but it also means "very expensive"—probably because salted meat was considered more valuable than poorly salted meat—and indeed, this hôtel particulier was extremely expensive to build.) Aubert, a nouveau riche who made his fortune as a tax collector,

displayed his rather ostentatious taste in the grandiose ironwork staircase, composed of winged figures bearing garlands of fruit framing medallions, and the Salon de Jupiter, with its cherubs, garlands, and two medallions with reclining gods. The decoration is the work of the sculptor Martin Desjardins.

Following Aubert's death, the hôtel was rented out to various parties, including the Venetian Embassy and Leclerc de Juigné. The last archbishop of Paris before the Revolution, he covered up the nude sculptures on the walls. The hôtel was pillaged during the Revolution, then sold and rented to two art schools, the École Centrale des Arts et Manufactures and the École des Métiers d'Art. The City of Paris acquired the mansion in 1964 and leased it to the State, which considered making it a costume museum. Picasso's death in 1973, however, prompted a search for a proper museum to display his works, and the Hôtel Salé was selected in 1976—appropriately, since the historic mansion corresponded to the artist's taste in architecture.

PICASSO—THE MAN AND HIS ART

Picasso liked to joke that he was the world's greatest collector of Picassos, and indeed he kept much of his own output during his nearly 80 years of artistic production. Born in Malaga in 1881, Picasso left Spain at the age of 23 for France. Because of his close affinity with France, he lived most of his life here.

After a 1934 visit to Spain, he vowed never to return because of his opposition to Franco.

After Picasso's death in Mougins, his heirs donated his artworks in lieu of paying estate duties, and this allowed the State to have first choice in selecting the works that now form the bulk of the museum's collection. Their choices were not necessarily the finest of Picasso's works but are representative of his prolific output. In all, they total 203 paintings, 158 sculptures, 28 tableaux reliefs, 16 paper collages, 88 ceramic pieces, and over 3,000 prints and drawings, ranging from "The Girl With Bare Feet" (painted in 1895, when Picasso was 14) to his later works. Picasso had kept many of his masterpieces, and although many of them had traveled for temporary exhibitions, some had never been seen, even by his friends. The artist left very few unfinished or abandoned works, and obviously took great care of his collection, as even the fragile cubist constructions were in good condition.

The number of works and their diversity mark the originality of this museum, which provides detailed descriptions as it traces the artist's career chronologically—the movement into his blue period followed the suicide of a friend, Casagemas; the rose period, when he accentuated volume and the simplification and disproportion of features typical of Iberian art; the impact of his discovery of African and Oceanic art at an exhibition at the Ethnological Museum at Trocadéro; his movement from Cézanne's cubism, with its simplified volumes, to his own more complex use of volume; his revolutionary incorporation of everyday items, or "real elements," to facilitate identification, unknown in the history of painting; his thematic works, which revolved around minotauromachy (minotaur fighting), crucifixion, and the *corrida* (bullfight); and his movement from painting and sculpture to paper collage and tableau relief, which transferred the characteristics of each medium onto the other.

The museum also shows his favorite models—Dora Maar, his wife Jacqueline, and Marie-Thérèse—in many forms, displaying his virtually unmatched skill as a draftsman. Picasso's own collection, including works by Paul Cézanne, Henri Matisse, Georges Braque, André Dérain, Pierre Renoir, and Douanier Rousseau, along with his collection of primitive art, is also exhibited. The splendid furniture and chandeliers are by Diego Giacometti, the Swiss artist Alberto's brother. ∎

One of Picasso's portraits of Dora Maar, "Femme Assise aux Bras Croisés" ("Seated Woman with Arms Crossed"), painted in 1937

Jewish Quarter

Jewish Quarter
- Map p. 105
- Centered on rue des Rosiers
- Métro: St.-Paul

Musée d'Art et d'Histoire du Judaïsme
- Hôtel de Saint-Aignan
  71 rue du Temple
  75003
- 01 53 01 86 53
- Closed Sat., some Jewish holidays

JEWISH PEOPLE HAVE LIVED IN PARIS SINCE THE SIXTH century, as recorded by Gregory of Tours. They were believed to have come with the Romans as merchants or craftsmen. The first Jewish quarter in Paris was not created, however, until 1119 along Rue de la Juiverie (now Rue de la Cité).

Following Philippe-Auguste's expulsion of the Jews in 1182, there was a new influx in 1198, with some returning to the Left Bank, and others gravitating toward the Right Bank and Rue St.-Bon. When it became compulsory for Jews to live within restricted areas of the city in 1294, they coalesced around Rue St.-Merry and the Seine.

Another Jewish quarter sprang up in the same period farther east, between Rue des Rosiers and Rue aux Juifs (today's Rue Ferdinand Duval). After a series of expulsions and returns, only a few Jewish people remained in Paris after 1394, when they were banished by Charles VI. They returned in the early 18th century and were granted citizenship in 1791 during the Revolution. In 1871 the Jewish community numbered 25,000.

In the late 19th century, an influx of Jews from Central and Eastern Europe settled in and around Rue des Rosiers. Sephardic Jews from Egypt, Algeria, Tunisia, and Morocco, arriving between 1950 and 1962, spread the community far beyond this initial area.

Today, the more traditional section of the quarter has been squeezed down to the western end of Rue des Rosiers. Jo Goldenberg's (No. 7) and Finkelstzan's (No. 27) are the traditional landmarks for herring, flanken, borscht, and other specialties. The old Jewish boys' school *(École de Hospitalières, 10 Rue de Hospitalières-St.-Gervais),* where 165 students were rounded up and deported, is nearby; N'OUBLIEZ PAS ("Do not forget") is engraved on the wall.

The newly opened **Musée d'Art et d'Histoire du Judaïsme** explores Jewish heritage with an emphasis on ceremonies, rites, and learning. It includes works by Chaim Soutine, Chagall, and Modigliani. ∎

Owner André Journo paints displays, adages, and maxims on the exterior walls of Chez Marianne, a deli and restaurant in the Jewish Quarter.

Musée Carnavalet

THIS RENAISSANCE-STYLE MUSEUM DEVOTED TO PARISIAN history is housed in the Hôtel Carnavalet, where celebrated letter-writer Madame de Sévigné once lived. Originally built for the president of the parliament in 1548, it was acquired by the widow of Henri III's tutor, Kernevenoy, who was nicknamed Carnavalet (a corruption of his name).

Musée Carnavalet

- Map p. 105
- 23 rue de Sévigné
- 01 44 59 58 58
- Closed Mon.
- $$
- Métro: St.-Paul, Chemin Vert

THE MUSEUM

As he was razing Paris and pushing the poor out toward the suburbs, Baron Haussmann (see p. 160–61) asked the City of Paris in 1866 to acquire the Musée Carnavalet for storing the interiors of buildings he dismantled. The mansion was expanded, Renaissance-style galleries were built, and architectural elements, such as the Nazareth archway (from the old Palais de la Cité), were added. The museum's collection is displayed in two buildings—the remodeled Hôtel Carnavalet has collections dating from the origins of Paris to the Revolution; and the adjacent Hôtel Le Peletier de St.-Fargeau has the world's largest collection of portraits, objects, and memorabilia from the Revolutionary period and after.

THE COLLECTIONS

The rooms are arranged chronologically to illustrate the changing face of Paris. Exhibitions range from the city's origins to the 16th-century Renaissance influence; through 17th-century decorative ensembles, to the French Revolution and its impact on the capital; the Second Empire; and the belle epoque. You'll also find Marcel Proust's bedroom, a scale model of a guillotine, a small piece of the Bastille, and objects belonging to Voltaire and Rousseau. Don't miss Charles Le Brun's painted ceiling in the Hôtel de La Rivière (Room 21), the Louis XV Bouvier collection (Rooms 37 to 48), Demarteau's salon by Boucher and Fragonard (Room 62), and the temporary exhibits and concerts (check schedule). ∎

STORE SIGNS

The entrance to the Musée Carnavalet has a superb collection of old store signs donated by previous proprietors. Such signs were plentiful during the Ancien Régime, as street and house numbering did not develop until the late 18th century (see p. 108). ∎

Art nouveau boutique of the jeweler Fouquet in the Musée Carnavalet

Great Parisian love affairs

Time seems to stand still for lovers in Paris. Passion—as intangible and ephemeral as the charms of the city itself—has created such timeless loves as sculptors Auguste Rodin and Camille Claudel (see p. 172) and writers Anaïs Nin and Henry Miller. The fame of these historic liaisons is such that for many, the capital is synonymous with love itself.

Love united in death:
Héloïse & Abélard

One of the earliest recorded pairs of lovers repose in the Père-Lachaise Cemetery. Sometime around 1118, a man named Fulbert offered scholar Peter Abélard (1079–1142) hospitality in his home on the Île de la Cité in exchange for ensuring Héloïse's (his 17-year-old niece) education. Despite their age difference (Abélard was 39), the two fell in love and married secretly. Outraged, Fulbert laid a trap for Abélard and had him castrated. Héloïse, who died 24 years after her lover, had arranged for the two to be united in death by being buried in the same coffin; a disapproving nun thwarted her plans and placed them in separate coffins. Héloïse's wish was finally granted in 1817, when their remains were united in the neo-Gothic tomb at Père-Lachaise (see p. 84).

Royal mistress:
Henri II & Diane de Poitiers

Although the initials of Henri II (1519-1559) and Catherine de Médicis carved throughout the south wing of the Cour Carrée in the Louvre seem to imply a great devotion between the monarchs, the intertwined letters "H" and "C" were actually an expression of Henri's deep attachment to his mistress, Diane de Poitiers, who was 20 years his senior. The insignia was therefore meant to be read as a double "D" for Diane, not "C" for Catherine. When Henri granted Diane the revenue from a tax on church bells, Rabelais famously quipped: "The king hung the bells of the realm around the neck of his mare." The queen was relegated to near obscurity until the king died, at which time she took her revenge by ousting Diane from her beloved château of Chenonceau in the Loire Valley.

Unrequited love:
Napoleon & Josephine

Napoleon Bonaparte, the man who conquered most of Europe, had trouble conquering the woman he loved. On March 9, 1796, he and Josephine de Beauharnais were married in a simple civil ceremony. What began as a marriage of convenience for Josephine—a widowed aristocrat seeking financial and political security in the troubled years after the Revolution—was a true affair of the heart for the future emperor of France, who was passionately in love with his wife. He ended one of his many ardent letters to her with these words: "I shall see you in three hours. Until then, *mio dolce amor*, a thousand kisses; but give me none in return, for they set my blood on fire." They spent their happiest moments together at the Château de Malmaison (see p. 232), but he divorced her in 1809 when she could not produce an heir. Napoleon continued to bankroll her extravagant lifestyle, however, while pleading with her to limit her lavish spending. Despite his continuing support, she owed three million francs at her death in 1814.

The Romantics:
George Sand & Frédéric Chopin

The 19th century was the era of the Romantics. A leading figure of the times, writer George Sand (born Amandine-Aurore-Lucie Dupin in 1804), led a wild, bohemian life in Paris after leaving her oafish husband in the countryside. She embarked on a tempestuous, short-lived love affair with French poet Alfred de Musset, followed by her most famous liaison with Polish composer Frédéric Chopin.

The two were part of the community of Romantic artists and writers who lived in the area known as La Nouvelle Athènes, just south of Montmartre. They broke off in 1847 when he fell ill with tuberculosis and grew impatient with her hovering maternal solicitude. Traces of this famous couple are visible at the Musée de la Vie Romantique (*16 Rue Chaptal, Tel 01 48 74 95 38, closed Mon., Métro: St.-Georges or Pigalle*), with Chopin memorabilia and a re-creation of her drawing room.

Above: Detail of Vigier du Vigneau's 1867 "La Rose de Malmaison," showing Empress Josephine with her friends and sisters-in-law in her Malmaison garden, receiving a rose from Napoleon

The eroticists: Henry Miller & Anaïs Nin

The film *Henry and June* (1990) shows something of the stormy ménage à trois between American writer Henry Miller, his wife June, and the French erotic writer, Anaïs Nin, during the 1920s. The three of them embarked on an exploration of sexual libertinism that developed a new form of literature, resulting in Miller's banned *Tropic of Cancer* and Nin's *Diaries* (in which she chronicled her sexual experiences) and *Delta of Venus*. Miller rented a house at 18 Villa Seurat, which he shared with Nin from time to time. ■

Star-crossed lovers Héloïse and Abélard, depicted in Jean de Meung's 14th-century miniature "Le Roman de la Rose, le Testament" (Condé Museum, Chantilly; see p. 232)

Madame de Sévigné gave vivid descriptions of aristocratic life under Louis XIV (represented here in the Musée Carnavalet's cour d'honneur) in letters to her daughter.

A walk around the old Marais

The sheer density of the historical and architectural wealth in Paris's best preserved quarter is overwhelming, requiring several days to visit all of its museums, hôtels particuliers, squares, and various sites.

Begin at Place de la Bastille and walk down Rue St.-Antoine, past Beaumarchais' statue on your right. Turn right on Rue de Birague to enter **Place des Vosges ➊** (see p. 106) via the king's pavilion, and right again under the arcades to visit the stores and galleries, noting the illustrious residences. Exit at No. 7 through the passageway into the gardens and building of **Hôtel de Sully,** now the Caisse National des Monuments Historiques et des Sites (the institution in charge of classified historic monuments and sites). The passageway may be closed at night; if so, return to Rue de Birague to reach Rue St.-Antoine.

Turn right on Rue St.-Antoine and right again on Rue Caron. Continue to **Place du Marché Ste.-Catherine,** once a 13th-century Augustinian priory. Cross the square and turn left on the tranquil Rue de Jarente. No. 6 leads to a charming, villagelike wing off the street. From there, turn right onto Rue de Sévigné, and then left onto Rue des Francs-

Bourgeois. (Rue des Poulies, "pulleys," between Rue Vieille du Temple and Rue Payenne was named for the looms of medieval weavers' workshops.) Number 23, now a chic shoe store, was a former belle epoque *boulangerie*.

Visit the **Musée Carnavalet ➋** (see p. 113) before continuing down Rue des Francs-Bourgeois. Note the lovely quadrangular watchtower bearing the letters S.C. on its base, marking the limits of the estates of the Convent of Ste.-Catherine-du-Val-des-Écoliers from which the land was bought. It is part of one of Le Marais' oldest mansions, the Hôtel de Lamoignon (now the Bibliothèque Historique de la Ville de Paris—the History Library of Paris). Hector Guimard built the synagogue at 10 Rue Pavée; he fled to the United States with his American-Jewish wife during the rise of Nazism.

Turn right on Rue Payenne. The **Square Georges Cain,** a splendid park with ruins and monuments, holds the **Musée**

Lapidaire de Paris (Stone Museum of Paris), a cemetery for old stones. Look through the **Musée Cognacq-Jay** ❸ (see p. 120) at No. 11 on the left side of the street; note the keel-shaped roof of the Swedish Cultural Center next door, where the governess of Marie-Antoinette's children once lived. The courtyard of No. 13 is particularly exquisite in summer.

Take a left on Rue du Parc Royal, opposite Square Léopold Achille, and continue to Place de Thorigny. **Hôtel Libéral Bruand** at 1 Rue de la Perle has a lock museum with locks, door handles, and metal fastenings from Roman times to the belle epoque, including refined pieces from various royal châteaux. Take a right onto Rue de Thorigny for the **Musée Picasso** ❹ (see pp. 110–11). Backtrack and continue down Rue de la Perle, taking a detour at the corner of Rue Vieille du Temple (left) for the **Hôtel de Rohan** ❺. Inside, you can see Robert Le Lorrain's magnificent "Horses of Apollo" bas-relief (open only for temporary exhibits and scheduled

tours). Walk along Rue des Quatre Fils (the continuation of Rue de la Perle after the Vieille du Temple intersection) toward the **Hôtel Guénégaud** ❻ on the right. This 17th-century mansion, now the Musée de la Chasse et de la Nature—Museum of Hunting and Nature (*60 Rue des Archives, Tel 01 53 01 92 40, closed Mon., Métro: Hôtel de Ville*), with its small, beautiful formal garden, is the only

---

- ⓜ See also area map p. 105
- ▶ Place de la Bastille
- ⟷ 1.5 miles (2.4 km)
- ⏱ Allow 3 hours
- ▶ Rue des Rosiers

NOT TO BE MISSED
- Place des Vosges
- Place du Marché Ste.-Catherine
- Musée Carnavalet
- Square Georges Cain
- Musée Picasso
- Rue des Rosiers

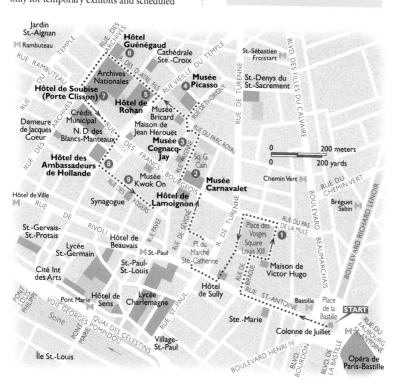

Mansart-designed hôtel particulier still fully intact. Turn left on Rue des Archives—No. 58 is the great **Porte Clisson** ⑦ (built between 1372 and 1375), flanked by two Gothic turrets. Built on Templar grounds, it was the gateway to the manor house of Olivier de Clisson, Constable of France and companion-in-arms to the warrior Du Guesclin, and it is one of the city's oldest vestiges. The Guise family, the most powerful in Le Marais, obtained the mansion in the 16th century, using it as their headquarters during the Wars of Religion; the St. Bartholomew's Day Massacre (see p. 21) was probably plotted here. The mansion was reconstructed by François de Rohan, Prince of Soubise, and the Clisson gateway was incorporated. In the early 19th century, the mansion became state property, and Napoleon annexed Rue des Quatre Fils and Rue des Archives to store the national archives in 1808.

Take a left on Rue des Francs-Bourgeois. On the right at No. 55 is the Mont de Piété or Crédit Municipal, a government-run pawnshop, auction house, and bank created in 1777. Enter the courtyard on the right to see the remains of one of Philippe-Auguste's 20 towers from the 800-year-old wall,

preserved thanks to Victor Hugo's intervention. Continue to the graceful Renaissance-style tower on the corner of Rue Vieille du Temple and Rue des Francs-Bourgeois, home of Jehan Hérouet, Louis XII's treasurer.

Turn right onto Rue Vieille du Temple, which has a stupendous door facade (No. 47) with Renaudin's Medusa head and the Hôtel Amelot de Bisseuil, also known as the **Hôtel des Ambassadeurs de Hollande** ⑧, where Beaumarchais lived and wrote *The Marriage of Figaro*. Although never an embassy, it was from 1720 to 1727 home to a Protestant chaplain from the Dutch embassy, who held services after the Edict of Nantes was revoked. One of Benjamin Franklin's relatives was wed here, and Madame Necker, the future Madame de Stael, a Protestant, was baptized here in 1766. Knock and you may be permitted inside to see a 1660 bas-relief of "Romulus and Remus" and four large sundials on the walls.

As you exit, turn right and then left onto **Rue des Rosiers** ⑨ (see p. 112), the heart of the medieval Jewish Quarter. Traces of the Philippe-Auguste Wall can be found at Nos. 8, 10, and 14. ∎

Jewish memorabilia and books can be found at Librairie du Marais Rosiers, Rue des Rosiers.

Place de la Bastille

THE GOLDEN SPIRIT OF LIBERTY GLEAMS IN THE SUN BY day, and the illuminated July Column shines beaconlike at night. Place de la Bastille is not significant for what stands here today—cafés, movie theaters, and an opera house (Opéra de Paris-Bastille) that looks like a beached silver whale—but for its history. Intended as a square for the people, it is still the scene of many political and social demonstrations. Every year, on July 14, the entire city celebrates Bastille Day, with major fireworks held on the 13th, and street dances and a military parade along the Champs-Élysées on the 14th.

The eight-towered fortress with its moat, drawbridge, and crenelated walls was built during the 14th century to ward off English attacks from the east and protect the Hôtel St.-Pol (Charles V's residence). The Café Français *(3 Place de la Bastille)* now stands where the medieval gate was. Pinkish cobblestones indicate the precise location of the Bastille, which never played a military role except during the Fronde (see p. 21); instead, it was a State prison from the days of Cardinal Richelieu.

A series of illustrious figures were imprisoned here in the 17th and 18th centuries, in surprisingly comfortable conditions—the Cardinal de Rohan hosted a dinner party for 20 here; the Marquis de Sade had his own wine brought in from Provence; and Voltaire praised the food upon his release. Because the prison was expensive to run, Necker, Minister of Finance to Louis XVI, planned to tear down the Bastille (and replace it with Place Louis XVI), but Revolutionary fervor did it for him.

THE JULY COLUMN

The July Column was inspired by Trajan's column in Rome, and commemorates those who died during the July 1830 Revolution. At night it is illuminated, and beneath the column is a spherical gallery where the victims' remains from the 1830 and 1848 Revolutions lie (see p. 25). ∎

The July Column, centerpiece of the Place de la Bastille, and the Opéra de Paris-Bastille. The opera was conceived "for the people," making it accessible to all—although the cheaper seats are often at vertiginous heights.

Place de la Bastille

🅰 Map p. 105

🚇 Métro: Bastille

More places to visit in Le Marais & Bastille

BASSIN DE L'ARSENAL

Leisure boats are docked in a basin that occupies what used to be part of the former ancient moats of the Bastille. The southern extremity of Canal St.-Martin flows underneath Place de la Bastille, offering a lovely garden on the eastern bank.

Map p. 105 ✉ Between boulevards Bourdon and de la Bastille Métro: Bastille

HÔTEL DE SENS

One of the few great medieval private residences in Paris, this beautiful, half-civilian, half-military mansion (circa 1475), overlooking the Seine, provides a fine example of the transitional period between Gothic and Renaissance styles. The architect remains unknown, although it was possibly a joint project of Tristan de Salazar, Archbishop of Sens at the time, and Martin Chambiges, who designed the transept for Sens cathedral. In 1605 Henri IV housed his former wife, Queen Margot, here, and it was later used for various businesses. The gable next to the tower on the left still holds the orange-size shell that was lobbed at the mansion during the 1830 Revolution.

The City of Paris purchased the Hôtel de Sens in 1911 and began to restore it in 1929. In 1961 it was turned into the Forney Library of Decorative and Fine Arts; its stunning reading room is open to the public.

Map p. 105 ✉ 1 rue du Figuier ☎ 01 42 78 14 60 🕐 Closed Sun.–Mon. 💲 Free; temporary exhibits $ Métro: St.-Paul, Pont Marie

MUSÉE COGNACQ-JAY

The museum, with its collection of 18th-century European paintings and furniture, was assembled by Ernest Cognacq and his wife, Louise Jay (founders of the Samaritaine department store). Some of the objects belonged to the Hôtel Denon; others were part of Cognacq's personal collection, which was bequeathed to the City of Paris in 1928 and includes works by Fragonard, Boucher, Chardin, Reynolds, Guardi, Canaletto, and Watteau. There is also an extremely rare collection of jeweled and enameled snuffboxes.

Map p. 105 ✉ Hôtel Denon, 8 rue Elzévir ☎ 01 40 27 07 21 🕐 Closed Mon. 💲 $ Métro: St.-Paul ∎

Leisure boats dock at the Arsenal Basin, but many people live on houseboats here year-round.

There are more than a hundred museums in Paris, yet the Louvre stands alone for its high-tech pyramid and scope of its collection. Paris spared no expense to adorn its masterpiece, the largest museum in the world.

The Louvre & Palais-Royal

The Louvre Pyramid

The Louvre & Palais-Royal

THE MONARCHY MAY BE LONG GONE, BUT ALMOST EVERYTHING IN THIS neighborhood is a reminder of centuries of royal rule. Although the Louvre is now a museum, it was originally constructed as a fortress to protect Paris from various foreign invaders. For nearly 600 years it was the royal residence; each king (and emperor, for that matter) altered, expanded, and renovated the work of his predecessors. It later became the royal family's shelter from Parisians during periods of civil unrest.

As the palace expanded, so did its surrounding streets. The gardens were extended westward; the Tuileries Palace was constructed outside the old city walls, then linked to the Louvre; the Palais-Royal, a former royal residence (see p. 141) was constructed; and Rue de Rivoli (see p. 142) was laid out.

As the Louvre museum was formed from royal collections, so the Bibliothèque Nationale (see p. 159) began as a royal library, when Charles V brought his personal library of 973 works to the palace in 1373. The library was dispersed after his death, but successive kings built it up again. The idea for the Bibliothèque Nationale took form during Louis XIV's reign. His finance minister, Jean-Baptiste Colbert, gathered the royal collection and stored it in a lavish palace on Rue de Richelieu. It expanded over the centuries, outgrowing its original premises; the books have been transferred to the new Bibliothèque de France (on Quai de la Gare), which opened in 1997, while prints, photographs, maps, medals, and musical scores remain in the older building.

During the 19th century, France wavered between royal rule and revolution, and much of the action was staged in and around the Louvre. Louis XVI was held captive in the Tuileries Palace before being beheaded, and revolutionaries gathered in the Palais-Royal gardens, where the first call to arms was sounded. During the Commune of 1870–71, the Tuileries Palace, the symbol of royal oppression, was burned down. Afterward, a relative peace settled over Paris, and this neighborhood once again attracted the rich and fashionable.

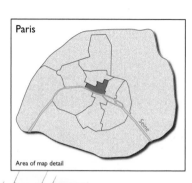

Paris

Area of map detail

Concorde

PLACE DE LA CONCORDE

Galerie National du Jeu de Paume

Musée de l'Orangerie

Jardin des Tuileries

PORT DES TUILERIES

Seine

QUAI

DES

TUILER

PONT DE SOLFERINO

PORT DES TUILE

R u e

Although the streets are now lined with tourist shops, a few exclusive establishments remain, including the Hôtel Meurice— once a 19th-century haven for a wealthy British clientele. While the city extends for miles from this center, it is easy to escape the noise of the nearby streets in the recently reno-vated Jardin des Tuileries (see p. 137), or the even more discreet gardens of the Palais-Royal, which are completely shut off from traffic.

The Louvre has been revived both above and below ground. I.M. Pei's controversial 1989 pyramid was the first of many manifes-tations of this major facelift. An entire subter-ranean city stretches out beyond the museum, with the Carrousel du Louvre—a vast, ele-gant, underground complex, complete with shops, parking, and a food court. An inverted glass pyramid echoes Pei's main entrance, pro-viding light to the entire underground area.

The Tuileries gardens lie west of the Louvre toward the Place de la Concorde and the eighth arrondissement. Two museums flank the gardens, overlooking the Concorde: the Jeu de Paume, now an exhibition center for contemporary art; and the Orangerie (see p. 140), which houses Monet's famous water lilies paintings, as well as 22 paintings by Soutine, 14 by Cézanne, and 24 by Renoir. ■

THE LOUVRE & PALAIS-ROYAL

1 Carrousel du Louvre

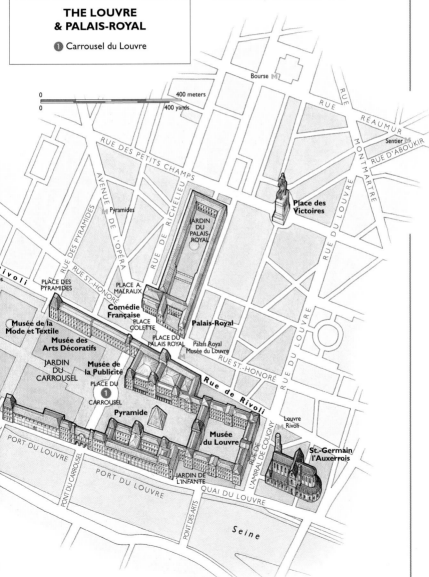

Musée du Louvre

Musée du Louvre
www.louvre.fr

▲ Map p. 123

✉ Main entrance: Pyramide du Louvre, Cour Napoléon.

☎ 01 40 20 53 17. Recorded information: 01 40 20 51 51.

🕐 Open 9 a.m.–6 p.m.; Closed Tues. Open late Mon. (limited access) & Wed. Rooms are closed on a rotation basis (check before visiting).

💲 $$. Reduced charge from 3 p.m. & all day Sun.; free 1st Sun. of each month & for under 18s. Guided tour: $. Audio guide: $$. To avoid long lines, purchase tickets in advance (Tel 08 03 80 88 03 or 08 03 34 63 46) or at 500 sales outlets in France (Fnac, Virgin Megastore, etc.). The newly opened tribal arts rooms are most easily accessed through the Porte des Lions.

🚇 Métro: Palais-Royal–Musée du Louvre

"I have nearly the whole of the Louvre in my head: room by room, painting by painting," Alberto Giacometti, quoted in *Dialogues of the Louvre* (1972).

THE HUGE "GRAND LOUVRE" MODERNIZATION PROJECT, initiated by President François Mitterrand in 1981, has transformed this magnificent museum both inside and out. The first step was I.M. Pei's glass pyramid, which created space, light, and a much needed main entrance; the next steps reorganized the collections and exhibition spaces.

The Louvre began in 1190, when King Philippe-Auguste constructed a massive fortress surrounded by a wall and towers on the western edge of Paris before setting out on a crusade. In the 14th century, Charles V commissioned Raymond du Temple to turn the medieval keep into a royal residence. It expanded under two visionary Renaissance builders: Kings François I, who tore down the medieval keep; and Henri IV, who constructed the immense gallery bordering the Seine, thus linking the Louvre to the Tuileries Palace begun in 1564 by Catherine de Médicis (for whom the Louvre was far too drafty and inelegant). The Louvre at this time consisted of a string of buildings that stretched over a quarter of a mile along the Seine—a long passageway linking the city palace to the country home. (At that time the Tuileries lay beyond the walls of Paris.)

In 1608, Henri IV opened up the palace to artists, granting them studio space, living quarters, and the status of official recognition. When Louis XIV moved his court to Versailles in 1682, the Louvre was overrun by sculptors, painters, and architects who left the palace in a pathetic state by the mid-18th century. Among them were Jean Honoré Fragonard, Jean Chardin, François Boucher, Jean-Louis David, and Guillaume Coustou, who, along with Antoine Coysevox, sculpted the famous "Horses of Marly," now wonderfully displayed in the glass-covered Cour Marly.

In 1793 the Musée Central des Arts was inaugurated at the Louvre, which then opened as a museum, marking a turning point in its history. Napoleon III realized Henri IV's dream of constructing the Richelieu Wing to mirror the Galerie du Bord de l'Eau.

The Louvre had finally achieved a state of architectural symmetry, but it didn't last long: The Tuileries Palace enclosing its western edge was burned to the ground in 1871 by the Commune.

The Louvre and its collection of royal artwork survived, the latter growing through donations and acquisitions. The museum's antiquities departments flourished in the 19th century, as government-sponsored excavations unearthed treasures in Egypt and the Middle East. Under the terms of a now questionable agreement, the archaeological finds were divided between the various countries involved. This form of looting was justified by the argument that without intervention, these prized works faced almost certain destruction.

I.M. Pei's controversial pyramid shocked many when it was unveiled in 1989 as the new main entrance to the museum, yet it is in keeping with a long tradition—architects have always been faced with the problem of integrating the palace's disparate elements.

THE COLLECTIONS

The Louvre's collections are divided into seven departments, displayed in three main sections: Sully (the Cour Carrée); Richelieu (enclosing the wing parallel to Rue de Rivoli); and Denon (the wing along the Seine), each accessible from the main entrance beneath the pyramid.

Despite the new organization, the Louvre can be a daunting experience. On a first visit, pick up one of the free maps or the guidebook "Louvre First Visit" in the main hall and choose a few works of art or periods before setting out (for example, the "Winged Victory of Samothrace "and the "Mona Lisa").

A good place to start is in the Sully Wing, at the foundations of Philippe-Auguste's medieval keep— it's in the heart of the Louvre, kids love it, and it leads straight to the Egyptian rooms.

A brilliant anomaly, the glass pyramid by I.M. Pei has virtually the same dimensions as the Egyptian pyramid of Cheops in Giza.

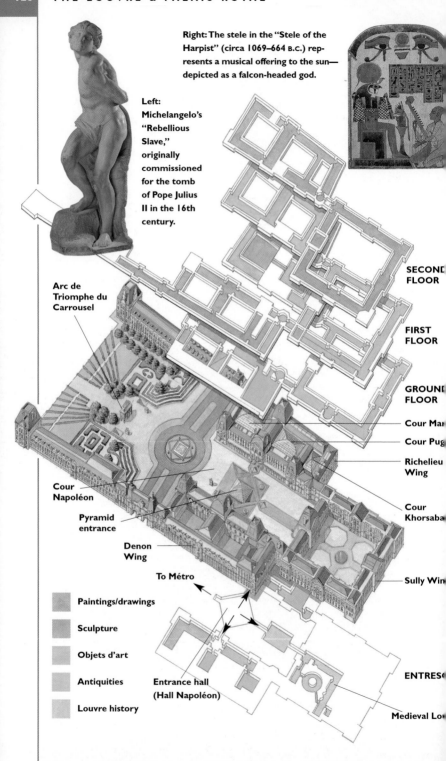

Right: The stele in the "Stele of the Harpist" (circa 1069–664 B.C.) represents a musical offering to the sun—depicted as a falcon-headed god.

Left: Michelangelo's "Rebellious Slave," originally commissioned for the tomb of Pope Julius II in the 16th century.

SECOND FLOOR

FIRST FLOOR

GROUND FLOOR

Arc de Triomphe du Carrousel

Cour Ma...

Cour Pug...

Richelieu Wing

Cour Napoléon

Cour Khorsaba...

Pyramid entrance

Denon Wing

To Métro

Sully Win...

Paintings/drawings

Sculpture

Objets d'art

Antiquities

Louvre history

Entrance hall (Hall Napoléon)

ENTRESO...

Medieval Lo...

ANTIQUITIES

The Louvre's Egyptian treasures are displayed in the Entresol level of the Denon Wing (Rooms A–3), and in Rooms 1–30 of the Sully Wing. Greek, Etruscan, and Roman antiquities can be found in the Entresol level of the Denon Wing (Rooms 1–3), and on the ground and first floors of the Denon and Sully Wings (Rooms A, B, and 4–44).

Egyptian Department

For years, this collection of nearly 55,000 objects (of which about one-tenth is exhibited), the largest collection of Egyptian antiquities after the Cairo Museum, was seriously cramped for space. The recently renovated and expanded section is now worthy of these masterpieces, which are so rich that curators have created a twofold display. The ground floor (Rooms 1–19) is arranged thematically and the upper floor (Rooms 20–30) is organized chronologically, from prehistory to the Roman conquest.

The first few rooms are devoted to specific aspects of Egyptian life—writing, fishing, farming, music, games, jewelry, and funeral rituals. A spectacular room follows, with a row of 20-foot-high (7 m) palm- and papyrus-shaped

columns of pink granite and huge statues of Ramses II (Room 12). While friezes are everywhere throughout the Egyptian collection, this room contains one of the loveliest, a painted-limestone relief of Ramses II among the gods (1275 B.C., 19th dynasty). The world of the dead is displayed in the dramatic Crypt of Osiris, providing a good overview of Egyptian religious practices. Animal mummies—from an 8-foot (3 m) crocodile to a tiny, mummified scarab—are featured in one of the last rooms in the thematic display.

The collection continues in chronological order on the upper floor. The first object is also one of the oldest: a predynastic ivory dagger from Gebel El-Arak. This sophisticated ceremonial knife was sculpted more than 5,000 years ago. The following rooms trace the rise of the First Kingdom, the era in which the pyramids were built, the cult of the pharaoh grew, and a centralized government developed. "The Seated Scribe" is in this section (Room 22), also a radiant, surprisingly tender, wooden sculpture, "Anonymous Couple." The famous Amarna period is illustrated by a colossal statue of Akhenaten (Room 25), the revolutionary pharaoh who overturned the centuries-old political and religious order by worshiping a single sun god. Although his reign lasted only 16 years, and his capital Amarna was destroyed, his influence can be seen in the more lifelike, expressive art of later dynasties. The New Kingdom (1554–1075 B.C.) was a golden age for the arts in ancient Egypt, especially during the reigns of the Tuthmoses, Amenophis,

Sandstone fragment of a colossal statue of Akhenaten (1353–1337 B.C.). The long nose and sensuous lips are characteristic of this renegade pharaoh who worshiped a single god, Aten.

French Father of Egyptology

Jean François Champollion (1790–1832) is considered the French father of Egyptology. He played a major role in deciphering the hieroglyphic text of the Rosetta Stone, thereby unlocking the mysteries of the Egyptian language. He was appointed the first curator of the Louvre's Egyptian Department in 1826. ∎

Painting inside a sarcophagus (New Empire, 18th Dynasty 1552–1199 B.C.) depicting the deceased person flanked by Maat, goddess of truth and divine order (right), and Anubis, the Egyptian god of the underworld (left)

ETYMOLOGY OF "LOUVRE"

No one knows the origin of the word "Louvre," or *Lupara* in Latin. Theories suggest it came from the words for leper house, watchtower, or Saxon fortress, or that it was named for a pack of wolves (*loups*) that lurked in the area. ■

SPELLS FOR THE AFTERLIFE

The Book of the Dead, known in ancient Egypt as the *Book to Come Forth by Day*, gives no inkling of life in the hereafter. It is actually a long litany of spells and incantations for surviving the perils beyond. ■

and Ramsesid kings, as illustrated by the painted limestone relief of Seti I and the goddess Hathor.

The Greco-Roman period began in 332 B.C. with the conquest by Alexander the Great, ending a period of Egyptian rule that lasted over 3,000 years. The final room contains one of the last masterpieces of Egyptian art, a magnificent gold jewel representing the Triad of Osiris (god of the dead), Isis (goddess of the throne), and Horus (god in the form of a falcon), their son.

To continue this chronological tour, visit the sections devoted to Egypt under Roman control (Room A) and to Coptic art (Rooms B and C) on the Entresol level at the Denon Wing entrance. There are a number of funerary statues and mummies, as well as the striking funerary portraits from Faiyum— so realistic that they were initially considered fakes. On the opposite side of the Cour Visconti is the collection of Coptic art, dating from the early centuries of the Christian era. Among the Louvre's most obscure treasures are the Coptic fabrics that date from the second century A.D., and include the brilliantly colored, complex "Sabine Shawl." The Bawit Room contains a reconstruction of the Coptic Church of Bawit (sixth–seventh centuries A.D.), discovered in 1900, and now believed to represent only a small part of the original monastery.

Greek antiquities

Two lovely women reign over this department: the "Venus de Milo" and the "Winged Victory of Samothrace." The former may be more famous, but the latter is quite simply breathtaking. She stands ready to take flight from the top of the monumental staircase, looking as though she had been sculptured by the wind itself.

The Louvre's collection stretches from preclassical Greece to the final years of the Roman Empire. The recently refurbished room on the Entresol level, Denon entrance, devoted to the preclassical era, has several remarkable examples from the Geometric (650–480 B.C.) and Archaic (circa 900 B.C.) periods. The Cycladic sculptures are especially striking: The pared-down, almost abstract idols look like sculptures from our own century. Two major pieces in the development of archaic Greek sculpture are the "Kore of Samos" and the "Dame d'Auxerre," a female figure with highly stylized drapery.

Antiquities from the classical and Hellenistic periods are on the ground floor of the Sully Wing (Rooms 8–17). During the classical period, the reputation of Greek artists spread, and they were in demand from Persia to Rome. Athens was flourishing, and state patronage of the arts was generous. Figures came to life—for example, in the Frieze of the Panathenaic Procession, 447–406 B.C. (Room 7), as artists explored the ideals of beauty, form, and emotional expression.

The Hellenistic period began with the death of Alexander the Great and the breakup of his immense empire. Artists had developed a canon of classical art and worked out the problems of anatomy, technique, and composition. This period ushered in a more experimental style, and sculptors worked to capture a broader range of human experience and movement, including childhood, old age, violence, and fear. The "Winged Victory of Samothrace," which commemorated a naval victory, is an incomparable example of this command of motion. It is dated at 190 B.C., but was only discovered in 1863. The sensuality,

The "Winged Victory," discovered in more than 300 fragments on the island of Samothrace in 1863, stands like a windswept Nike on a pedestal shaped like a ship's prow.

TREASURES IN WARTIME

Evacuated during World Wars I and II, the Louvre's treasures were packed up in unmarked crates and moved to safety (many works went to the Château of Chambord in the Loire Valley). During World War II, almost all the works had left Paris by September 1, 1939. ∎

The terra-cotta "Sarcophagus of a Married Couple," dating from the late sixth century B.C., was discovered in Cerveteri, Italy. It combines an archaic Greek style with graceful Etruscan features.

dignity, and simplicity of the "Venus de Milo" (Room 12) circa 100 B.C., on the other hand, echoes the ideals of the earlier classical era.

The Greek collection continues on the first floor, with displays of bronzes and stoneware (Rooms 32–44). Among the fine works is a cache of 109 pieces of silver and gold found at Boscoreale, near Pompeii, as well as the collection of Greek ceramics in the recently opened Campana Gallery. No examples of Greek painting have survived, but these vases, from the geometric-style funerary urns and amphorae of the eighth century B.C. to the classical masterpieces, give some indication of what it may have looked like. The golden age of Greek pottery was from the mid-sixth to the mid-fifth century B.C., with the development of the so-called "red-figure" technique (replacing the earlier "black-figure" technique). A krater (bowl for mixing wine and water) illustrated by Euphronios (510 B.C.) shows the refinement in painting at this time, with atten-

tion to anatomical detail and emotional expression.

Etruscan antiquities

There's something intriguing about the distant, cheerful smiles on the faces of many Etruscan sculptures, and their civilization remains a compelling mystery. It thrived for ten centuries, from about 1000 B.C. to the early years of the Christian era, and was the most sophisticated culture in pre-Roman Italy. This country of 12 to 14 city-states north of Rome flourished through trade and mining. Although the Etruscans developed at the same time as the Greeks, they developed a unique artistic style. This was revealed in their skill with bronze- and metalworking, and is best seen in their delicate jewelry and elegant bronze mirrors detailed with engraved or repoussé scenes.

The painted terra-cotta "Sarcophagus of a Married Couple" (Denon Wing, Room 18) is another of the Louvre's masterpieces; equality between husband and wife, as reflected in this sculpture, was one

of the more extraordinary aspects of their society; women had more independence there than anywhere else in classical antiquity.

Roman antiquities

Although Roman artists constantly copied Greek sculptures, their art was more than just a watered-down version of Hellenistic Greek art. The empire encompassed many different countries and cultures, and Rome itself was filled with foreign artists. They integrated elements from both the Etruscan and Greek cultures, adapting the styles to their own less mythical, more factual concerns, namely the glorification of the State and the great families.

Portraiture took on a new dimension in Roman art, as the classical ideal of abstract beauty was replaced by more realistic and representative images. Portraits were so popular that the heads were often sculpted separately and placed on a kind of standard-issue body (for example, the statue of "Augustus," Room 27).

Wealthy Romans decorated their homes with lavish frescoes and mosaics. The mosaic on the floor of Room 31 once decorated the Constantine Villa near Antioch; it dates from the fourth century A.D.

PAINTING

The Louvre's paintings are divided into four sections: French works from the 14th through the 19th centuries, Italian, Northern European, and other European paintings.

"The Death of Sardanapalus" (1827) by Eugène Delacroix depicts the Oriental king after his defeat in battle, with his worldly goods (and women) being destroyed by his slaves.

The extreme emotion and contrasting lights and darks in Théodore Géricault's "Raft of the Medusa" (1819) are characteristic of the Romantic painters.

LOUVRE STAFF

A staff of 1,600—curators, guards, and technical specialists, among others—keep the Louvre running. Close to 60 curators watch over the 350,000 works of art, of which only about 30,000 are on display at any one time. ■

French painting

The French paintings on the first floor of the Denon Wing and the second floor of the Sully and Richelieu Wings cover every major period, from the early medieval and Renaissance periods through the mid-19th century. (Works after this date are found in the Musée d'Orsay, see pp. 174–78.) The collection starts with the oldest surviving easel painting, "Portrait of Jean le Bon" (circa 1350). The Renaissance came to France via King Charles VIII and King François I (portrait of François I by Jean Clouet, Room 7). Although Italy and France battled incessantly, the French kings easily admitted the superiority of Italian culture, bringing both its art and artists (such as Leonardo da Vinci) back to France. French painting in the 17th century moved toward realism, illustrated especially in Room 28 with George de la Tour's "The Cheat."

Rooms 50–73 concentrate on the first half of the 19th century. The last few rooms (63–73) contain landscapes by painters like Jean-Baptiste Corot, who prefigured the Impressionists.

The French collection does not end with this chronological sequence, however; large-format paintings hanging in two adjoining rooms (75 and 77) in the Denon Wing (first floor) illustrate the two conflicting schools of painting in the 19th century—neoclassicism and Romanticism. Painters clashed over the merits of the two: the idealized, cold, and rational beauty of the first (represented by Jacques-Louis David, the court chronicler for the Napoleonic era; in "The Oath of the Horatii," 1784, and "The Coronation of Napoleon I," 1804), and the emotion and individualism of the latter (as spearheaded by Eugène Delacroix in "The Death of Sardanapalus," 1827). The Romantics sought their subjects

RESTORING ORIGINAL COLORS

Veronese's "Marriage Feast at Cana" was recently restored to its original colors using advanced techniques in paint analysis and X rays. Just a few years ago, the green cloak worn by the figure in the foreground was red. ∎

from contemporary events: Théodore Géricault created an international scandal by illustrating an actual shipwreck in the "Raft of the Medusa" (Room 77), with its accompanying themes of treachery and cannibalism.

European painting

Northern European painting is exhibited in the Richelieu Wing, and includes 15th-century Dutch works by Jan van Eyck, the artist who is widely credited with the invention of painting with oils. The Galerie Médicis contains a rather overwhelming series of canvases (nearly 330 square yards, or 275 sq m) by Peter Paul Rubens, created for the Luxembourg Palace, ordered by Marie de Médicis. There are also a number of works by Rembrandt

van Rijn, including the lovely "Bathsheba," and two masterpieces by Jan Vermeer, "The Lacemaker" and "The Astronomer."

The Italian collection (Denon Wing, first floor, Rooms 1–11) begins with the painters Giovanni Cimabue and Giotto, whose work profoundly influenced the development of the Renaissance. Thirty years after Cimabue's "Virgin and Child," Giotto's "Saint Francis of Assisi Receiving the Stigmata" created a new style, placing more realistic figures within space, using rudimentary notions of perspective (defined by Filippo Brunelleschi in the 1420s). The collection continues with the Quattrocento artists: Paolo Uccello, Andrea Mantegna, and Domenico Ghirlandaio.

There are several paintings by

Leonardo da Vinci, the archetypal Renaissance genius, was both a painter and a scientist; the "Mona Lisa" marks the apogee of both these talents. It was commissioned around 1503 by the model's husband, Francesco del Giocondo, but Leonardo neither signed nor delivered the work. Indeed, once painted, it never left his side, and entered the French royal collection only upon his death in 1519.

Leonardo da Vinci in the Grande Galerie: "The Virgin and Child with Sainte Anne" and "Saint John the Baptist," for example—as intriguing as the "Mona Lisa," and usually fairly free of tourists. The Salles des États (the former State Room), where the "Marriage Feast at Cana" by Veronese dominates one entire wall, represents the best in 16th- and 17th-century Italian painting, with several Titians, a Caravaggio, and of course, the "Mona Lisa" (Room 6).

ORIENTAL ANTIQUITIES

Covering northern Africa to the borders of India, the Oriental antiquities encompass the world's earliest known civilizations, from which sprang many technological and philosophical inventions—wheeled vehicles, astronomical models, musical systems, and the birth of writing, not to mention a set of laws (recorded on the *Code of Hammurabi* in the Cour Khorsabad, Room 3) that formed the basis of the Greek and Roman legal systems.

The Louvre's collection covers four distinct regions and periods: Mesopotamia; ancient Iran; the Levant (all located on the ground floor in the Richelieu and Sully Wings; Rooms A–D and 1–21); and the Islamic arts (on the Entresol level of the Richelieu Wing; Rooms A and 1–11). Most of the displays came from 19th-century French excavation projects that unearthed long lost palaces and cities, including the winged bulls from the palace of King Sargon II of Assyria (720 B.C.) and the winged archers and monumental, bull-headed capitals from the palace of Darius in Susa (late sixth century B.C.).

SCULPTURE

Even on a gloomy winter's day, the Marly and Puget courtyards, covered by skylights, create an ideal setting for outdoor sculpture. Those in the Cour Marly were created for Louis XIV's private château at Marly. During the Revolution, the "Horses of Marly" were placed on the Place de la Concorde, but they were moved to the Louvre in 1984; cast models now stand in their original setting.

French sculpture begins in rooms around the Cour Marly with works from the 12th century and continues through the Romanesque and Gothic eras; many came from French churches. One of the oddest pieces is the actual-size funeral cortege of the 15th-century "Tomb of Philippe Pot" (Room 10), with eight hooded mourners bearing the deceased.

The Denon Wing houses a smaller collection of sculpture from Italy, Germany, the Netherlands, and Spain, including Michelangelo's two "Slaves" and other celebrated Italian work from the 16th and 17th centuries, such as Gian Lorenzo Bernini's "Angel Bearing the Crown of Thorns."

The Marly courtyard in the Richelieu Wing is a showcase for 18th-century French sculpture, with the marble "Horses of Marly" series by Antoine Coysevox ("Fame" and "Mercury," 1702) and Guillaume Coustou ("Horses Restrained by Grooms," 1743).

OBJETS D'ART

The objets d'art collection here contains works ranging from the Middle Ages through the 19th century. Many of the early pieces come from the cathedral of St.-Denis (see p. 220), although the department has grown through royal donations and other bequests. The term "objets d'art" designates everything from religious relics and enamels to tapestries, jewels, and furniture—in other words, the "everyday" items of the aristocracy. All the objets d'art are located on the first floor of the Richelieu and Sully Wings, with the exception of the glittering Galerie d'Apollon in the Denon Wing, which contains the French crown jewels.

Part of the objets d'art department and one of the Louvre's more obscure treasures are the Napoleon III apartments, opened to the public when the Finance Ministry moved to the Quai de Bercy *(open until 6 p.m.; groups until 3 p.m.).*

PRINTS AND DRAWINGS

Few visitors know of this department's temporary displays of select works, nor that it is possible to see specific works on paper with prior written authorization from the Louvre. The collection located on the first floor of the Denon Wing (Rooms 8–10), has some 120,000 works representing almost every period of art—illuminated manuscripts, drawings by Leonardo da Vinci, Delacroix's Moroccan sketchbook, and studies by Rembrandt.

The Chalcographie shop, which sells engravings made from original copper plates, is more accessible; it is located under the pyramid. ■

The sumptuous Napoleon III apartments in the Richelieu Wing, replete with silk fabric, gilt-and-red-velvet furniture, and chandeliers, were restored and opened to the public in 1983.

Three museums of the arts

Rohan & Marsan Wings of the Louvre

🅰 Map p. 123

✉ Palais du Louvre, 107 rue de Rivoli

🕐 Closed Mon.

☎ 01 44 55 57 50

💲 $

🚇 Métro: Palais-Royal—Musée du Louvre, Tuileries, Pyramides

The Advertising Museum houses posters such as this one for Le Chat Noir, the cabaret where the Montmartre *chansonnier* tradition was born. Major artists such as Aristide Bruant performed here.

THREE MUSEUMS OCCUPY THE ROHAN AND MARSAN Wings of the Louvre: the Decorative Arts Museum, the Fashion and Textile Museum, and the Advertising Museum, all administered by the Union Centrale des Arts Décoratifs (UCAD, or Central Union for the Decorative Arts). Along with the rest of the Louvre, these museums have been refurbished and redesigned to add more exhibition space.

MUSÉE DES ARTS DÉCORATIFS

The Decorative Arts Museum, part of the Louvre since 1905, presents an extraordinarily rich collection of some 220,000 works from the Middle Ages to the 20th century—including ceramics, glassware, jewelry, furniture, wallpaper, drawings, and toys.

Partially reopened in 1998, the nine rooms devoted to the Middle Ages and the Renaissance illustrate religious and everyday life from the 13th to the 16th centuries. The exhibition is not arranged in strict chronological sequence; it is instead organized into a fine arts section and a decorative arts section. Visitors will discover period rooms followed by others containing religious objects. The entire collection, from the 17th century to the present opened in 2000.

MUSÉE DE LA MODE ET DU TEXTILE

The Fashion and Textile Museum's permanent collection explores major trends in fashion through the ages. Clothing from the 17th to the 19th centuries, fashion accessories, and rare fabrics are on display, as are major contributions from 20th-century haute couture artists and contemporary fashion designers. The curators rotate the collection with thematic displays that are changed each year. A recent exhibit devoted to exoticism explored this theme through luxury products and interior design.

The museum also has a documentation center that is open to researchers, professionals, and by appointment, to the public.

MUSÉE DE LA PUBLICITÉ

The Advertising Museum, originally kept in the city's tenth arrondissement, was created in 1978. It contains posters from the UCAD library, a collection that has expanded over the years through numerous donations. It now contains nearly 40,000 posters from around the world, ranging from the mid-18th century to 1949; in addition, it has 45,000 contemporary posters donated by agencies and designers, and 20,000 contemporary publicity films. ■

Jardin des Tuileries

THE VIEW FROM THE LOUVRE WEST ENCOMPASSES ONE OF the most impressive alignments of monuments in any city. This symmetry starts with the Arc de Triomphe du Carrousel framed by the two wings of the Louvre and continues past the Luxor Obelisk at the Place de la Concorde to the Arc de Triomphe and the Grande Arche de La Défense, 5 miles (8 km) to the west.

Jardin des Tuileries
Map p. 122–23
Métro: Palais-Royal, Tuileries, Pyramides, Concorde

When the Tuileries was created by André Le Nôtre in 1666, it was outside the city walls—a place where aristocrats came to see and be seen and enjoy royal festivities and fireworks. As part of the Grand Louvre project, completed in late 1997, the adjoining gardens were given a face-lift to emphasize the east–west axis and link the new Louvre parvis (square) to the gardens on the west.

The original design, which called for a more formal garden near the Louvre gradually becoming more wooded toward Place de la Concorde, was reinstated. The beginning of the gardens' eastern edge, marked by the Arc de Triomphe du Carrousel added by Napoleon, is enclosed within the long wings of the Louvre. Seen through this arch, the Luxor Obelisk (see p. 146) and the Arc de Triomphe are perfectly aligned. Replanting has restored Le Nôtre's original design, and cafés, pony rides, and a summer funfair give a pleasure garden atmosphere.

Hidden away among hedges of yew near the Louvre is a sculpture garden with 20 bronzes by Aristide Maillol. ■

The Tuileries is like a throwback to another time: Children pilot their boats across the ponds, and classic green metal chairs are sprawled from one end of the gardens to the other.

Bridges & quays of Paris

Stand on the Pont de la Concorde at night, with the Assemblée Nationale illuminated at one end and the imposing Madeleine Church in the far distance at the other, and you can see why Paris is called the City of Light. Or wander along the quays to explore the 36 other bridges spanning the Seine, where lovers, traffic, history, politics, and art all converge. The city's splendor and its traditions are reflected, quite literally, in the waters of the Seine.

Paris's two islands, the Île de la Cité and the Île St.-Louis, are connected by a total of eight and five bridges respectively, with one footbridge—the Pont St.-Louis—joining the two islands behind Notre-Dame. The Pont de Sully, at the quaint eastern tip of the Île St.-Louis, took its name from the celebrated duke, minister, and friend of Henri IV, who masterfully directed the royal finances in the late 16th century.

Majestic Pont Neuf

Just west of the Latin Quarter, between the Quai des Grands Augustins and the Quai de la Mégisserie and straddling the western end of the Île de la Cité, sits the majestic Pont Neuf and its 12 perfect arches. One of Paris's loveliest bridges, it is also the oldest remaining one—despite its name, which means "new bridge." It was inaugurated in 1607 under the direction of Henri IV, who is immortalized in bronze on horseback on the bridge. The Pont Neuf was the first bridge to be lined with sidewalks rather than dwellings; it immediately became the center of Paris, a fashionable strolling place. For the Fête de la Musique in the mid-1990s, the eccentric artist Christo chose this bridge to wrap in miles of cloth, and the fashion designer Kenzo decorated the crossing with 100,000 flowers.

Unusual & artistic bridges

The Pont des Arts, a few hundred yards farther west, is a wooden footbridge that attracts the city's romantic souls, especially at sunset. It is in line with the ornate, gilded dome of the world-renowned Institut de France, founded by Mazarin as the center of France's great science and art academies.

The 348-foot-long (106 m) Passerelle de Solferino, one of the city's ambitious projects, to join the Louvre complex with the Musée d'Orsay, creates a direct link via the Jardin des Tuileries. The new, metal arched-suspension bridge includes a two-tiered walkway built from exotic wood; it is the only Parisian bridge accessible from both the river and street levels.

Winged horses, cherubs, nymphs, gold-leaf swords (regilded for the 1989 bicentennial and repainted in gold in 1997), and other art nouveau details grace the Pont Alexandre III. Paris's most celebrated and photographed bridge, the Pont Alexandre III was named after Tsar Alexander III, who laid the first stone in 1896 (see p. 150).

Cult bridges: the Pont de l'Alma & the Pont de Bir-Hakeim

The area around the Pont de l'Alma and the tunnel that passes underneath it is now heavily visited by tourists drawn to the site where Diana, Princess of Wales, was killed in 1997. The Pont de l'Alma has a sculpture of a Second Empire soldier, known as the Zouave, which is used to measure the level of the Seine. During the major flood of 1910, the water reached as high as his beard.

At the foot of the bridge on the Right Bank sits the gold-encrusted Statue of Liberty flame, cast from the original mold. A scale replica of the entire statue now greets river visitors to Paris as they sail under the Pont de Grenelle.

Farther west, the Seine is straddled by the gray-metal stanchions of the Pont de Bir-Hakeim. In the 1970s, it gained cultlike status with the movie *Last Tango in Paris*. ■

Top: The quai and Pont de la Tournelle (seen here in an oil painting, circa 1646) were rebuilt many times in wood before the stone bridge was constructed in 1656. Right: The recently restored Pont Neuf is the oldest bridge in Paris. Henri III placed the first stone in 1578 and it was inaugurated nearly 30 years later.

Below: For decades, the sculptured figure of a soldier, known as the Zouave, on the Pont de l'Alma has been used to measure the water level of the Seine.

Musée de l'Orangerie

Musée de l'Orangerie

Map p. 122

Jardin des Tuileries, place de la Concorde

01 42 97 48 16

Closed for renovation, reopening Jan. 2002

$$

Métro: Concorde

Monet was inspired by Japanese prints of floral designs shown during the Universal Expositions of 1878 and 1889, and began painting water lilies at the turn of the century.

CLAUDE MONET'S WATER LILIES HAVE MADE THE MUSÉE DE l'Orangerie famous throughout the world. However, this small gem of a museum also boasts 144 masterpieces by other school of Paris artists—from the Impressionists to artists of the 1930s.

The Orangerie building was constructed in 1852 as a winter shelter for the orange trees lining the Tuileries walkways. In the early 20th century, it became a temporary exhibition center, and was renovated in 1984 to display the remarkable Walter Guillaume Collection. Paul Guillaume amassed this collection of works by the school of Paris painters and opened a gallery in 1914 in Paris, enthusiastically supporting such avant-garde painters as Chaim Soutine and Maurice Utrillo. The exhibit reflects his pioneering stance as a collector and supporter of modern art, with 22 works by Soutine, and others by Cézanne, Matisse, Modigliani, and Picasso. Guillaume's wife,

Domenica, donated the works to the government in 1977 on condition that the paintings remain together.

Monet's Water Lilies, at the end of the exhibition, are the highlight. The French politician Georges Clemenceau helped Monet get the commission to paint these murals in 1914 as a gift to France. Throughout World War I, and despite his failing eyesight and periods of self-doubt, Monet remained absorbed by the elusive patterns and luminous colors of this theme. The specially designed oval rooms containing the murals, often referred to as the Sistine Chapel of Impressionism, were inaugurated in 1927, less than a year after the painter's death. ■

Galerie National du Jeu de Paume

Napoleon III constructed the Jeu de Paume between 1861 and 1862 as an indoor tennis court. Used as an exhibition space in 1909, it was co-opted by the Nazis as a temporary storehouse for their plundered art. Immediately after the war, it became one of the world's finest Impressionist museums. In 1986 the collection was moved to the Musée d'Orsay, and its light, spacious rooms now hold temporary exhibitions of contemporary French and international artists. ■

Galerie National du Jeu de Paume
- Map p. 122
- ✉ Jardin des Tuileries, place de la Concorde
- ☎ 01 42 60 69 69
- 🕐 Closed Mon.
- 💲 $$
- 🚇 Métro: Concorde

Palais-Royal

The original palace (not the gardens behind) was built by Cardinal Richelieu in 1636, thus its name, the Palais Cardinal. Louis XIV lived here as a child for some time, before fleeing to escape the Fronde (see p. 21). He was never fond of Paris and was happy to hand over the property to his brother, Philippe d'Orléans. Much to the disdain of Philippe's aristocratic kin, his deeply debt-ridden son (also named Philippe) went on to construct 180 arcades and shops on the site.

This new Palais-Royal opened with great fanfare in 1784 and soon drew merchants, intellectuals, and houses of ill repute. When the puritanically minded Louis-Philippe was crowned in 1830, he closed down this hotbed of vice, causing fashionable Parisians to move to other neighborhoods.

By the time Colette and Jean Cocteau had become residents (at 9 Rue de Beaujolais and 36 Rue de Montpensier, respectively), the gardens had become an island of serenity in the heart of Paris. The former palace, burned down during the Commune and restored, is now home to government institutions.

The Palais-Royal's most recent controversy was the installation of Daniel Buren's black-and-white striped columns at the south end of the gardens. At the other end is one of Paris's loveliest restaurants, the elegant 18th-century Grand Véfour (see p. 247). Between these, today's gardens form one of the city's most peaceful public parks, overlooked by quaint arcaded shops. ■

Palais-Royal
- Map p. 123
- ✉ place du Palais-Royal
- 🚇 Métro: Palais-Royal–Musée du Louvre

CANNON AT NOON
In 1786 a small cannon replaced the sundial in the Palais-Royal gardens; a guard still fires it every day at noon. ■

Daniel Buren's black-and-white columns in the main courtyard of the Palais-Royal

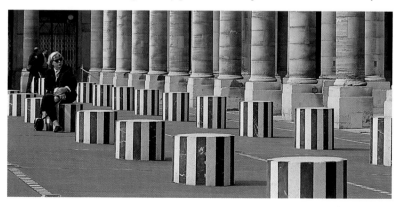

Mosaic medallions and arabesques decorate many of the arcades along Rue de Rivoli.

More places to visit around the Louvre & Palais-Royal

COMÉDIE FRANÇAISE
Created in 1680 by Louis XIV and based here since 1799, this state-subsidized company performs classic and modern French plays (see p. 259 for information).
🅼 Map p. 123 ✉ 2 rue Richelieu ☎ 01 44 58 15 15 🚇 Métro: Palais-Royal–Musée du Louvre

PLACE DES VICTOIRES
Maréchal de la Feuillade, a fawning court follower, created this square solely as a backdrop for a gilded statue of Louis XIV. Melted down during the Revolution, the statue was replaced in 1822. Now mainly a quiet shopping area, the square's shops have been colonized by Japanese designers, including Kenzo.
🅼 Map p. 123 🚇 Métro: Louvre-Rivoli, Bourse

RUE DE RIVOLI
Always packed with tourists because of its proximity to the Louvre, Rue de Rivoli was built by Napoleon to provide the city with another east–west axis to ease the traffic along the existing Rue St.-Honoré. The covered arcades, completed in 1835, were an innovation at the time, providing pedestrians with protection from both the weather and carriages. Today, souvenir shops share the elegant facades with old-time luxury hotels like the Meurice. Two English bookshops, W. H. Smith and Galliani, are also here, as well as the Angélina tearoom at No. 226, famous in particular for its hot chocolate.
🅼 Map p. 122–23 🚇 Métro: Concorde, Tuileries, Palais-Royal–Musée du Louvre

ST.-GERMAIN L'AUXERROIS
This church, opposite the eastern end of the Louvre, was the royal parish for the Valois kings while they resided in the palace across the street. Most of the original decoration has disappeared, with the exception of the superb Flamboyant Gothic porch (circa 1435), the only original one left in Paris.
🅼 Map p. 123 ✉ place du Louvre 🚇 Métro: Louvre-Rivoli ■

Whether it's the bicentennial celebration of the French Revolution, a military parade, or the finish line of the Tour de France, the Champs-Élysées—long called the Triumphal Way—is where Paris best puts itself on display.

Champs-Élysées

Fountain statue on Place de la Concorde

Champs-Élysées

NO FIRST-TIME VISITOR TO PARIS WANTS TO MISS THE MYTHICAL CHAMPS-Élysées, the famous Arc de Triomphe, or the glitter of lights around the Place de la Concorde, which symbolize the French sense of grandeur in the most ostentatious way. Though once the promenade of elegant aristocrats and the bourgeoisie, the avenue is today overwhelmed with movie theaters, fast-food emporiums, airline agencies, and megastores.

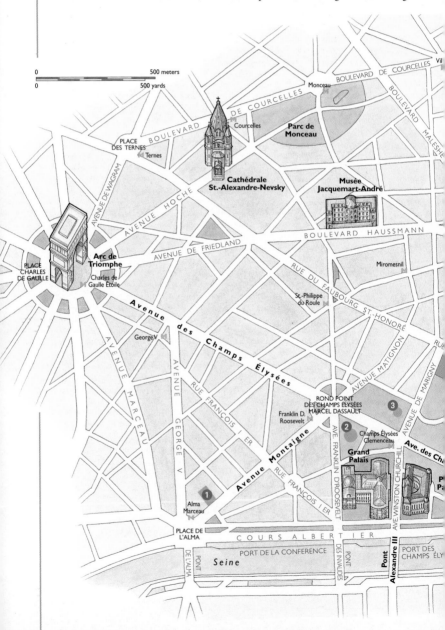

The entire area is a relatively recent neighborhood, developed mostly during the Second Empire (1852–1870). Napoleon III returned from London determined to bring the space and greenery of British gardens to the French capital; supervised by Adolphe Alphand, he overhauled the Champs-Élysées (see p. 147). Alphand's gardens and parks (such as the Parc de Monceau; see p. 152) transformed the western edge of Paris into a respectable, residential neighborhood.

The gardens hosted endless entertainments in the form of theater and concert venues, and panoramas—which often depicted battle scenes in the round to give the spectator a sense of standing in the midst of the action. The fad for panoramas that swept Paris in the mid-1850s soon fell out of fashion, but one of the original buildings still survives as the Théâtre du Rond-Point, which in the early 1980s was home to the legendary couple of French theater, the actors Jean-Louis Barrault and Madeleine Renaud. A second panorama stood on the site of the present-day Théâtre Marigny. Another venue—the Théâtre des Champs-Élysées at 15 Avenue Montaigne—is now among the best concert halls in Paris.

HEART OF HAUTE COUTURE

The international heart of haute couture was created in Paris's eighth arrondissement by Englishman Charles Worth during the Second Empire, and is still firmly clustered around the Champs-Élysées. Paul Poiret, who was once an apprentice to Jacques Doucet (the other innovative tailor of the period), opened a shop on what is now Avenue Franklin D. Roosevelt; his revolutionary designs did away with constraining corsets, allowing women a new freedom of movement and inspiring a row of other shops that still line Avenue Montaigne (see p. 152) and Avenue George V (all south of the Champs-Élysées). The Faubourg St.-Honoré, running parallel to the Champs-Élysées to the north, is lined with art galleries and elegant shops, including Hermès at No. 24 (leather goods, silk scarves, and clothes). At No. 55 is the Palais de l'Élysée, the official presidential residence since 1873. This palace was originally purchased in 1753 by Louis XV's mistress, Madame de Pompadour, who invested immense sums to redecorate it to her highly extravagant tastes. It is open to the public during the Journées des Patrimoine (National Heritage Weekend), usually around the second weekend of September.

CHAMPS-ÉLYSÉES

1 Théâtre des Champs-Élysées
2 Théâtre du Rond-Point   3 Théâtre Marigny   4 Palais de l'Élysée

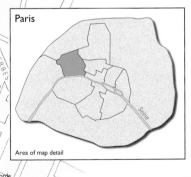

Paris

Area of map detail

UNIVERSAL EXPOSITION MONUMENTS

Few of the monuments built for the Universal Expositions (see p. 168) of the late 19th and early 20th centuries that were held on both sides of the Seine, from the Champ de Mars to the Champs-Élysées, were made to last, but the Grand Palais, Petit Palais, and the Pont Alexandre III survived (see p. 150). ∎

Place de la Concorde

Place de la Concorde
🔲 Map p. 145
🚇 Métro: Concorde

ONCE THE SITE OF REVOLUTIONARY BLOODBATHS, TODAY'S Place de la Concorde is framed by the American Embassy and the luxurious Hôtel Crillon, and offers a breathtaking view up the Champs-Élysées toward the Arc de Triomphe.

The obelisk on the Place de la Concorde is surrounded by two fountains— allegories of sea and river navigation— and figures representing France's eight leading cities.

The Place de la Concorde was laid out in 1757 by the royal architect Jacques-Ange Gabriel as a backdrop for an equestrian statue of Louis XV. As opposed to Paris's other royal squares (Place des Victoires and Place Dauphine, for example), which were enclosed, Gabriel constructed buildings on one side only, leaving intact the view from the Tuileries Palace up the Champs-Élysées to the Rond-Point. His two colonnaded buildings—now the Crillon hotel and the Ministère de la Marine (where Marie-Antoinette once kept a secret apartment)— mirror the facade of the National Assembly across the river. Louis's statue was pulled down during the Revolution, and the Place Louis-XV was rebaptized the Place de la Révolution. During the Terror, over 1,200 people were guillotined here, including Louis XVI, Maximilien Robespierre, and Marie-Antoinette.

THE OBELISK

After a series of name changes, the square was renamed the Place de la Concorde in 1795. Louis-Philippe erected statues and fountains representing the great cities of France, and placed a central monument in the square—a 3,300-year-old obelisk, a twin of the one that stands in front of the Temple of Luxor, given to France in 1829 by Egyptian Viceroy Mohammed Ali— which had no link to the royal or revolutionary past.

Some 200,000 Parisians cheered as the engineer Le Bas and his 120-strong team raised the obelisk in 1836. Their exploit is recorded on the obelisk's base, which is the best place to appreciate the square's sweeping view of the Louvre's pyramid (to the east), and the Champs-Élysées extending west toward La Défense, framed by copies of the "Horses of Marly." The originals are now in the Louvre (see p. 134). ■

Champs-Élysées

WHEN IT WAS CREATED BY ANDRÉ LE NÔTRE IN 1667 FOR Louis XIV, the Champs-Élysées was meant to be a visual extension of the Tuileries gardens. It was not yet the classy neighborhood it was to become, and the fields and undergrowth served as a meeting place for the city's riffraff. The Champs-Élysées is divided into two sections: the pretty, garden-lined avenue that leads from Place de la Concorde to the Rond-Point, and the commercial area from the Rond-Point to the Arc de Triomphe.

Champs-Élysées

🅰 Map pp. 144—45

🚇 Métro: Concorde, Champs-Élysées—Clemenceau, Franklin D. Roosevelt, George V, Charles-de-Gaulle-Étoile

In the 1830s, architect Jacques Hittorff began to transform this unpopulated area of Paris. Over 1,200 gas lamps were installed, and the area became a giant playground, filled with formal gardens, fountains, restaurants, and concert-cafés. All that remains of these former pleasure pavilions are two expensive restaurants, Ledoyen (see p. 250) and Laurent. The gardens of the Élysées Palace (the presidential residence) border the northern edge of Avenue Gabriel.

During the 1914 Occupation of Paris, the Allied armies divided the city between the Russians and the British. The latter camped in the Tuileries Gardens and at the Place de la Concorde, while the Cossacks set up their tents along the Champs-Élysées, effectively devastating the area; it took the city two years to repair the damage.

West of the Rond-Point stretches what the French like to call the most beautiful avenue in the world, still considered the obligatory route for all important gatherings, departures, and returns. For example, the July 14 military parades, with their low-flying jets, pass here; it marks the finish line of the annual Tour de France bicycle race; and the starting point of the Paris Marathon.

However, the Champs-Élysées' reputation tends to outshine its reality. Despite a recent face-lift that removed parking and expanded the already huge sidewalks, it has been invaded by flashy car dealerships, fast-food restaurants, and giant movie complexes. ■

When Bismarck arrived with his Prussian army in 1871, he was so impressed by the Champs-Élysées that he ordered a copy built in Berlin—the Kurfürstendamm.

French fashion

France remains the world capital for luxury, particularly when it comes to fashion and fragrances. Despite heated competition from designers and multinationals in New York, London, and Milan, Paris is the only true center for haute couture, and it clings tenaciously to its reputation.

Fashion in the 1990s

The 1990s will most likely go down in history as a time when minimalism reigned, when consumers from Long Island to Shanghai clamored for the pared-down look of Gap basics and the clean, urban lines of Armani, Gucci, Prada, and Calvin Klein. American street style and "Cool Britannia" will be counted among the top exports of their countries. The ascent of British designers John Galliano and Alexander McQueen to the top of the houses of Dior and Givenchy, respectively (both the property of Louis Vuitton Moët Henessy), probably heralded the biggest fashion watersheds of the early 21st century.

Parisian haute couture

Nowhere is it clearer that Paris is still the center of creative fashion than in the twice-yearly haute couture shows held since 1994 at the Louvre's Cour Carrée. While today's haute couture proceeds from its legends—which include Coco Chanel, Christian Dior, Yves Saint Laurent, Daniel Hechter, and Pierre Cardin—it still distinctly demonstrates the difference between what is French and what is the Rest of the World.

New York fashion tends to be about practicality and versatility, with American fashion magazines chiefly concerned with clothing that travels from office to evening; London fashion is filled with fanciful expressions of eccentricity; and Milan fashion focuses on the beauty, quality, and salability of fabrics—which leaves the out-and-out romantic glamour to Paris.

Wearability and sales are of secondary importance to the designers—after all, few can afford extravagances such as handmade

Supermodel Kate Moss has filled out a little since her "waif" days in the early 1990s. Here, she is modeling Chanel.

designs that sell for 50,000 francs (around $8,700) and higher. Prêt-à-porter labels, accessory spin-offs, and fragrances pick up and cash in on all the important trends. What counts is the range of expression, virtuosity in technique, detail, color, and most of all, the "theater of the moment"—the *spectacle*. ∎

As stylish as ever: Chanel has retained its old verve under the direction of Karl Lagerfeld.

Do whatever you want, but do it with style

French style—the much admired way French women have of carrying themselves, wearing a scarf, and pulling a look together in a seemingly effortless, innate manner—is the subject of much study and imitation; it can sometimes be learned, but it can never be bought.

As with many other countries, the French have embraced the American fashion influence, but their approach to style as an art form can be seen as much on Parisian streets as on the catwalks at fashion houses. For example, the lofty house of Chanel quietly introduced (and quickly sold out of) silver all-purpose cross-trainers a few seasons ago. Unlike her Anglo-Saxon counterpart—whose buying habits tend toward quantity and all-purpose wear—the French woman (particularly Parisian) usually buys fewer, higher-ticket items, such as an excellent pair of shoes, a top-quality handbag, or a brand-name cardigan, and has no qualms about wearing the same thing twice or more in one week, as a designer piece will look just as chic on the hundredth wearing. Accessories do not have to match, and the sharpest dressers adhere to the no-more-than-two-colors rule.

Fortunately, France is not a country where dressing for success has become politicized. Most French women dress to accent their femininity, even playing it to their advantage in a business context: They don't worry that high hemlines or figure-revealing clothes might interfere with being taken seriously, any more than the average French man worries whether offering a compliment will result in being slapped with a lawsuit. ■

The Alexandre III Bridge has a single 358-foot (109 m) span.

Universal Exposition Monuments

THESE THREE LEGACIES OF THE 1900 UNIVERSAL Exposition were conceived as monuments to the glory of French art. The 1889 Universal Exposition was so successful that immediately after it closed, plans were laid for another in 1900. This time, the city decided to build permanent structures.

GRAND PALAIS

The Grand Palais, which replaced the obsolete Palais de l'Industrie of 1885, is an immense iron-and-glass structure with a classical stone facade. Exuberant ironwork, the colossal bronze statues of Apollo's chariot drawn by flying horses, and a seemingly endless glass roof are characteristic of the art nouveau style of its time.

Since opening, the Grand Palais has hosted many major exhibitions, such as the 1905 Salon d'Automne that launched the fauves (wild beast) group of artists. The annual book fair and the International Fair of Contemporary Art (FIAC) have been held here.

The **Galeries Nationales du Grand Palais** host international art shows. At the **Palais de la Découverte,** the Grand Palais

science museum, interactive exhibits—popular with children—explore such diverse topics as animal communication, the Earth's origins, and meteorology.

PETIT PALAIS

The Petit Palais was also built for the 1900 exposition; it now belongs to the City of Paris and houses a mixed collection ranging from Chinese porcelain to 19th-century paintings.

PONT ALEXANDRE III

Another vestige of the 1900 exposition is the Pont Alexandre III, an extravagant metal structure with gilded statues dedicated to the friendship between Russia and France. Tsar Nicholas II laid the first stone on October 7, 1896, and it was completed two years later. ■

Arc de Triomphe

PARISIANS STILL CALL THE SQUARE SURROUNDING THE Arc de Triomphe l'Étoile ("the star"), despite its name changing in 1970 to the Place Charles-de-Gaulle. It gets its name from the 12 avenues radiating from it. At its center stands the Arc de Triomphe, the ultimate symbol of French pride and military power—a striking landmark in the middle of Paris's longest vista.

In 1806, Napoleon commissioned a monument from the architect Jean-François Chalgrin to honor his Grande Armée and the victory of Austerlitz. In keeping with the Napoleonic sense of grandeur, the Arc de Triomphe is 164 feet high (50 m) and 147 feet wide (45 m)—the largest arch of its kind ever built. It was finally completed in 1836.

Its bas-relief sculptures include the famous "Départ des Volontaires," or "La Marseillaise," a winged figure leading soldiers into battle, by François Rude; and its friezes depict the departure of the French armies (eastern side) and their return (western side).

The 12 avenues radiating out from the arc and the 12 matching *hôtels* (residences) surrounding the Place were not part of the original design, but were introduced by Baron Eugène Haussmann (see p. 160). The result is perhaps monumental in a way he never intended: The 12 streets converging at the Étoile now create a huge traffic jam.

Over the years, the Arc de Triomphe has symbolized all that is great and glorious in France: Napoleon's ashes passed under the arch on their way to Les Invalides, as did Victor Hugo's funeral cortege. The conquering armies—the Prussians in 1871 and the Germans in 1940—that marched here were succeeded by France's heroic liberators, such as Gen. Charles de Gaulle, who led the Allied victory march before thousands of jubilant Parisians on August 26, 1944.

An unknown soldier's tomb was placed here in 1920, and every evening at 6:30 veterans relight the flame. An underground walkway at the end of the Champs-Élysées leading underneath the Place Charles-de-Gaulle provides a safe passage to the Arc de Triomphe, where the view from the top overlooks Haussmann's ambitious design and the traffic below.

Beneath the viewing platform is a small museum with an exhibition on the history of the building of the monument and mementoes of Napoleon and World War I. ∎

Arc de Triomphe
🗺 Map p. 144
✉ place Charles-de-Gaulle
☎ 01 55 37 73 77
💲 $$ (includes museum)
🚇 Métro: Charles-de-Gaulle-Étoile

The Arc de Triomphe is engraved with the names of great French military victories, along with the names of 666 senior officers who participated in the Revolution and wars of the Empire.

More places to visit along the Champs-Élysées

AVENUE MONTAIGNE

Home to one of the most famous *bals populaires* (dance halls) in the mid-1800s, the ultra-chic Avenue Montaigne is lined with luxury shops, palatial hotels, and the haute couture houses of some of France's leading fashion names, including Christian Lacroix and Christian Dior. Givenchy's shop is on the nearby Avenue George V, which also includes the princely Hôtel George V.

Map p. 144 Métro: Franklin D. Roosevelt, Alma-Marceau

CATHÉDRALE ST.-ALEXANDRE-NEVSKY

The heart of Little Russia, this onion-domed, Russian Orthodox cathedral was constructed in 1861 and is based on a Greek-cross floor plan. The inside is lined with impressive frescoes and icons, and the tympanum is covered with mosaics on a gilded background.

Map p. 144 12 rue Daru 01 42 27 37 34 Open 3 –5 p.m. Tues., Fri., & Sun. Métro: Courcelles

MUSÉE JACQUEMART-ANDRÉ

This little known museum in the home of Edouard André and his wife, Nélie Jacquemart, reflects the couple's lifetime devotion to building a showcase for their art collection. Famous for its Italian Renaissance works, the collection includes a rare fresco ceiling by Tiepolo, "Henri III Received in Venice by the Doge Cantarini," and Uccello's "Saint George Slaying the Dragon." There are also French and Flemish paintings (with Rembrandt's "Pilgrims of Emmaus," "Amalia von Sohms," and "Doctor Tholinx"). The museum reopened in 1997 after the mansion was renovated; it is a perfect representation of a 19th-century architectural vogue.

Map p. 144 158 boulevard Haussmann 01 42 89 04 91 $$ Métro: Miromesnil, St.-Philippe du Roule

PARC DE MONCEAU

This park is farther afield but is linked in spirit to the Second Empire, when it and much of the area surrounding the Champs-Élysées became a fashionable neighborhood. It retains something of its former 19th-century bourgeois aura, with its picturesque park, grottoes, and rockery, along with several extravagant follies (decorative constructions).

Map p. 144 boulevard Courcelles Métro: Monceau, Courcelles ■

The Parc de Monceau was first laid out by the Duc de Chartres in the 18th century, then transformed into an English-style garden during the Second Empire.

Les Grands Boulevards, from the Madeleine to Bastille, were created in the 19th century for the up-and-coming bourgeoisie. These broad streets encompass the Opéra, the biggest department stores, theaters, and show halls.

Les Grands Boulevards

Ornamental detail, facade of Opéra Garnier

Les Grands Boulevards

LES GRANDS BOULEVARDS BEGIN NEAR THE MADELEINE QUARTER AND RUN eastward as far as Bastille. These wide thoroughfares form a shopping and cultural hub, including the ostentatious Opéra Garnier, luxury food stores and designer boutiques, fashion houses, cafés, theaters, and galleries.

"*Là est la vie!*" ("That's where life is!") proclaimed novelist Honoré de Balzac, referring to Les Grands Boulevards, in vogue throughout the 19th century. They became the center of entertainment after the prudish Louis-Philippe closed down the bordellos and gambling dens at the Palais-Royal. Crowds flocked to the boulevards, the wealthy to the west of Rue Montmartre, the poor to the east. Les Grands Boulevards ("boulevard" being derived from the Middle-Dutch word *bollwerk*, meaning "rampart") were created by Louis XIV in the 1670s, following a string of military victories rendering the city's ramparts obsolete. Part of the Charles V Wall and ramparts built by Charles IX and Louis XIII were razed, the moats were filled in, and broad thoroughfares built.

The Boulevard des Capucines, Boulevard des Italiens, and Avenue de l'Opéra converge at the Opéra Garnier (see p. 157) in the Place de l'Opéra designed by Baron Haussmann (see pp. 160–61) to enhance the opera, one of the largest theaters in the world. It is also one of Paris's most brilliant illustrations of the Napoleon III style. Napoleon III crowned the Colonne d'Austerlitz on Place Vendôme (see p. 156) with an imperial effigy of his uncle (Napoleon I) dressed as Julius Caesar. Ancient Greece inspired the series of temples previously commissioned by Napoleon I as well: La Madeleine church, a temple of glory to the Grande Armée, and La Bourse, or

Paris stock exchange, a temple to finance.

The Madeleine Quarter, where Les Grands Boulevards begin, is also a modern-day temple to luxury. Rue de la Paix and Place Vendôme were tranquil bourgeois corners until the late 19th century, when the lavish boutiques of jewelers and fashionable tailors, including the *maison de couture* of Englishman Charles Frederick Worth (the first to display *couture* designs on a live model—his wife), moved in. Jeanne Lanvin, another fashion pioneer, set up shop at No. 22

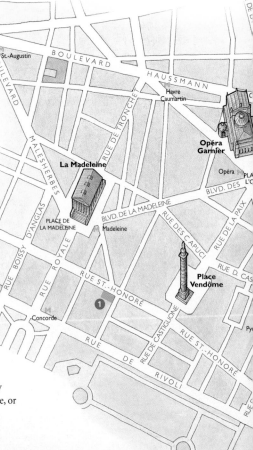

on the Faubourg St.-Honoré in 1890, creating designs for her daughter.

Artists of various media were drawn to the area: The first Impressionist exhibition was held at 35 Boulevard des Capucines, the first showing of the Lumière brothers' film shorts was at No. 14 (now the Hôtel Scribe) in 1895. Musicians such as Lully (the 17th-century court composer who established French opera) gravitated to the area around the Opera House of Paris, which was torn down by Charles X following the assassination of his heir, the Duc de Berry, during a performance of *The Carnival of Venice* in 1820.

The elegant Square de Louvois, near the Bibliothèque Nationale (see p. 159), with its magnificent Labrouste Reading Room (most of the books and manuscripts have been moved to the Bibliothèque de France, 13th arrondissement), now stands in place of the old Opera House. Across the street are the Vivienne and Colbert Galleries, in one of the area's remaining 19th-century covered arcades, where people could shop without worrying about the elements. Today, these galleries have various stores, a restaurant, and a tearoom.

Place Vendôme is studded with the world's leading jewelers, the Ritz Hotel, and the Justice Ministry. Luxury shops, such as Fauchon's, Hédiard's, and Maison de la Truffe, where white truffles from Italy sell for more than 20,000 francs per kilo (about $1,500 per pound), are scattered around the Madeleine, as are the famous flower markets. ∎

LES GRANDS BOULEVARDS

① Église Notre-Dame de l'Assomption
② La Bourse ③ Passage des Panoramas
④ Passage Jouffroy ⑤ Passage Brady

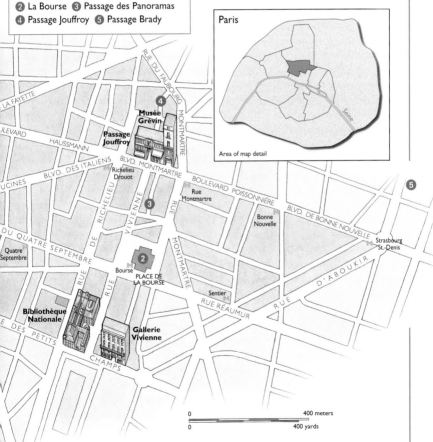

La Madeleine

La Madeleine

 Map p. 154

✉ place de la Madeleine

🕐 01 44 51 69 00

🚇 Métro: Madeleine

FEMINIST REVOLT

Women led by feminist Théroigne de Méricourt massacred nine aristocrats and paraded their heads around on pikes during the Revolution. ■

The Madeleine, formally the church of Saint Mary Magdalene, is one of the most famous monuments in Paris, particularly interesting for its colossal exterior—the 64-foot-high (20 m) Corinthian columns are higher than any in Greece or Rome. The interior is dark and lugubrious, with light coming from three domed skylights in the nave and a semicircular apse. Here celebrity weddings, funerals, and memorial services (as well as regular religious services) are held. In the vestibule is the "Baptism of Christ" (far left), a masterpiece by François Rude.

The church was planned as part of J.A. Gabriel's layout for the Place Louis XV (today's Place de la Concorde). The original construction begun in 1764 was razed in favor of a building modeled on the Panthéon until work was halted by the French Revolution. In 1806, Napoleon commissioned a temple of glory to his Grande Armée and the existing structure was once more razed. However, in 1814 Louis XVIII confirmed that it should be a church and devoted the building to his guillotined brother, Louis XVI. ■

Place Vendôme

Place Vendôme

 Map p. 155

🚇 Métro: Opéra

The jeweler Chaumet, Place Vendôme

The Place Vendôme is superlatively spacious and luminous at night, with an imposing, imperial air. The square (called Place Louis le-Grand until the Revolution) was originally created by Louis XIV to rival Place

des Vosges. In 1792, the square's statue of Louis XIV by François Girardon was destroyed, and replaced in 1810 by the Colonne d'Austerlitz to glorify Napoleon's military campaigns. The bronze spiral wrapped around the stone column—inspired by Trajan's column in Rome—was made from the 1,200 cannon captured at the Battle of Austerlitz (1805). During the Commune, Courbet led a movement to pull down the column; Communards photographed in front of the razed column were executed, and Courbet was forced to finance the column's rebuilding. Napoleon's triumphant, Caesarlike figure has remained ever since.

Opened in 1898 overlooking the square, the Ritz was the first hotel to have private bathtubs. Scott and Zelda Fitzgerald lived here in the 1920s. Ernest Hemingway claimed to have "liberated" the hotel with Allied soldiers in August 1944, while Coco Chanel, who was condemned for having "close" contacts with the Germans, died here. ■

Opéra Garnier

THE OPÉRA GARNIER, BUILT UNDER NAPOLEON III, NOW features ballet primarily, with opera mostly staged at the Opéra de Paris-Bastille. Following Felice Orsini's attempt on Napoleon III's life in 1858 near the narrow street, Salle Le Peletier, the emperor moved the Opéra to a more secure, open site. Architect Charles Garnier was selected from over 170 contestants, having resolved the dilemma of building the Opéra over a lake—it still lies underneath the Opéra, and the fountains and pools in the basement are said to have inspired *The Phantom of the Opera.*

Despite Haussmann's approval of Garnier's project in 1861, Empress Eugénie complained: "What is this style? It is no style at all, neither Greek nor Louis XVI." To which Garnier reportedly replied: "Those styles have had their day. It is Napoleon III, and for this you complain?"

The Opéra indeed epitomizes Napoleon III style: baroque, eclectic, and ridiculously extravagant, with its Apollo-crowned dome and statues of music and dance, including a copy of Carpeaux's "La Danse." The bacchanalian sculpture to the right of the entrance was branded an "ignoble saturnalia" and an "offense to public morals" (the original work is now in the Musée d'Orsay). The Emperor's Pavilion on Rue Scribe, which once featured a ramp to allow the king to enter the royal box directly from his carriage, now provides access to a museum of props and scores.

The Opéra's interior is filled with gold leaf, precious stones, frescoes, marble, and a grandiose foyer and staircase. The five-tier auditorium has only 2,131 seats, some with no visibility, but the huge stage can accommodate up to 450 performers. The false ceiling painted by Chagall in 1964 can be seen when performances or rehearsals are not in progress.

Honey made in the beehives on the Opéra roof is sold in the boutique, at a price. ■

Opéra Garnier

- Map p. 154
- place de l'Opéra
- Switchboard: 01 40 01 17 89. Tour information/museum: 01 40 01 22 63. Box office: 08 36 69 79 68
- Closed for visits on days when there is a matinée performance or special event. Guided tours by prior arrangement
- $$ (for tour)
- Métro: Opéra

The Opéra Garnier, which has been compared to a gilded wedding cake, was modeled after Victor Louis' opera house in Bordeaux and took 13 years to complete.

A walk along Les Grands Boulevards

As you stroll along Les Grands Boulevards, originally laid out as tree-lined promenades in the 17th century, you can still get an impression of what the area looked like in its heyday.

Begin your walk at the 19th-century **Café de la Paix** on the Place de l'Opéra (built by Charles Garnier), frequented by Émile Zola and Guy de Maupassant. Next, visit the landmark **Opéra Garnier** ① (see p. 157).

Exiting the Opéra, turn right down Boulevard des Capucines. The Hôtel Scribe at No. 14 is where, in 1895, the Lumière brothers first showed a series of film shorts, including "*L'entrée en gare du train de La Ciota*." The entirely refurbished **Olympia** concert hall, at No. 28, is where Edith Piaf, Jacques Brel, and the Beatles once performed.

Continue straight on Boulevard des Capucines to **La Madeleine** ② (see p. 156). On the eastern side are the wonderful, wood-paneled art nouveau public rest rooms (women's side only), with mirrored columns, stained glass, and yellow and green floral tiles (*Closed between 11:30 a.m. & 12:30 p.m.*). Go around the church past the flower market (circa 1834) to **Fauchon's** at No. 26 Place de la Madeleine—Paris's most extravagant food store—then on to the more discreet **Hédiard** at No. 21 Place de la Madeleine, on the opposite side of the church. Hédiard is renowned for miniature and exotic fruits and vegetables, including six different kinds of peppers, great teas, and the first fruit of the season. Also on Place de la Madeleine are the Maison de la Truffe (No. 19) and Caviar Kaspia (No. 17) for caviar and pepper vodka.

Circle back in front of the church; Marcel Proust lived at No. 9 Place de la Madeleine, where the restaurant Lucas Carton is located. Head down **Rue Royale** ③ and within a few paces pass the Cité Berryer, which has a good wine shop. You're in the lap of luxury here, with the Ladurée tea salon and pastry shop, Maxim's restaurant, Lachaume florists, Lalique crystal, and Christofle flatware all nearby.

Turn left on Rue St.-Honoré. The Nain Bleu toy shop (No. 408), for label-conscious kids, is on the left. Farther on the right is the 17th-century **Église Notre-Dame de l'Assomption** ④, the former chapel of the Convent of the Sisters of the Assumption (now the Polish Church in Paris). Continue until you reach a passage just before Rue de Castiglione, and cut left through the passage to Place Vendôme, leading to **Rue de la Paix.** The 19th-century's most glamorous shopping street was called Rue Napoleon until it was renamed Rue de la Paix after the signing of the Treaty of Amiens in 1802.

Past the north side of the square, turn right

Galeries such as the Galerie Vivienne were forerunners of French department stores.

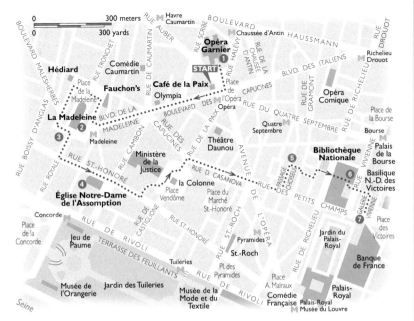

on Rue Danielle Casanova (which becomes Rue des Petits Champs). Look to the right toward **Rue du Marché St.-Honoré** to see the glass-and-steel Marché St.-Honoré—part of Paribas (a bank), it houses offices, a few galleries, and upscale shops. At No. 40 Rue des Petits Champs, turn left into the **Passage Choiseul 5**. Built in 1825 by Bertrand Tavernier, the glass-roofed gallery itself is attractive, although it is now a tacky arcade.

Turn right down perpendicular Passage Ste.-Anne at the Lavrut art supplies store, which leads to Rue Cherubini and Square Louvois. Cross Rue de Richelieu and enter the courtyard of the **Bibliothèque Nationale 6** (*58 Rue de Richelieu, Tel 01 47 03 81 26, Closed Mon., Métro: Bourse*). Temporary exhibitions display some of the treasures of this library, initially founded with royal collections in 1666. The books have been transferred to the Bibliothèque Nationale de France–Site Tolbiac, located along the Seine in the 13th arrondissement, but the maps, musicals scores, medals, prints, and photographs remain here. Turn right and enter the main building to see the spectacular **Labrouste Reading Room** created by Henri Labrouste in 1868; it's not open to the public, but you

See also area map pp. 154–55
► Café de la Paix, place de l'Opéra
◄► 1.6 miles (2.6 km)
🕐 3 hours
► Galerie Vivienne, rue Vivienne

NOT TO BE MISSED
- Opéra Garnier
- Art nouveau rest rooms
- Hédiard
- Bibliothèque Nationale
- Galerie Vivienne

Take this walk during the day, as it explores several passageways that close around 7 p.m.

can peek through the glass doors. Continue down the corridor of the main building and exit right through the gardens. Directly opposite is the entrance to the 19th-century arcade of **Galerie Vivienne 7**; the Galerie Colbert is perpendicular to the right. The belle epoque Grand Colbert restaurant is located here, and the tea salon in the Galerie Vivienne, Priory Thé, is good for brunch on Sundays. ■

Nineteenth-century urban renewal

At the turn of the 19th century, France was coming to terms with the Revolution and the end of the monarchy, and was about to embark on an industrial revolution that would transform its society and alter the city almost beyond recognition.

Impact of the industrial revolution

The development of steam-powered trains, iron wheels, and tracks in the early 19th century created a railway network that linked cities. Suddenly, architects had to find a way to integrate train stations—vast, industrial buildings—into the heart of the city. New materials, including cast iron and sheet glass, solved the problem. Metal was lightweight, strong, and flexible, and glass created uniform, overhead lighting. Glass-and-iron structures were therefore perfect for museums, stations, and marketplaces. The first passageways in Paris used this type of design, as did the marketplace at Les Halles.

Portrait of Baron Haussmann (1809–1891, A. Yvon), who was ousted by Napoleon III in 1870, allegedly for financial misdealings.

As industry thrived in the mid-19th century, workers from the provinces poured into the capital looking for work. Land seized from the Church and the aristocracy during the Revolution was divided up by speculators and developers, and a building boom was soon underway. By the time Louis-Napoleon Bonaparte came to power in 1848, Paris's population had doubled, and the congested city had serious housing, water supply, sanitation, and transportation problems. Inspired by the large parks and wide avenues of London, where he had lived in exile, Napoleon envisaged a new Paris. This was to be created by his prefect of the Seine, the Alsatian Baron

Georges Eugène Haussmann. Political concerns also motivated his decision. Just a few years earlier, barricades set up in the city center by rebellious Parisians had led to the downfall of his predecessors Charles X and Louis-Philippe. Haussmann's intention was to rid the capital of the intricate warren of tiny streets and replace them with broad, clean avenues, which were much easier to control and patrol.

Haussmann's transformations

Haussmann's plan to link the great train stations with wide avenues coincided with a changing view of the city. The newly created bourgeois classes wanted to live, work, and play in the center of the city, to enjoy the wealthy classes' privileges of theaters, museums, libraries, and department stores. Haussmann gave them what they wanted, and more. The entire urban structure was ripped apart and remodeled. The social ramifications of this upheaval were even more brutal. Those not wealthy enough to afford apartments in the lavish new neighborhoods— political troublemakers in Napoleon's eyes— were banished to outlying areas in Paris or to the suburbs.

A major aim was to facilitate traffic flow, which Haussmann did by opening up the area and slicing wide boulevards straight through the city (including Avenue de l'Opéra, Boulevard St.-Germain, and Boulevard Haussmann) and creating large squares, such as Place de la République. These new avenues were often designed to showcase a monument, for example, the exuberant Opéra Garnier at the end of Avenue de l'Opéra. Haussmann's sweeping vision of urban renewal was contested as Paris became a gigantic, muddy construction site.

With the exception of the major monuments, most of the Île de la Cité was destroyed. Entire blocks of centuries-old buildings collapsed under Haussmann's demolition crews. His methods were brutal—even unscrupulous—yet his ability to see the entire city as interlinking elements was a revolutionary new approach to city planning. Nearly 25,000 houses were destroyed, replaced by 50 boulevards and streets, 75,000 new buildings, and 3 new parks: Parc Monceau,

Parc Montsouris, and Parc des Buttes-Chaumont. Sewers, sidewalks, schools, hospitals, markets, and new parks went in. The new streets were lined with Haussmannian buildings, distinguished by their coherence and architectural unity (a result of strict building codes that defined every architectural element from overhangs to door widths). Haussmann also reorganized the political structure of the city, creating a town hall for each arrondissement. In just 17 years, he remodeled the entire city—a phenomenally expensive project that, for better or for worse, transformed Paris from a filthy warren of medieval streets to a modern, functioning metropolis. ■

The 12 streets radiating from the Arc de Triomphe epitomize Haussmann's vision.

More places to visit along Les Grands Boulevards

OTHER PASSAGES & GALLERIES

Described as "human aquariums," the glass-roofed passages and galleries of Paris run from north to south off Les Grands Boulevards, linking one area to the next. The arcades allowed shoppers to browse without fear of being splashed by mud from passing vehicles. Although there are now only about 20 left, more than 100 existed in the early 19th century.

Passage des Panoramas

This is the first gaslit passage and second oldest arcade in Paris. (The Passage du Caire, with its three heads of Hathor reflecting the Egyptomania following Napoleon's Egyptian campaigns, is the oldest.) Opened in 1800, the Passage des Panoramas is named after the giant, circular trompe l'oeil "panorama" paintings (such as those by the American Robert Fulton) of Rome, London, and other world capitals, which once decorated the

entrance. It branches off into a labyrinth of arcades—Galerie St.-Marc, Galerie des Variétés, and Galerie Feydeau. Note the Stern Engraving Company's (founded 1840) impressive store sign (No. 47) and the Napoleon III decor of the L'Arbre à Cannelle tea salon.

🅰 Map p. 155 ✉ Entrances on 11 boulevard Montmartre and 10 rue St.-Marc 🚇 Métro: Grands Boulevards

Passage Jouffroy

Adjacent to the Musée Grevin, this busy passage has storefronts containing miniatures, handcrafted toys, collector walking canes with ivory heads of dogs and recumbent lions, tea salons, and bistros; the continuing Passage Verdeau has books and lithographs.

🅰 Map p. 155 ✉ 12 boulevard Montmartre 🚇 Métro: Richelieu Drouot

Passage Brady

Passage Brady is a passage to India and South Asia, featuring exotic spices, fruits, vegetables, and inexpensive restaurants.

🅰 Map p. 155 ✉ Between 46 rue du Faubourg-St.-Denis and 43 rue du Faubourg St.-Martin 🚇 Métro: Château d'Eau

MUSÉE GRÉVIN

The Musée Grévin (wax museum) had a great impact in 1882—an age devoid of television or media images—as it enabled people to discover what celebrities looked like.

Figures include Serge Gainsbourg, Johnny Hallyday, President Clinton, and historic figures like Charlemagne, Napoleon III, and Marat, whose stabbed effigy lies in the actual bathtub in which he was killed.

Don't miss the Palais des Mirages sound-and-light show (held at regular intervals throughout the day), first featured at the Paris Universal Exposition of 1900. It's a kaleidoscope of images, music, and sound effects.

🅰 Map p. 155 ✉ 10 boulevard Montmartre ☎ 01 47 70 87 99 💲 $$ 🚇 Métro: Grands Boulevards ∎

Passage des Panoramas, an early example of a Parisian shopping arcade

The seventh arrondissement, where embassies, antique shops, and ministries occupy former aristocratic mansions, has a quiet elegance—with the best known Parisian monument, the Eiffel Tower, looming above.

Tour Eiffel & Les Invalides

Inside the Eiffel Tower, looking up

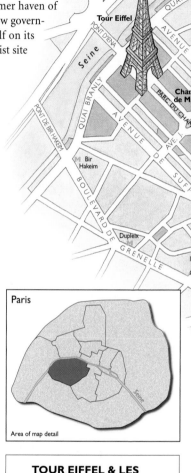

Tour Eiffel & Les Invalides

EXTENDING WEST OF ST.-GERMAIN-DES-PRÉS, the elegant seventh arrondissement—a former haven of aristocratic mansions, many of which are now government buildings and embassies—prides itself on its wealth of museums and on the greatest tourist site of them all, the Eiffel Tower.

In the early 17th century, this area was a large expanse of mostly empty land; it was far from the city center and very hard to reach. A ferry carried passengers across the river at Rue du Bac (meaning "ferryboat"), and the nearest bridge was the Pont Neuf downstream, a notorious hangout for vagrants and thieves. The Pont Royal, constructed in 1689 to replace the 1632 Pont Rouge footbridge, linked Rue du Bac on the Left Bank to the Jardin des Tuileries (see p. 137), thus providing easier access to the Right Bank.

Louis XIV's death in 1715 ushered in a new era of development for this neighborhood. The many nobles who had followed the king to Versailles were delighted to return to Paris at the end of his 72-year-long rule, and several moved to this area, building ornate mansions and palaces (see p. 22). During the Restoration, most of them fled and only returned to recover their properties in the Regency, although very few could afford to maintain them then. Many of these former mansions are now embassies and government ministries, including the magnificent Palais-Bourbon, built for the Duchesse du Bourbon (Louis XIV's daughter by Madame de Montespan) and now the home of the Assemblée Nationale (see p. 169); and the beautiful Hôtel Matignon at 57 Rue de Varenne, the official residence of the prime minister.

The former Hôtel Biron at 77 Rue de Varenne is today the Musée Rodin (see pp. 172–73), where you can visit the artist's former studio or enjoy a stroll through the sculpture-studded gardens.

The other major museum is the Musée d'Orsay (see pp. 174–78), which is devoted to 19th-century art and holds some of the world's best known Impressionist paintings.

TOUR EIFFEL & LES INVALIDES

1 29 Avenue Rapp **2** Les Égouts
3 Rue Cler **4** Hôtel Matignon

Next door to the Orsay is the little known Musée de la Légion d'Honneur, displaying a collection of the red-rosette buttonhole decorations instituted by Napoleon. France's famous emperor is forever linked to the neigh-

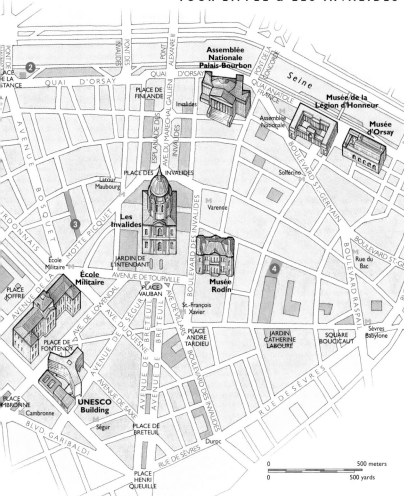

borhood, as his ashes are enthroned under the gilded dome of Les Invalides, originally built by Louis XIV (see p. 170).

The world's most famous monument, the Eiffel Tower (see p. 166) soars 1,051 feet (320 m) above the grassy expanse of the Champ de Mars (see p. 168), on the western edge of the neighborhood.

The Y-shaped UNESCO Building behind the École Militaire (see p. 168) was designed by an international team of architects; it was considered revolutionary when inaugurated in 1958. The collection of artworks reflects the institution's international ambitions: A giant Calder mobile and a Henry Moore sculpture,

"Silhouette," adorn the esplanade outside, while works by Karel Appel, Jean Arp, Matta, and Picasso are inside. Isamu Noguchi designed the lovely Japanese Zen garden, restored in 1998.

There are a few places with a more human scale—for example, the street market on Rue Cler is lined with exquisite upscale shops, and the entrance to 29 Avenue Rapp nearby is one of Paris's best examples of art nouveau architecture. For a subterranean view of the city, visit the famous Égouts (sewers; see p. 72), the entrance to which is on Place de la Résistance, opposite the Pont de l'Alma on the Left Bank. ∎

Tour Eiffel

PARISIANS TYPICALLY GREET ANY NEW MONUMENT IN their urban landscape with a mixture of horror, criticism, and public dismay for a few years, after which it becomes a cherished national symbol—the Eiffel Tower is a perfect example.

In 1887, Gustave Eiffel's cast-iron monument design was selected to showcase the 1889 Universal Exposition celebrating the centennial of the French Revolution. He used the same techniques for construction as in his bridges in France and abroad: All 15,000 metal parts were prefabricated and numbered for assembly, and most of the 2.5 million rivets were already in place before the tower went up. His well-laid plans and technological

"the hollow candlestick" and "a disgusting column of bolts and sheet metal." Guy de Maupassant was so distressed at the sight of it that he ate in its second-floor Le Jules Verne restaurant, claiming it was the only place in town he couldn't see it. Although it was slated for demolition 20 years after the exposition closed, it was unexpectedly saved by the invention of radio (or wireless) transmission, as its height made it an unrivaled antenna.

Tour Eiffel

⬛ Map p. 164
✉ Champ de Mars
☎ 01 44 11 23 23
💲 $$
🚇 Métro: Bir Hakeim

wizardry ensured that, with 300 steelworkers toiling 7 days a week for 26 consecutive months (and without a single fatal accident), the world's tallest building was completed just 7 days before the exhibition opened.

The Eiffel Tower was the largest and most innovative structure of its time, sending a clear message that France and French engineers intended to lead the world into the 20th century. Some critics, however, were less than enthusiastic, calling it

The tower offers a superb view that extends up to 45 miles (73 km) on a clear day. Ticket price varies, depending on how high you want to go, and whether you walk or take the elevator: You can walk up to the second platform. Its five million annual visitors rarely include Parisians, who often snub it as the ultimate in kitsch, but the one-star Le Jules Verne restaurant (see p. 252–53) is gradually luring them back. It's expensive, but has a wonderful view and excellent cusine. ∎

Above: The new medium of photography documented the Eiffel Tower as it took form in 1888.

Right: Recently redesigned, the new lighting makes the tower glow from within.

Champ de Mars & École Militaire

THE CHAMP DE MARS SPREADS OUT LIKE AN IMMENSE green carpet to the base of the Eiffel Tower; it actually predates the tower by 140 years. Today, it is a pleasant expanse of open grass, where children play soccer and throw frisbees, and families picnic.

Ecole Militaire

🗺 Map p. 165

✉ École Militaire, avenue de la Motte Picquet

🚇 Champ de Mars, Tour Eiffel, École Militaire

The Champ de Mars was initially laid out as a parade ground for the École Militaire, a military school founded to educate members of the impoverished nobility. Young Napoleon Bonaparte spent a year at the school (1784–85).

The first Bastille Day was celebrated here on July 14, 1790, when crowds gathered to watch Louis XVI pay allegiance to the new constitution (see pp. 23–24). In the late 18th century, the Champ de Mars was transformed from parade ground to playground when the sport of horse racing was introduced from England, and it remained a racecourse until 1855.

French city planners have always had a penchant for majestic vistas, and one of the best is from the École Militaire (not open to the public), across the Champ de Mars toward the Eiffel Tower, with the outstretched wings of the Palais de Chaillot in the background. ■

A great deal of new construction was carried out for the Universal Exposition of 1900, including the single-span Alexander III Bridge (visible in the foreground).

Expositions Universelles

England astonished the world in 1851 with the Crystal Palace, built for the first Great Exhibition to showcase British goods and technical know-how. The French immediately began planning their own world's fair. The first of five *expositions*, most of which were based around the Champ de Mars, was held in 1867 (see p. 150).

The greatest French fair was the one held in 1889, when 28 million visitors came to marvel at the glittering cast-iron and glass structures covering the site and to look up amazed at the Tour Eiffel. ■

Assemblée Nationale

THE LOWER HOUSE OF THE FRENCH PARLIAMENT (Assemblée Nationale) is housed in the Palais-Bourbon; the Upper House (Sénat) is in the Palais du Luxembourg (see p. 82). Visitors can view the Hémisphère (where political debates take place) and the library, decorated by Delacroix's "History of Civilization."

The Palais-Bourbon was constructed by the aristocracy but is now a symbol of democracy.

The Palais-Bourbon, which now houses the 577 elected deputies of the Assemblée Nationale (the legislative body of the government), was built between 1722 and 1728 for the Duchesse de Bourbon; she ceded part of her property to her lover, the Marquis de Lassay, who constructed the magnificent Hôtel de Lassay next door. After the duchesse's death, various members of the royal Condé family lived in and remodeled the two buildings; the last Condé linked the two, investing great sums of money in the property. The work was completed in 1788, just before the Revolution broke out, and the Condé prince lost everything.

The government confiscated the buildings in 1795, making them the seat of the elected assembly. Such extensive remodeling was done, including a semicircular Council Chamber to replace the formal reception rooms, that only the courtyard of the original gracious mansion remains.

Napoleon deserves the credit—or blame—for the heavy neoclassical facade. The original did not line up perfectly with the Place de la Concorde, and he approved Bernard Poyet's 1806 plan to slap an immense colonnaded false front onto the building, intended to mirror the Madeleine across the river.

The Hôtel de Lassay was spared somewhat and has served as the residence of the president of the Assembly since 1843. Most of the 18th-century interior remains, but the building is closed to the public (except for one day each year, the Journée Porte Ouverte). The Palais-Bourbon is open for visits when the chamber is not in session. ∎

Assemblée Nationale

- Map p.165
- 126 rue de l'Université
- 01 40 63 60 00
- Guided tours for groups require appointment. Individual tours on Saturday (10 a.m, 2 p.m., 3 p.m. etc.). Meet 30 minutes before start of tour at 33 Quai d'Orsay. Passport or identity card required.
- Métro: Assemblée Nationale

Les Invalides

LES INVALIDES IS GENERALLY LINKED TO NAPOLEON, BUT it was originally built by Louis XIV as a hospital for his veterans. After Versailles, Les Invalides ranks as the most important architectural project of Louis XIV's reign. The king longed to create an institution to care for the infirm soldiers and aging veterans of his army, the poorest of whom were encamped in the notorious Pont Neuf district. In 1670 he commissioned Libéral Bruant to build a military hospice on the far western edge of the Faubourg St.-Germain, where his retired veterans could be kept out of sight.

Four years later the soldiers were moved into their new home, where the discipline was so rigorous that many must have missed the freedom, if not the poverty, of their previous quarters. They were promised full pension and medical care, and though their days were strictly regulated, and any violations were punished by imprisonment, the infirmary was nevertheless a success. Originally intended for only 1,500 invalids, by 1690 some 6,000 men were clamoring to enter, and monarchs throughout Europe began modeling their own military hospitals on it.

NAPOLEON'S RESTING PLACE

The dome of the church at Les Invalides, designed by Jules Hardouin-Mansart and completed in 1706, is a gleaming landmark in the Parisian landscape. What was designed as a royal chapel became an imperial mausoleum in 1840 when the body of Napoleon I was returned to France from Saint Helena. In 1861, his ashes were laid to rest in a porphyry tomb, inside a glass-topped crypt in the center of the dome.

MILITARY MUSEUMS

Three museums are housed within the grounds of Les Invalides. The **Musée de l'Armée,** founded in 1905, is one of the most complete military museums in the world. Its collection ranges from antiquity to World War II, including paintings, armor, artillery, uniforms, and, of course, numerous Napoleonic souvenirs. The **Musée des Plans-Reliefs** is an intriguing museum of three-dimensional scale models of fortified towns, a collection that began in 1668, making it the oldest museum within Les Invalides's walls. The **Musée de l'Ordre de la Libération** honors all those who fought for France during World War II. The Order of the Liberation was created by General de Gaulle in November 1940. ∎

Les Invalides

- 🄰 Map p. 165
- ✉ Esplanade des Invalides
- ☎ 01 44 42 37 72
- 🕐 Closed Jan. 1, May 1, Nov. 1, Dec. 25
- 💲 $$
- Ⓜ Métro: Varenne, Latour Maubourg

Left: Napoleon's remains lie within six coffins, one inside the other, made respectively of iron, mahogany, lead (two), ebony, and oak.

Right: During World War II, the Germans set up quarters in Les Invalides; in 1942, the Resistance rigged up an escape route under their noses for Allied pilots shot down over Normandy.

Musée Rodin

AUGUSTE RODIN'S SCULPTURES FILL THE LUXURIOUS garden and interiors of the 18th-century Hôtel Biron, the most charming and intimate spot in this otherwise grandiose neighborhood. No fewer than 27 bronzes and 40 marbles by Rodin are scattered in the midst of the lovely rose gardens.

Musée Rodin
- Map p. 165
- 77 rue de Varenne
- 01 44 18 61 10
- Closed Mon.
- $
- Métro: Varenne

The figures in "The Kiss" (right) first appeared on "The Gates of Hell" as Paolo and Francesca, a pair of adulterous lovers from Canto V of Dante's *Inferno*. Caught in adultery, they were put to death by the enraged Gianciotto.

Rodin is generally credited as the founding father of modern sculpture. A self-taught artist, he vehemently rejected academic conventions throughout his life.

He was almost 38 when his first important work, "The Age of Bronze," was exhibited in 1878 amid great controversy. It was so perfectly modeled that critics accused him of taking plaster casts directly from his model. He was finally vindicated, and the ensuing publicity catapulted him into the public eye. Two years later he received a commission for "The Gates of Hell" (a work never completed in his lifetime), and by the time he had reached his mid-40s, he had achieved international fame. Yet nearly all of his major works created controversy, from "The Burghers of Calais" (1895) to his statue of Victor Hugo (1909), shocking his patrons with their realism, power, and emotional content. His statue of Balzac, wearing his legendary dressing gown, was considered so inappropriate that it was initially refused by the Société des Gens de Lettres (an institution of literary figures), and it remained hidden from public view for 41 years. In 1939, "Balzac" was finally placed at the Carrefour Vavin in Paris, where it now stands.

Rodin's Home & Studio
- Villa des Brillants, 19 avenue Auguste Rodin, Meudon (on the southern edge of Paris)
- 01 41 14 35 00
- Open May to Oct., Fri., Sat., & Sun. only 1:30 p.m.–6 p.m.
- $

Camille Claudel

Rodin said of Camille Claudel: "I showed her where to find gold, but the gold she found was truly hers." She came to Rodin's studio as a student in 1883 and soon became his model and lover. Her face appears in some of Rodin's best work, including "The Kiss," "The Gates of Hell," and "Fugit Amor." Their liaison lasted through 1898, when it became clear that Rodin would never break his long-term relationship with Rose Beuret. Claudel retreated into madness, living alone in her studio on the Île St.-Louis. She was interned in a mental institution in 1913, where she remained until her death in 1943. In his will, Rodin stipulated that her work be exhibited in his museum, which has such intensely emotional pieces as "Sakountala" (perhaps her most important work), "Waltz," and "L'Age Mûr," created during her separation from Rodin. ■

HÔTEL BIRON

The rococo-style Hôtel Biron was completed in 1730, and, after the Revolution, it housed the Russian Embassy and then a religious school. By 1905, it was in a dilapidated state, and its future uncertain.

During negotiations, a few artists were allowed to use the building as a temporary studio— Austrian poet Rainer Maria Rilke (Rodin's secretary at the time), Henri Matisse, Jean Cocteau, and lastly, Rodin, who moved there in 1908. This situation became permanent when the State purchased the property in 1911. In the early 20th century, at the height of his career, Rodin's dream of creating a museum of his work in the Hôtel Biron was approved by the State, but he died before his museum was officially inaugurated.

Rodin donated all of his own work to the State, as well as his collection of paintings and Greek and Roman sculptures. All of his major pieces are represented here, plus a number of studies.

His home and studio, in Meudon, contain thousands of his terra-cotta and plaster models. ■

"The Gates of Hell" was originally commissioned in 1880 for a future decorative arts museum in Paris (it was never built). Many of Rodin's major works appeared first on the gates.

Musée d'Orsay

ALTHOUGH THE IMPRESSIONIST PAINTINGS ARE PROBABLY the greatest draw for visitors to the Musée d'Orsay, the museum also features decorative arts, photography, and the performing arts.

Musée d'Orsay

◩ Map p. 165
✉ 1 rue de Bellechasse
☎ 01 40 49 48 84; www.musee-orsay.fr
🕐 Closed Mon.
💲 $$
Ⓜ Métro: Solferino

The Musée d'Orsay's building rose from its ashes. The former Palais d'Orsay, home of the Conseil d'État and the Cour des Comptes, was burned during the Commune, and the blackened ruins were left standing for nearly 30 years. On the eve of the Paris Universal Exposition of 1900, the government agreed to allow the Orléans Railway Company to construct a train station on the site of the ruins, providing a station that was more central than the remote Austerlitz.

The station and hotel were inaugurated on July 14, 1900, and their lobby was so luxurious that the painter Edouard Detaille called it—prophetically—a "Palace of Fine Arts." Train stations around the world were modeled after Orsay, including Grand Central Terminal in New York and Union Station in Washington, D.C. For nearly 40 years, the Orsay station was the hub for traffic bound for southwest France. By 1939, however, long-distance trains no longer stopped

The Orsay train station, which was in service for some 30 years, epitomized academic architecture, using stone and stucco to cover steel structures of amazing strength.

The problem of integrating the train terminus with its aristocratic environment was solved by Victor Laloux in 1898, who suggested hiding the cast-iron train structure under finely cut stone. He incorporated the most up-to-date technology inside—elevators, ramps, luggage elevators, electric traction, and even a 370-room hotel surrounding the station along the length of Rue de Bellechasse, Rue de Lille, and part of the quay.

here as the platforms were too short for the longer modern trains.

The building was then put to a number of different uses, becoming a mailing center during World War II, a holding center for returning prisoners of war, a film set (featured in Orson Welles' adaptation of Kafka's *Trial* in 1962), and a temporary auction house. In the 1960s, plans to destroy the building and replace it with a modern hotel complex had already been approved when critics lobbied to have it classified as a historical monument. It was saved in 1977 when President Valéry Giscard d'Estaing proposed transforming it into a museum devoted to all forms of 19th-century art (from 1848 to 1915), thus filling a historical gap between the Louvre Museum and the Beaubourg project.

The ACT architecture group transformed the building itself, and a team of architects under Italian Gae Aulenti worked on its interiors. The masterful result incorporates Laloux's original cast-iron pillars and stucco decoration in a space suitable for the museum's requirements. The huge, luminous central entrance hall is divided by stone partitions and lined with galleries on either side.

The Musée d'Orsay was officially inaugurated on December 1, 1986, by President François Mitterand and it became the new home for Impressionist works that had been displayed at the Jeu de Paume. The Louvre transferred

The train station's initial decor was so luxurious that Italian architect Gae Aulenti chose to preserve the glass roof and coffered ceilings for the museum, making it look like an ancient basilica.

Salon paintings and works by artists born after 1820, and Post-impressionist works came from the Musée National d'Art Moderne.

THE COLLECTIONS

The period covered by the Musée d'Orsay is important in the history of contemporary art. Academic conventions were overturned, new themes were introduced, and a radical approach to painting and photography regarding color and composition appeared. The museum is organized in broad chronological sequences, beginning on the ground floor, continuing to the top, and finishing on the middle floor.

Ground Floor

The period represented here, from 1848 to 1870, is less known than that of the Impressionists, yet it was these artists who broke new ground for the generations to come. At that time, the yearly Salon (an official exhibition of art sponsored by the French government), with its staid and predictable historical and mythological paintings, was the standard by which artists were measured. Ingres and Delacroix, who belonged to the earlier years of the century, continued as leading figures, and several of their later works (in the first rooms to the right of the entrance) illustrate the transition in academic painting. Thomas Couture and Alexandre Cabanel exemplified the languid, classical, and uncontroversial subjects of the *pompiers* (as in "pomp" and "pompous"), although they were highly regarded in their day. To the left of the entrance are landscapes from the Barbizon school (Jean-Baptiste Camille Corot, Charles Daubigny, and Théodore Rousseau), whose work was based on an idealization of nature and a rejection of academic convention. Jean-François Millet's painting,

"Gleaners," perhaps best represents this humanistic spirit.

Honoré Daumier was a major figure in Realism, the movement that opposed the *pompier* style. Although better known as a cartoonist, his real masterpieces (on display) are the 26 painted clay busts that ruthlessly caricatured contemporary politicians. The Realist leader was Gustave Courbet, who portrayed scenes from contemporary life with an unsentimental yet sympathetic eye (as in his "Burial at Ornans"). His most sensational painting, the sexually explicit "Origins of the World," only recently acquired, was so realistic that it has never before been shown in public.

This floor also exhibits works by Impressionist artists painted before 1870, including Édouard Manet, whose "Olympia" caused a scandal at the 1865 Salon des Refusés (created for those turned down by the official Salon). However, it was his subject matter—criticized as an obscene portrayal of a prostitute—that shocked the critics, not his technique, and although sympathetic to other Impressionists, Manet remained aloof from them. Works by Monet, Degas, and Fréderic Bazille illustrate their early experiments in solving the problems of light and shadow, and their work pioneered a new vision of painting.

The central aisle emphasizes 19th-century sculpture in the neoclassic tradition; the most interesting are those by Jean-Baptiste Carpeaux, whose "Dance" for the facade of the Opéra Garnier was called "an offense to public morals."

Upper Floor

Escalators go straight to the upper galleries, where room after room contains treasures from the years 1874 to 1886—a period that revolutionized painting as artists began seeing in a new way. After the Prussian Wars (1870–71), Renoir, Monet, and Pissarro, along with Berthe Morisot and Alfred Sisley, banded together in opposition to the official Salons. The first exhibition by the Impressionist painters, held in 1874, was where the term "Impressionism" was coined, when critic Louis Leroy used it to mock Monet's painting, "Impression: gallery. Note especially "The Card Players" and "Apples and Oranges." He was less interested in the Impressionist experiments with light, working instead on structure, color, and composition. Ridiculed by critics, Cézanne was ultimately vindicated as the forerunner of 20th-century painting; both Picasso and Matisse were heavily influenced by his work.

Sunrise" (now in the Marmottan Museum, see p. 183). The artists adopted the name themselves, continuing to exhibit until 1886.

The first gallery on this floor exhibits the Moreau-Nélaton Collection, dominated by Manet's "Déjeuner sur l'Herbe," the masterpiece of the 1863 Salon des Refusés. The next rooms are devoted to Manet and James Whistler and to the spread of Impressionism, with works by Degas ("Blue Dancers"), Monet ("Gare St.-Lazare"), Renoir ("Le Bal du Moulin de la Galette"), and others.

Paul Cézanne's works are displayed in a room in the upper

Cézanne appears again in the room devoted to Dr. Gachet's collection (Gachet was doctor and friend to Cézanne) in the Bellechasse Gallery, which includes such masterpieces as van Gogh's "Église d'Auvers-sur-Oise," "Portrait of the Artist," and "l'Arlésienne."

The innovative tendencies of the next generation—Gauguin and the Pont-Aven painters Odilon Redon and Paul Signac—are exhibited in the following rooms of the Bellechasse Gallery; these include Gauguin's "La Belle Angèle," "On the Beach," and "The White Horse," Signac's "The Red Buoy," and Redon's "Decorative Panels."

Thomas Couture's "Romans in the Period of Decadence" (1847)

Van Gogh painted "The Midday Siesta" (1889–1890), a copy of a drawing by Jean-François Millet, during his self-internment in St.-Rémy in southern France.

Middle Floor

It may seem that the galleries on this floor hold solely genre works and the monumental decorations of the Third Empire, but they actually encompass a wide range of painting, decorative arts, and sculpture, with nearly a quarter of the sculpture terrace devoted to Rodin. Several works are on loan from the nearby Musée Rodin (see pp. 172–73), including the plaster versions of "The Gates of Hell" and "Balzac." Commissioned for a decorative arts museum that was never built, "The Gates of Hell" was based on Dante's "Divine Comedy."

The nabi painters—Pierre Bonnard, Édouard Vuillard, and Maurice Denis—occupy several rooms on the south side of this level. They aimed to establish painting as a decorative art for embellishing day-to-day existence.

Several rooms are also dedicated to the art nouveau movement that

spread throughout Europe under various names—Modern Style, Jugendstil, and Arte Joven—in the late 19th century. Objects of all kinds, from chairs to furniture, glassware, and stained glass, illustrate what was a radically new approach to design at the time. One of the most beautiful examples is the Charpentier Dining Room (circa 1900), a luscious interior of mahogany, oak, and poplar, with the chacteristic floral decoration.

PHOTOGRAPHY

The museum also has several thousand remarkable images from the earliest days of photography. These are presented in rotation in exhibition rooms: Dossier 3 (ground floor) and Dossier 5 (upper floor).

The early photographs of Eadweard Muybridge, who was critical in the transition from still to moving pictures, are also in the collection. ∎

With the Trocadéro museums, Chaillot Palace, and such well-heeled quartiers as Passy, the 16th arrondissement has long been the preserve of the capital's more monied citizens.

The 16th arrondissement

Bronze statue outside the Palais de Chaillot

The 16th arrondissement

DESPITE ITS REPUTATION AS A REFUGE FOR THE RICH AND AS AN OPULENT but boring neighborhood, the 16th arrondissement has a wealth of museums, a few remaining traces of its former village life, and the most concentrated number of art nouveau and art deco buildings in Paris. Comfortably wedged between the Seine on one side and the Bois de Boulogne on the other, the 16th arrondissement—far from the fray of the city center—is the neighborhood favored by both old and new money. Much of the area, especially near the Champs-Élysées, is occupied by banks, multinationals, overpriced hotels, and fashion designers. The southern part of this arrondissement, including the former villages of Passy and Auteuil, is just as snooty but still has a neighborly feel, however exclusive.

This part of Paris has lured the upper classes for centuries. Catherine de Médicis often stopped on Chaillot Hill (the present-day Trocadéro, a semicircular square in front of the Palais de Chaillot) on her way from St.-Germain-en-Laye to Paris, gradually expanding and remodeling the lodge that stood on the site. Later, nobles traveling to Louis XIV's Versailles found that Passy and Auteuil were convenient places at which to break their journey.

Wine and water also contributed to the area's fame. The wine produced by the Abbey of Passy and the Minimes de Chaillot was famous throughout the region, and vineyards lined the hills sloping down toward the Seine. In the 17th century, the curative powers of Passy's spring brought upper-crust clientele anxious to sample its highly reputed thermal spa; today, its source still provides crystal-clear water to nearby areas.

ARCHITECTURAL GEMS

More than half of Hector Guimard's art nouveau buildings are in the 16th arrondissement, particularly in Auteuil. Best known for his superb glass-and-iron Métro entrances (especially the one at the Porte Dauphine), Guimard also designed the flamboyant Castel Béranger, an art nouveau masterpiece, and several other buildings along Rue de la Fontaine. The streamlined art deco style followed in the 1920s and '30s; its chief Parisian proponent, Robert Mallet-Stevens, designed a series of town houses on an Auteuil street that now bears his name. Several small alleyways off Rue Boileau (*Métro: Exelmans*), including the Villa Cheysson and the Villa

Mulhouse—originally built to house mill-workers—are lined with charming houses and gardens; although reminders of their former more modest inhabitants, they are now highly prized homes.

The villages of Passy, Auteuil, and Chaillot were annexed to the City of Paris in 1860. This was the era of lavish *Expositions Universelles* (see p. 168), and the Third Republic's officials chose Chaillot Hill as the site for an immense Moorish palace, built for the 1878 Universal Exposition. Most Parisians hated it, and for the 1937 exposition it was replaced by the present, enormous Palais de Chaillot (see p. 182), built in neo-classic style, and decorated with sculptures and bas-reliefs. It now contains three museums, a theater, and the Cinéma-thèque Française, a repository for both classic and contemporary films. Its enormous esplanade is the meeting place for the city's skateboarders, and it has a breathtaking view of the Eiffel Tower.

East down Chaillot Hill are two major museums: the Musée Guimet (see p. 184), which is devoted to Asian Arts, and, just across the street, the lively Musée d'Art Moderne de la Ville de Paris (see p. 182), housed in the neoclassic Palais de Tokyo, which was built for the 1937 Universal Exposition. ■

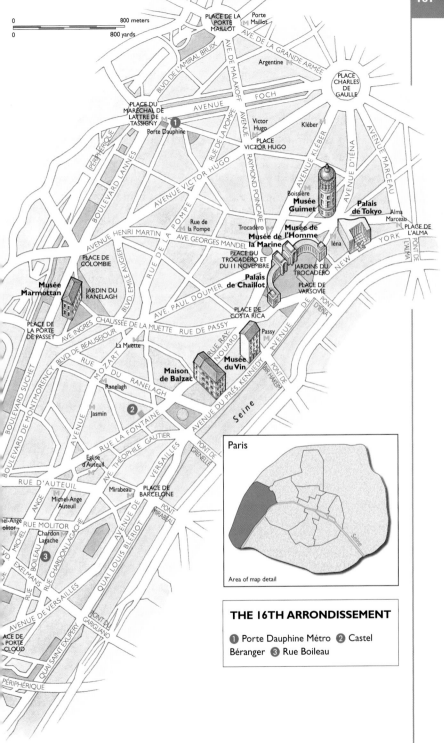

THE 16TH ARRONDISSEMENT

① Porte Dauphine Métro ② Castel
Béranger ③ Rue Boileau

Entrance to the temporary exhibits at the Museum of Modern Art

🅰 Map p.181

Trocadéro Museums
✉ Palais de Chaillot, 17 place du Trocadéro
☎ Musée de l'Homme: 01 44 05 72 72. Musée de la Marine: 01 53 65 69 69.
🕐 Closed Tues.
💲 $$
Ⓜ Métro: Trocadéro

Théâtre Nationale de Chaillot
✉ I place du Trocadéro
☎ 01 53 65 30 00
Ⓜ Métro: Trocadéro

Musée d'Art Moderne de la Ville de Paris
✉ II avenue du Président Wilson
☎ 01 53 67 40 00
🕐 Closed Mon.
💲 $
Ⓜ Métro: Iéna

Palais de Chaillot & Trocadéro Museums

THE VIEW FROM THE TERRACE OF THE MONUMENTAL Palais de Chaillot across the river from the Eiffel Tower and the École Militaire is one of the best in Paris. However, the museums inside this monument are less well known—the Musée de l'Homme, the Musée de la Marine, and, scheduled to reopen in 2003, the Musée des Monuments Français, a remarkable collection of casts and reproductions of French monumental sculpture and architecture. The Cinémathèque Française *(Tel 01 56 26 01 01)*, also in the Palais de Chaillot, schedules daily projections of classics and more obscure films. The palace still holds the Théâtre National de Chaillot, which presents the classics of French theater. Down the hill from the Palais du Chaillot is another small museum, the Musée d'Art Moderne de la Ville de Paris.

MUSÉE DE L'HOMME
The Musée de l'Homme is an ethnology and anthropology museum, with a demographics exhibition—"Six Billion People"—and a chronological display in the prehistory gallery called "The Mists of Time," tracing human evolution from prehistory to the present.

MUSÉE DE LA MARINE
Created in 1748 from the personal collection of Louis Henri Duhamel de Monceau, Inspector General of the French Navy, this is one of the oldest marine museums in the world. It contains intricate scale models of warships dating from the 17th century to the present and splendid examples of the famous tall sailing ships.

MUSÉE D'ART MODERNE DE LA VILLE DE PARIS
The Museum of Modern Art of the City of Paris, inaugurated in 1961 in the sober Palais de Tokyo, represents many artists of the school of Paris along with a rich collection of exuberant fauvist and cubist works. Its Contemporary Art Department (ARC) regularly organizes ambitious temporary shows, highlighting young international artists and the themes of current art trends. ∎

Musée Marmottan

ALTHOUGH THE MUSÉE MARMOTTAN IS NOW FAMOUS throughout the world for its Impressionist paintings, including Monet's "Impression: Sunrise," the museum was initially devoted to an entirely different theme: the Napoleonic era.

Jules and Paul Marmottan, father and son, were responsible for this collection, housed in a former hunting lodge, which was entirely remodeled by Marmottan senior. At the turn of the 19th century both men were interested in Napoleonic memorabilia, a time when everyone else either ignored or despised it, and they amassed a superb collection of Empire furnishings. While Jules made his fortune as manager of a coal company, Paul endured a short-lived career as a functionary until his father's death made him a wealthy man. After this, he became a recognized expert on Empire art. When he died in 1932, he left his mansion and entire art collection to the Institut de France.

Several later bequests transformed the Marmottan into a world-renowned Impressionist museum. The first bequest included "Impression: Sunrise," while a second in 1966, from Claude Monet's son Michel, brought 65 works by the painter, including some of his best paintings.

A number of the magical Water Lilies paintings are exhibited downstairs, along with the images of smoke-filled train stations and brilliant fields of flowers and other works such as Alfred Sisley's "Spring in the Environs of Paris" and "Apple Trees in Bloom," Pierre-Auguste Renoir's "Claude Monet Reading," and Paul Gauguin's "Bouquet of Flowers."

The ground-floor room contains a collection of medieval illuminated manuscripts from the Georges Wildenstein collection. ∎

Musée Marmottan
- Map p. 181
- 2 rue Louis Boilly
- 01 42 24 07 02
- Closed Mon.
- $$
- Métro: La Muette

"Bouquet of Flowers" (1897) is one of the few works painted by Paul Gauguin in Tahiti that now hangs in a French museum.

More places to visit in the 16th arrondissement

MAISON DE BALZAC

In 1840, Honoré de Balzac, writer of *La Comédie Humaine* (*The Human Comedy*), was on the brink of financial ruin. He moved to this house in Passy, where he lived under the pseudonym of Monsieur de Breugnol. A museum since 1960, it displays many of his personal objects, including his writing desk, where he sometimes worked for 24 hours at a stretch. As he wrote to Madame Hanska, whom he married just before his death at the age of 51, this desk "witnessed my anguish, my miseries, my distress, my joys, my everything."

porcelain from China. The museum at 6 Place d'Iéna is scheduled to open in the fall of 1999, after major renovations; however, the galleries of the Buddhist pantheon at 19 Avenue d'Iéna, devoted to the history of Far Eastern religions, remain open.

🗺 Map p. 181 ✉ 19 avenue d'Iéna
☎ 01 40 73 88 11 🕐 Closed Tues. 💲 $
🚇 Métro: Iéna

MUSÉE DU VIN

Just a few steps from the Trocadéro is a 15th-century hideaway enclosing the wine

The Musée du Panthéon Bouddhique contains Émile Guimet's Far Eastern finds, including a fine collection of Buddhas and bodhisattvas.

🗺 Map p. 181 ✉ 47 rue Raynouard
☎ 01 55 74 41 80 🕐 Closed Mon. 💲 $
🚇 Métro: Passy

MUSÉE GUIMET–GALERIE DU PANTHÉON BOUDDHIQUE

The museum's original collection came from Émile Guimet, who gathered a fantastic amount of objects during his trips to the Far East in the late 19th century. A national museum since 1928, it exhibits Guimet's collection, which ranges from Afghan to Japanese works and spans 2000 B.C. to the 19th century, including examples of Khmer artwork, bronze statues from India, and antique jade and

cellars of the former Minimes de Chaillot monastery, which distilled one of Louis XIII's favorite vintage wines. Most of the buildings were destroyed during the Revolution, and the cellars were forgotten until the 1950s, when they were reopened. They were eventually made into a wine museum in 1984. Visitors can now explore the former limestone quarries that house objects used in the making and drinking of wine. Entrance to the museum is free if you eat in the restaurant (open for lunch only).

🗺 Map p. 181 ✉ rue des Eaux, 5 square Dickens ☎ 01 45 25 63 26 🕐 Closed Mon.
💲 $$ (including a glass of wine)
🚇 Métro: Passy ■

Montmartre has retained a certain village charm, its narrow, sinuous streets snaking downward toward Pigalle. In the heart of it all, the dome of Sacré-Coeur, visible from nearly all points in Paris, stands out bright white.

Montmartre

Montmartre poster

Montmartre

THERE IS NO OTHER PLACE IN PARIS QUITE LIKE MONTMARTRE. HIGH ON A hill (known to Parisians as the "Butte"), it has a unique village atmosphere, enclosing both Pigalle's neon lights and the lyrical, winding streets and charming houses just steps away. Music, art, and wine—along with a touch of the licentious and an irreverence for authority and tradition—have all contributed to the myth of Montmartre. But its roots are much older than its legendary 19th-century cabarets, which include the famous Moulin Rouge.

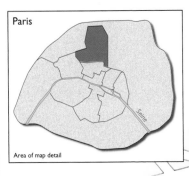

Paris

Area of map detail

MONTMARTRE

1 Lapin Agile 2 Allée des Brouillards
3 Place des Abbesses 4 Folies-Bergère

The start of the grape harvest is celebrated at Montmartre vineyard on the first Saturday in October.

The Butte of Montmartre has been a place of worship since earliest history: The Druids celebrated their priestly rites here, and it was also the site of a Roman temple, probably dedicated to Mercury. This area has escaped real estate development largely because the ground is riddled with tunnels from old quarries, where gypsum and limestone have been mined since Roman times.

Montmartre's hill is also punctuated with Christian edifices, such as the Royal Abbey of St.-Denis, constructed in 1133 by Louis VI and his wife, Adelaide de Savoy, in honor of the martyred saint (see p. 16). Its lands extended south into the present-day ninth arrondissement, and north toward the abbey. After the Revolution, the abbey's lands were sold and its buildings dismantled, except the Romanesque St.-Pierre de Montmartre Church (see p. 188), which continued to be the villagers' favored place of worship even after work on the Basilica of Sacré-Coeur

(see p. 188) began in 1876. The villagers' long history of independence was demonstrated when, infuriated by Thiers's capitulation to the Prussians in 1871, they refused to hand over the cannon guarding the city, setting off a series of events that produced the Commune (see p. 26). The generals dispatched by Thiers to recover the cannon were killed, an act that would be commemorated on a plaque behind the basilica (on Rue Chevalier-de-la-Barre).

Montmartre's social structure was transformed when trainloads of people from the provinces came to the capital during the industrial revolution to look for work, and ended up living in this inexpensive neighborhood. The wall of the Fermiers Généraux, or toll road, where the present-day Place Pigalle is, effectively cut Montmartre off from the city. Incoming goods were levied on Pigalle's tollgate; therefore, outside the walls, wine—produced in abundance on the hills of Montmartre—was cheaper and the demand

was heavy. The village was incorporated into the City of Paris in 1860 as the 18th arrondissement.

By the late 19th century, the area's numerous cabarets, brothels, and nefarious underworld activities had earned Montmartre an enduring reputation for depravity that inevitably attracted artists, writers, and bourgeois Parisians in search of new thrills. Artists of all types, from Eugène Delacroix, Hector Berlioz, and Vincent van Gogh to contemporary painters, have come to the Butte for its

charm, light, and, in the past, low rents.

Montmartre today is much as it has always been: a mix of romance, poetry, sex, and commercialism. The Moulin Rouge (see p. 193) is still packed every night, and the Place du Tertre is inundated with portrait painters and the pervasive smell of crepes from the food stands. But glimpses of a more lyrical era still survive in the labyrinth of steep, tree-lined streets encircling the Butte. From its vantage, the busy capital below seems miles away. ∎

Sacré-Coeur

RISING LIKE A GIANT WEDDING CAKE IN NORTHERN PARIS,
the Basilica of Sacré-Coeur stands on the highest point of the city and
is thus the most visible of Montmartre's monuments, though one of
its most recent. One of Sacré-Coeur's most striking aspects is its per-
petually sparkling white stone, despite the dirt and grime of city pollution. The stone, from the Seine and Marne regions, produces a
white-lime deposit when it rains, although those parts that remain
unexposed have actually turned darker.

Sacré-Coeur

- Map p. 187
- Métro: Anvers, Abbesses, Lamarck Caulaincourt

Basilica

- place du Parvis du Sacré-Coeur
- Basilica: free. Crypt and dome: $.

St.-Pierre de Montmartre

- 2 rue du Mont-Cenis

THE BASILICA

The impetus for the construction
of this Romano-Byzantine church
came from the French Catholics'
vow to build a basilica devoted to
the Sacred Heart of Jesus after the
country's humiliating defeat in the
Franco-Prussian War of 1870.

Work began in 1876. The architect, Paul Abadie (a student of
Eugène Viollet-le-Duc), died in
1884, and the project was completed by Lucien Magne, who added
the 275-foot (84 m) campanile.
Preparation of the foundations
alone was an enormous engineering
feat: 83 wells were dug 147 feet
(45 m) deep and filled with mason-
ry, then connected by a series of
underground arches to stabilize the
subsoil and compensate for the

quarried tunnels riddling the hill-
side. Twenty-eight horses were
needed to draw the wagon carrying
up Montmartre's hill the Savoyarde
bell, one of the world's largest bells,
which resonates at a high C note.
Today, visitors can climb to the
stained-glass gallery in the dome
for a view of the church's interior.

ST.-PIERRE DE MONTMARTRE

The residents ignored Sacré-Coeur
and continued to worship in the
Church of St.-Pierre. Situated
between the basilica and the Place
du Tertre, this is one of the oldest
churches in Paris. Open the doors
of the 18th-century facade to discover the beauty of its 12th-century,
Romanesque-style nave within. ■

Place du Tertre

THE PLACE DU TERTRE AND ITS SURROUNDING STREETS
are lined with souvenir shops, overpriced cafés, and portrait painters,
all vying for your francs.

PLACE DU TERTRE

Early in the morning, before the crowds arrive, you can see traces of old Montmartre in this village square, which once housed the post-Revolution town hall. It was also here, at La Mère Catherine restaurant, that the word "bistro" was coined when Russian soldiers during the occupation of Paris in 1814 banged on the table shouting "bistro!"—Russian for "quick."

MUSÉE DE MONTMARTRE

The Musée de Montmartre is just behind the Place du Tertre. In the late 19th century, a number of French artists lived in this 17th-century building, including Dufy, Renoir, and Suzanne Valadon (mother of Impressionist painter Maurice Utrillo). The museum's memorabilia re-creates the unique atmosphere of Montmartre's past.

Don't miss the reproduction of one of the great artistic jokes played on the Montmartre art scene when the author Roland Dorgelès—who despised modern art—attached a paintbrush to the tail of the donkey that belonged to the owner of the Lapin Agile Cabaret. The resulting canvas, "Sunset Over the Adriatic," received critical acclaim. ■

Map p. 181

Musée de Montmartre

✉ 12 rue Cortot

☎ 01 46 06 61 11

🕐 Closed Mon.

💲 $

🚇 Métro: Lamarck Caulaincourt

André Gill painted the cabaret's sign of the quirky rabbit leaping from the saucepan.

A walk through Montmartre

This bohemian area of Paris may have lost some of its romantic appeal, but there are times when a stroll around the quaint old streets can take you back a hundred years or more to an age when it was a renowned artists' quarter.

As the steps and steep streets may make this rather a strenuous walk, another option is to take the small train that leaves Place Blanche (opposite the Moulin Rouge at 82 Boulevard de Clichy) for a 40-minute guided tour of the Butte, although some of the sites below can only be reached on foot.

Begin at the **Place Pigalle** (*Métro: Pigalle*), whose late 19th-century dance halls and cabarets lured Parisians in search of flash and flesh. A less classy ambience still reigns among the garish, neon-lit sex shops and seedy boulevards.

Walk east on Boulevard de Clichy and turn left up Rue des Martyrs, the street once

The ubiquitous portrait painters on the Place du Tertre make this square one of the more renowned tourist traps in Paris.

climbed by many illustrious Christian pilgrims on their way to the Basilica of Sacré-Coeur, to reach 9 Rue Yvonne le Tac. Here Saint Denis was supposedly beheaded in the third century (see p. 16), and Ignatius of Loyola founded the order of the Jesuits in 1534. At the end of Rue Yvonne le Tac, turn right on Rue des Trois Frères, then left at the

Place Charles Dullin, past the **Théâtre de l'Atelier** (1822).

Continue to Rue de Steinkerque, over which Sacré-Coeur looms, and turn left up the street. The streets and the nearby Place St.-Pierre are lined with shops offering the best prices and widest selection of fabrics in Paris. From here, the only way to go is up—climb the steps that zigzag up the middle or the set of steps just past the funicular, or if you prefer to ride, take the funicular off to the left side (fare: one Métro ticket).

After enjoying the view and visiting **Sacré-Coeur** basilica ❶ (see p. 188), follow the tourists heading up Rue Azais to **Place du Tertre** (see p. 189), an unavoidable tourist stop on any tour of Montmartre. Take the time to explore the church of **St.-Pierre de Montmartre** ❷ (see p. 188), one of Paris's few remaining Romanesque churches.

Walk past the church down Rue du Mont Cenis (past Rue St.-Rustique) to explore the real charms of old Montmartre. Turn left on Rue Cortot to reach the **Musée de Montmartre** ❸ at No. 12 (see p. 189). Continue onto Rue des Saules, and turn right past Montmartre's last remaining vineyard, whose harvest festival takes place on the first Saturday in October. Straight ahead is the legendary **Lapin Agile** ❹ (*22 Rue des Saules, Tel 01 46 06 85 87*), the cabaret whose regulars once included Picasso, Apollinaire, and Modigliani.

Backtrack up the hill and turn right onto Rue de l'Abreuvoir. The postcard-perfect, pink house at No. 2 was immortalized by the painter Maurice Utrillo. Continue down the mysterious **Allée des Brouillards,** across the street from where Renoir and his family used to live. The fountain in the nearby Square Suzanne-Buisson is reputedly where Saint Denis stopped to wash off his severed head before continuing down the hill. Go to **Avenue Junot** ❺ and turn left. Number 15, built by the Viennese architect Adolf Loos in

1926, is a good example of art deco architecture. At No. 25 is the **Villa Léandre,** a row of impeccable houses built in 1926.

Go through the gate at No. 23 and walk down the steps to Rue Lepic. Turn left here to see one of the two remaining windmills on the Butte Montmartre—the **Moulin de la Galette** 6 of Renoir's famous painting is now a restaurant. Turn right down Rue d'Orchampt to reach **Place Émile Goudeau** 7. Here Picasso, Max Jacob, and others lived in the Bateau-Lavoir, an old wooden warehouse, during the early 1900s. The original building was replaced by a block of studios at 6 Rue Durantin (to the right).

Continue along Rue Durantin to Rue Tholozé and turn left down the hill to No. 10. The Studio 28 Cinema made headlines in 1930 when shocked spectators pelted the screen with eggs and ink during the premiere of Luis Buñuel's classic surrealist film, *L'Age d'Or*; Buñuel's and Jean Cocteau's footprints are embedded in the hall of the cinema, which is

still a local art theater.

Turn left on Rue des Abbesses, where you can end the walk at any one of the local cafés. Or go on to the Métro at **Place des Abbesses** 8. ■

> 🗺 See also area map pp. 186–87
> ▶ Place Pigalle (Métro: Pigalle)
> ↔ 3 miles (4.8 km)
> 🕐 Allow 2½–3 hours
> ▶ Place des Abbesses
>   (Métro: Abbesses)

NOT TO BE MISSED
- Place Pigalle
- Sacré-Coeur
- Place du Tertre
- St.-Pierre de Montmartre church
- Musée de Montmartre
- Allée des Brouillards

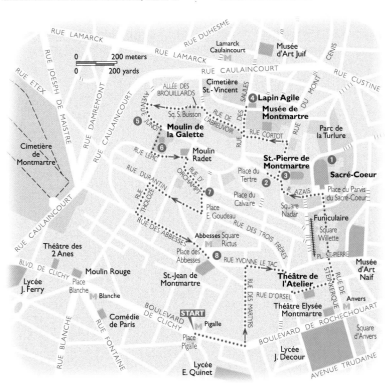

Cabaret

Paris has continually invented and re-invented new forms of entertainment, perfecting the art of whetting both the appetite and the eye. The *cafés chantants* or *goguettes* popular during the Revolution gave way during the Second Empire and belle epoque to concert-cafés, the forerunners to the 20th-century music halls and irreverent *cabarets artistiques* launched in Montmartre at the turn of the century.

A fine French tradition

Talents such as balladeers Léo Ferré and Georges Brassens debuted in cabarets during the 1950s. In the 1960s, a new form of expression surfaced in the café-théâtres, which combined comedy and satire performed in close-quartered cafés (initiated by Le Royal in Montparnasse and La Vieille Grille in the Latin Quarter). The café-théâtre was responsible for launching such diverse talents as the late comedian Coluche, Gérard Depardieu, and the Théâtre du Splendide troupe (featuring Anémone and Gérard Jugnot). The tradition is alive and well today.

However, the most typically French tradition in this hub of hedonism is the legendary music hall revues—throwbacks to the champagne nights of the belle epoque era. The Crazy Horse Saloon on Avenue George V evolved from a Wild West-style barroom, with swinging doors and signs like "Check Your Guns Here," into a theater flaunting the wildest of risqué apparel, with features such as Betty Buttocks and Nouka Bazooka, and a Canadian Mountie bouncer at the door. (During the 1950s, one Crazy Horse Saloon routine featured the whip-cracking, blond dominatrix Dodo d'Hambourg, and Bertha Von Paraboum—clad merely in boots, helmet, and a swastika G-string. This made a somewhat unfortunate impression on Parisians, whose memory of German occupation was a bit too recent.)

Exoticism and extravagance

On the Champs-Élysées, the Lido and its glittering Bluebell Girls are the closest you'll get to Las Vegas this side of the Atlantic, with extravagant megaproductions featuring lasers, video, fountains, and fire-breathing dragons. The Paradis Latin, staged in a theater designed by Gustave Eiffel, supposedly offers a traditional Parisian cabaret, driven by a feathered Latin beat.

In 1926, Josephine Baker descended onto the stage of the Folies Bergère from a flower-covered bubble, thrilling viewers as she danced on a large mirror.

The Folies Bergère, inaugurated in 1869, is the oldest music hall; it features jugglers, wrestlers, dancers, and magicians in a series of exotic decors. Although the Folies are closely associated with the legendary black cabaret *artiste*, Josephine Baker, she actually debuted in *La Revue Nègre* at the Théâtre des Champs-Élysées in 1925. Born in St. Louis, Missouri, she became the star attraction of the Folies. Her set featured pink backdrops with hams and watermelons, and she entered wearing only a pink flamingo feather between her legs, or a string of bananas around her waist. She became a French citizen and remained in France until her death in 1975.

Moulin Rouge

We couldn't fail to mention the kitsch Moulin Rouge, where today only the red windmill is original, but the feathered Doriss Girls still offer up a cancan or two. The Moulin is usually associated with the cancan (which originated in Montparnasse) due to Toulouse-Lautrec's paintings of Jane Avril and Yvette Guibert, but it is believed that it was the striptease that actually originated here in 1893. Supposedly, dur-

The best place to see the French cancan is at the Moulin Rouge, where the feather-clad Doriss Girls can change costumes faster than you can say "Toulouse-Lautrec."

ing a contest between artists' models at the yearly Bal des Quat'z Arts held by the Fine Arts School students at the cabaret, one of them leapt up on a table and threw off her clothes. Outraged upon learning of this new phenomenon, the president of the Ligue Contre la Licence des Rues—the league in charge of cleaning up the streets—took the case to court. The model was arrested, thus sparking protests by students demanding the right to "artistic nudity." The publicity surrounding the case led to a spate of risqué sketches in neighboring cabarets, such as the Divan Fayouau, where the star, Yvette, undressed and got ready for bed each night on stage—at least in the spectator's imagination; another *demoiselle* perused her body in a most sensual way as she searched for a flea bite in "La Puce."

Check *Pariscope* for information on cabarets, addresses, and telephone numbers. ∎

More places to visit in Montmartre

MUSÉE GUSTAVE MOREAU

Situated south of Montmartre, the Musée Gustave Moreau offers a rare glimpse into the intimate world of an artist and his workplace. It was created by and for the artist, who planned the layout and collections before his death. Considered a precursor of the surrealist movement, Moreau was a shy, financially independent painter who shunned exhibitions of his own work, instead teaching at the Fine Arts School. Among his most celebrated pupils were Georges Rouault and Henri Matisse. A marvelous clutter hangs on the museum's walls and fills the rooms of the meticulously organized family mansion. The ornate, double-spiral staircase is one of its more unique features; the nearly 6,000 drawings and paintings include watercolors and large, mythological themes, such as "Apollo and Pegasus," "The Unicorns," and "The Descent From the Cross."

🅜 Map p. 187 ✉ 14 rue de la Rochefoucauld
☎ 01 48 74 38 50 🕐 Closed Tues. 💲 $
🚇 Métro: Trinité ∎

Moreau commissioned Albert Lafon to build this elaborate staircase linking the third and fourth floors of the museum.

Montmartre vineyards

The Butte was once covered with vineyards, but by the 1920s grapes were no longer harvested here. In 1929, when a vacant lot opposite the Lapin Agile was earmarked for real estate development, a group of drinking buddies came up with a plan to save the property by creating a park.

Again threatened with a building project five years later, the plotters proposed replanting the hill with vines. However, they didn't realize that the vines needed to mature for four years before producing fruit, so they gaily made plans for a harvest festival the first year. With the vines bare and the festival approaching, the good-natured but visibly incompetent group was saved when French wine growers shipped in more than 30 tons of grapes, distributed during the festivities.

Today, the vineyards produce about 75 gallons of wine each year (reputedly of dubious quality), which are auctioned off along with a painting by a local artist, with the proceeds going to charity. ∎

Paris proper, which is contained within the Périphérique ring road, is framed by two vast landscaped parks, former outlying villages, and one of the world's most ambitious urban projects, at La Défense.

In & around the Périphérique

At the Science Museum (Cité des Sciences et de l'Industrie)

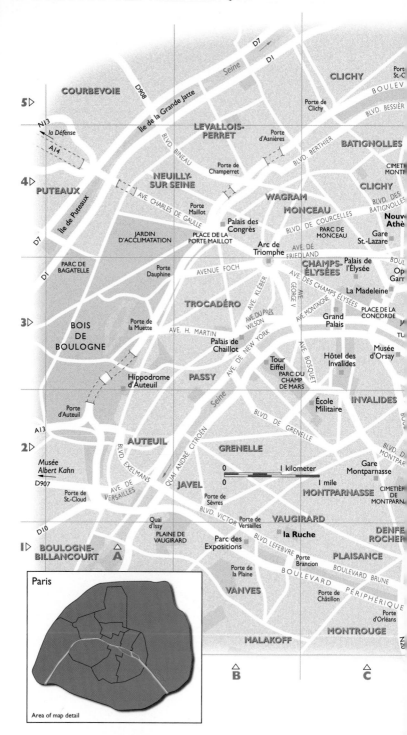

5▷

COURBEVOIE

D908

Seine

D7

D1

D7

CLICHY

Port St-C

BOULEV

Porte de Clichy

BLVD. BESSIÈR

Île de la Grande Jatte

LEVALLOIS-PERRET

N13

la Défense

A14

BLVD. BINEAU

Porte d'Asnières

BATIGNOLLES

BLVD. BERTHIER

CIMETI
MONTI

4▷

PUTEAUX

Porte de Champerret

NEUILLY-SUR SEINE

AVE. CHARLES DE GAULLE

Île de Puteaux

D7

JARDIN D'ACCLIMATATION

Porte Maillot

PLACE DE LA PORTE MAILLOT

Palais des Congrès

WAGRAM

MONCEAU

BLVD. DE COURCELLES

PARC DE MONCEAU

Arc de Triomphe

AVE. DE FRIEDLAND

CLICHY

BLVD. DES BATIGNOLLES

Nouv Athè

Gare St.-Lazare

3▷

PARC DE BAGATELLE

D1

Porte Dauphine

AVENUE FOCH

CHAMPS-ÉLYSÉES

AVE. DES CHAMPS ÉLYSÉES

Palais de l'Élysée

Op Garr

BOUL

BOIS DE BOULOGNE

Porte de la Muette

AVE. H. MARTIN

TROCADÉRO

AVE. KLÉBER

AVE. DU PRÉS. WILSON

AVE. GEORGE V

AVE. MONTAIGNE

La Madeleine

PLACE DE LA CONCORDE

JA

TU

Palais de Chaillot

AVE. DE NEW YORK

Grand Palais

Hippodrome d'Auteuil

PASSY

Seine

Tour Eiffel

PARC DU CHAMP DE MARS

AVE. BOSQUET

Hôtel des Invalides

Musée d'Orsay

Porte d'Auteuil

A13

BLVD. DE GRENELLE

École Militaire

INVALIDES

BOU

2▷

Musée Albert Kahn

D907

AUTEUIL

BLVD. EXELMANS

QUAI ANDRÉ CITROËN

GRENELLE

0   1 kilometer

0   1 mile

Gare Montparnasse

BLVD. D MONTPAR

Porte de St-Cloud

AVE. DE VERSAILLES

JAVEL

Porte de Sèvres

BLVD. VICTOR

Porte de Versailles

VAUGIRARD

MONTPARNASSE

CIMETIÈR DE MONTPARN.

Quai d'Issy

PLAINE DE VAUGIRARD

Parc des Expositions

BLVD. LEFEBVRE

la Ruche

DENFE ROCHER

1▷

D10

BOULOGNE-BILLANCOURT

△ **A**

Porte Brancion

PLAISANCE

BOULEVARD BRUNE

Porte de la Plaine

BOULEVARD

PÉRIPHÉRIQUE

VANVES

Porte de Châtillon

Porte d'Orléans

MONTROUGE

N20

Paris

Area of map detail

△ **B**

△ **C**

MALAKOFF

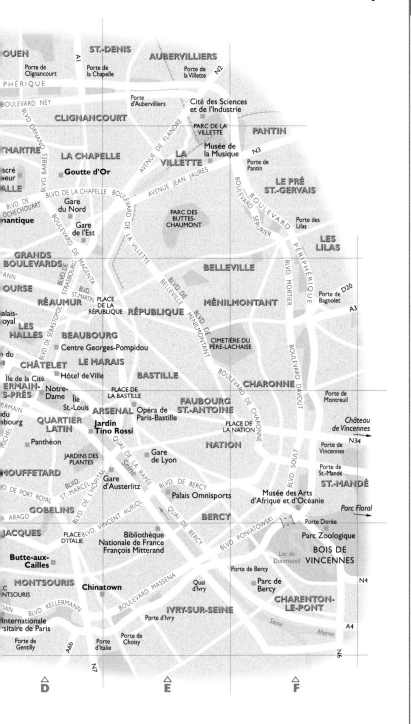

OUEN

ST.-DENIS

AUBERVILLIERS

Porte de Clignancourt

Porte de la Chapelle

Porte de la Villette

N2

PHÉRIQUE

BOULEVARD NEY

Porte d'Aubervilliers

Cité des Sciences et de l'Industrie

BLVD ORNANO

CLIGNANCOURT

PARC DE LA VILLETTE

PANTIN

AVENUE DE FLANDRE

TMARTRE

LA CHAPELLE

LA VILLETTE

Musée de la Musique

N3

acré eur

Goutte d'Or

Porte de Pantin

LE PRÉ ST.-GERVAIS

BLVD. BARBÈS

ALLE

BLVD. DE ROCHECHOUART

BLVD. DE LA CHAPELLE

BOULEVARD

AVENUE JEAN JAURÈS

BOULEVARD SÉRURIER

mantique

Gare du Nord

PARC DES BUTTES-CHAUMONT

Porte des Lilas

Gare de l'Est

BOULEVARD DE LA VILLETTE

LES LILAS

GRANDS BOULEVARDS

BELLEVILLE

PÉRIPHÉRIQUE

ANN

BLVD. DE STRASBOURG

BOULEVARD DE MAGENTA

BLVD. DE BELLEVILLE

BLVD. MORTIER

OURSE

RÉAUMUR

BLVD. ST-MARTIN

PLACE DE LA RÉPUBLIQUE

MÉNILMONTANT

Porte de Bagnolet

D20

alais-oyal

RÉPUBLIQUE

A3

LES HALLES

BEAUBOURG

BLVD. DE SÉBASTOPOL

BLVD. DE MÉNILMONTANT

CIMETIÈRE DU PÈRE-LACHAISE

du e

Centre Georges-Pompidou

BOULEVARD DAVOUT

CHÂTELET

LE MARAIS

BASTILLE

CHARONNE

Île de la Cité

Hôtel de Ville

Notre-Dame

PLACE DE LA BASTILLE

Porte de Montreuil

ERMAIN-S-PRÉS

Île St.-Louis

BOULEVARD DE CHARONNE

ERMAIN du bourg

ARSENAL

Opéra de Paris-Bastille

FAUBOURG ST-ANTOINE

Château de Vincennes

N34

QUARTIER LATIN

Jardin Tino Rossi

PLACE DE LA NATION

Porte de Vincennes

MICHEL

Panthéon

NATION

Porte de St-Mandé

JARDINS DES PLANTES

Gare de Lyon

BLVD. VAL DE

ST-MANDÉ

MOUFFETARD

Gare d'Austerlitz

QUAI DE LA RAPÉE

BLVD. ST-MARCEL

BLVD. DE BERCY

Musée des Arts d'Afrique et d'Océanie

Parc Floral

D. DE PORT ROYAL

Palais Omnisports

Seine

BLVD. DE L'HÔPITAL

GOBELINS

QUAI DE BERCY

BERCY

Porte Dorée

ARAGO

BLVD. VINCENT AURIOL

BLVD. PONIATOWSKI

JACQUES

PLACE D'ITALIE

Bibliothèque Nationale de France François Mitterand

Parc Zoologique

Butte-aux-Cailles

Lac de Daumesnil

BOIS DE VINCENNES

MONTSOURIS

Chinatown

Quai d'Ivry

Parc de Bercy

N4

C NTSOURIS

BOULEVARD MASSENA

CHARENTON-LE-PONT

OAN

BLVD. KELLERMANN

Porte de Bercy

Internationale sitaire de Paris

IVRY-SUR-SEINE

Seine

Marne

A4

Porte de Gentilly

Porte d'Italie

Porte de Choisy

Porte d'Ivry

A6b

△ D

△ E

△ F

In & around the Périphérique

THE PÉRIPHÉRIQUE RING ROAD THAT ENCLOSES PARIS SHARPLY DEFINES the city's limits. Many areas of the arrondissements bordering the Périphérique are somewhat off the beaten track, but form entities in and of themselves, with a degree of independence that survives to this day. If you have enough time, they are well worth a visit.

The Bois de Vincennes is one of the best places to view the changing seasons.

Diversity has been inherent in Paris for centuries, owing in part to the various outlying villages that were eventually incorporated into the city.

Butte-aux-Cailles (see p. 202) is typical of old Paris with its narrow cobbled streets, obscure passageways, and small vine-covered town houses. Belleville, with its hamlet Ménilmontant (see pp. 206–207), served as the vineyard for the great abbeys of Paris, and a place for Parisians to go on Sundays to drink a glass of *guinguet* (a sour-tasting wine). Both were active during the Commune (see p. 26), and have been bastions of working-class agitation, especially after Baron Haussmann's

urban projects (see pp. 160–61) drove the proletariat from the center of the city in the 19th century. Belleville has traditionally drawn waves of immigrants from the world over, and its population is the most diverse and cosmopolitan in the city, with Chinese, Arabic, African, and Turkish quarters, and colorful, ethnic markets.

The former slaughterhouses at La Villette (see pp. 208–209) are now part of a huge park, a recent addition to the vast, city-park system that includes the great Bois de Vincennes (see p. 203) and Bois de Boulogne (see p. 199) flanking eastern and western Paris respectively. ■

Bois de Boulogne

AN IMMENSE PARK OF 2,132 ACRES (863 HA), THE BOIS DE Boulogne draws people from all over the city. The two lakes (Lac Supérieur and Lac Inférieur) within the park are at different levels, connected by means of a superb waterfall.

🅰 196 B3

Jardin d'Acclimatation
✉ avenue Mahatma Gandhi
☎ 01 40 67 90 82
💲 $
Ⓜ Métro: Sablons

Jardin Shakespeare
✉ route de Suresnes
Ⓜ Métro: Porte Maillot, then bus No. 244

Bagatelle Gardens
✉ route de Sèvres
☎ 01 40 67 97 00
🕐 Open daily
💲 $
Ⓜ Métro: Porte de Neuilly, then bus No. 43; or Porte Maillot and bus No. 244

Roland-Garros Stadium
www.fft.fr
✉ 2 avenue Gordon-Bennett
☎ 01 47 43 48 00
🕐 French Tennis Open, late May–early June
💲 $
Ⓜ Métro: Porte-d'Auteuil

The Bois de Boulogne was commissioned by Napoleon III for the fashionable neighborhoods extending west from the city center. The elegant and sophisticated world met there in the day, while a more dubious underworld congregated at night—and still does, so certain areas are best avoided after sunset.

Graceful avenues and paths lead to the lakes, through a pine forest and several oak groves. The **Jardin d'Acclimatation** has rides, miniature golf, and other activities.

The **Jardin Shakespeare** in the heart of the Bois encompasses a small, 300-seat open-air theater (performances in English and French). Nearby is the romantic (and expensive) **Le Pré Catalan** restaurant (see p. 254).

The **Bagatelle Gardens** is a spectacular showcase in the spring and summer with nearly 9,000 rosebushes. There is also an impressive water lily and iris garden.

At the southern edge of the Bois, near the **Roland-Garros Stadium** (venue of the French Tennis Open), is an unexpected haven: the greenhouses of Auteuil, which contain exotic plants, a tropical greenhouse, and a palmarium under the central dome. ∎

The Comte d'Artois (the future Charles X) built the Bagatelle in seven weeks in 1775, thus winning a 100,000-franc bet with his sister-in-law, Marie-Antoinette.

La Défense

La Grande Arche
✉ parvis de la Défense
☎ 01 49 07 27 57
$ $$

⚑ 196 B4

LA DÉFENSE, WITH ITS GRANDE ARCHE COMPLETING THE monumental east–west axis cutting through Paris, is the French response to the Manhattan skyline.

The Grande Arche is the third triumphal arch in the axis that runs from the Louvre's Arc du Carrousel to La Défense.

Conceived in 1950 and begun in the early 1960s, this commercial district was designed on an American model as a functional and modern international business center for Paris.

In the early 1970s, it became a symbol of the inhumanity of modern architecture; companies snubbed the project, yet the 1980s brought a recovery with the construction of the gigantic Quatre-Temps shopping center and a new IMAX theater.

Some berate La Défense as inhuman and sprawling; others praise it as innovative and futuristic. But it remains one of the most ambitious urban developments in Europe. Designers initially modeled their plan on similar structures in U.S. cities such as Manhattan and Chicago, but went further by eliminating traffic. The result is a two-tiered development, with the above-ground commercial and residential buildings linked by an immense esplanade, and a network of roads, trains, parking lots, and Métros below.

One of the first structures was the CNIT building, with a record-breaking 759-foot roof span. Major trade fairs used to be held here, before moving to the Porte de Versailles. It now houses smaller shows, a hotel, and various stores and restaurants.

Concrete, glass, and steel are the rule here, but the esplanade has been brightened up with works of art that include a gigantic sculpture by Alexander Calder, a piece by Nikki de Saint-Phalle, and several playful fountains.

The crowning work, however, is **La Grande Arche.** The rooftop, at 300 feet (91.5 m), is open to the public and houses an exhibition tracing the construction of the Arche. Faced with Carrara marble, this vast, empty cube is large enough to frame Notre-Dame. ∎

Denfert-Rochereau

THE 14TH ARRONDISSEMENT IS A GOOD PLACE TO GET A
feel for everyday Parisian life by exploring the streets, markets, parks,
(particularly Montsouris), and the nearby Montparnasse cemetery.

196 D1

In the center of Place Denfert-Rochereau stands the "Lion of Belfort," a copy of a lion sculpted by Auguste Bartholdi as a tribute to the courage of the Alsatians during the Franco-Prussian War. North of the Place, at 261 Boulevard Raspail, stands the **Cartier Foundation** (*Tel 01 42 18 56 50, closed Mon.*). Constructed in 1994, the sleek, glass-and-steel structure stands in a beautiful garden and hosts contemporary art shows.

The strangest necropolis in all of Paris is the **Catacombs** (entrance on Place Denfert-Rochereau), the resting place for more than six million skeletons (and parts thereof) moved from inner-city cemeteries in the 18th century because of the stench. Stacks of bones line miles of corridors under the city streets. Clandestine parties are sometimes organized underground, a tradition begun in 1897 with an illicit concert held for a group of journalists. ■

The original lion by Bartholdi is in Belfort, Alsace.

Catacombs
✉ place Denfert-Rochereau
☎ 01 43 22 47 63
🕐 Closed Mon.
💲 $
🚇 Métro or RER: Denfert-Rochereau

Wallace Fountains

Parisians can thank Sir Richard Wallace for the city's first free drinking fountains. As public hygiene became a prime concern under the Second Empire and Third Republic, the first of the Wallace fountains was inaugurated in 1871 on Boulevard de la Villette.

Sixty-six of these elegant, green cast-iron fountains are scattered throughout Paris; they are easily recognizable by their four caryatids of Simplicity, Charity, Sobriety, and Abundance, which support a dolphin-topped dome. The fountains are typical of the 19th-century style of street furniture, including benches, street lamps, and onion-domed Morris columns used to bill plays and concerts. ■

Butte-aux-Cailles

PAST AND PRESENT COEXIST IN THIS WORKERS' QUARTER, which was one of the city's many outlying villages. Locals were called *pieds mouillés* or "wet feet" as they waded barefoot across the Bièvre River (now channeled under the Rue Corvisart) into intramuros (within the city walls) Paris to avoid paying tolls.

Butte-aux-Cailles
- 197 E1
- Between rue de la Butte-aux-Cailles and rue des Cinq Diamants
- Métro: Corvisart

The 18th-century Butte-aux-Cailles quarter, with cobblestone streets and narrow, sloping impasses, remains little changed.

The Butte-aux-Cailles became famous on November 21, 1783, when physicist Pilâtre de Rozier landed his hot-air balloon between the Moulin des Merveilles and Moulin Vieux windmills, having left the Château de La Muette 25 minutes earlier. It was the first ever manned free flight in a hot-air balloon, reaching an altitude of roughly 3,100 feet (945 m). At the time, the butte was a marvelous natural belvedere, overlooking the swamps, prairies, and water-mills of the Bièvre Valley and the steeples of Paris.

This working-class neighborhood was one of the first to rebel during the Commune, and it still has a strong independent streak, represented by Le Temps des Cerises restaurant (one of the rare anarchist establishments in Paris until the 1980s) and Le Merle Moqueur (dating from the Commune). The area served as a refuge for communards, and even today the Association des Amis de la Commune holds regular meetings, selling books and documents that revive the spirit of the period.

In addition to being one of the bastions of the Paris Commune, the Butte-aux-Cailles also became famous for having the last cows in Paris; there was a farm and cows near the Passage Barrault well into the first half of the 20th century. Small houses, cobbled streets, and winding lanes stand next to apartment buildings against the ultra-modern backdrop of high-rises in Paris's premier **Chinatown** and the Place d'Italie, which used to be an ancient Roman crossroads.

Explore the charming, picturesque Rues Buot, Michal, de la Butte-aux-Cailles, and des Cinq Diamants, as well as the Villa Daviel, with its scenic miniature villas and cottages, and farther away, the town-house-lined Square des Peupliers.

Near Place Verlaine is an indoor-outdoor public swimming pool. Built in 1924, it was recently renovated and repainted a brilliant yellow and red. It is fed by an artesian well 1,870 feet (570 m) deep and receives over 1.585 million gallons (6 million liters) of sulfurous water at 82°F each day. ■

Bois de Vincennes & Château

THIS PARK IS STILL THE MOST POPULAR IN THE EASTERN section of Paris. Like the Bois de Boulogne, it has a racetrack; the International Buddhist Institute (housing a highly colorful, Tibetan-style temple) is also located on the grounds of the park, as well as a lake, zoo, museum, children's play area, and, of course, a château.

Once the Bois de Boulogne had been painstakingly landscaped and given to the city in 1852, Napoleon III decided to make a grand gesture in 1860 for "the workers of the 11th and 12th arrondissements," by commissioning a matching park to the east, the Bois de Vincennes. Four lakes were created, complete with romantic islands dotted with restaurants and secret grottoes.

The park's main attractions include the large **Daumesnil Lake** and the nearby **Vincennes zoo** (*53 avenue de St.-Maurice, Tel 01 44 75 20 10*). Also at the Porte Dorée is the **Musée des Arts d'Afrique et d'Océanie,** housed in an art deco building designed for the 1931 Colonial Exhibition. The permanent collection includes African masks and art from Oceania. A small aquarium occupies the basement. Less well-known is the **Parc Floral,** a magnificently landscaped park within the park. A separate children's play area includes rides, climbing frames, and a go-cart track, while various pavilions house special exhibitions and classical and jazz concerts in spring and summer.

Finally, the **Château de Vincennes** was a royal abode for centuries. There is a museum in the 14th-century keep, and the 16th-century chapel still has beautiful stained glass. ■

Bois de Vincennes

- 🅰 197 G1
- ✉ avenue Daumesnil or avenue de Gravelle

Tibetan Temple (Kagyu Dzong)

- ✉ route de la ceinture du Lac Daumesnil
- ☎ 01 40 04 98 06
- 🕐 Closed Mon.
- Ⓜ Métro: Porte Dorée

International Buddhist Institute

- ✉ route de la ceinture du Lac Daumesnil
- ☎ 01 43 41 54 48
- Ⓜ Métro: Porte Dorée

Musée des Arts d'Afrique et d'Océanie

- ✉ 293 avenue Daumesnil
- ☎ 01 44 74 85 00
- 🕐 Closed Tues.
- 💲 $$

Parc Floral

- 🅰 197 G2
- ✉ Entrance near the Château de Vincennes
- ☎ 01 43 43 92 95
- 💲 $
- Ⓜ Métro: Château de Vincennes

Château de Vincennes

- 🅰 197 G2
- ✉ avenue de Paris
- ☎ 01 48 08 31 20
- 💲 $
- Ⓜ Métro: Château de Vincennes

In 1763 the Marquis de Sade was imprisoned at the Château de Vincennes.

Parks & gardens of Paris

Parisians often complain about the lack of open space in this dense city, yet more than 400 parks, gardens, and squares dot the urban landscape, ranging from André Le Nôtre's formal French design for the Tuileries in the 17th century, to the recent color-coded, postmodern André Citroën Garden at the edge of the 15th arrondissement.

Great Parisian parks

Until the 19th century, the great gardens—Luxembourg, Palais-Royal, Tuileries—were part of royal domains. But under the Second Empire, enormous parks and small neighborhood squares began to appear all over Paris, under the impetus of Jean-Charles Alphand, Baron Georges Haussmann's chief park director. He transformed what remained of the Rouvre Forest into the Bois de Boulogne and created the Bois de Vincennes, along with the Buttes-Chaumont and Parc Montsouris.

By the early 20th century, planners were using up available land for housing, and few new parks were opened up. It wasn't until the 1980s that the authorities shifted their attention back toward open spaces. In the last 20 years alone, nearly 250 acres (101 ha) of new parks have been opened, affording plenty of places to escape the noise and congestion of the city.

Lesser known parks

Created by Jean-Charles Alphand during the Second Empire from a dismal gypsum quarry, the Buttes-Chaumont (*rues Botzariss Manin, and de Crimée, Métro: Simon Bolivar or Buttes-Chaumont*) in northeast Paris is a romantic park with steep slopes and intertwining paths, grottoes, and a famous belvedere perched at the top of a hill. There is a small lake, a bandstand for summer concerts, children's activities, and a spectacular view of the city.

Parc Montsouris (*avenue Reille/boulevard Jourdan, RER: Cité Universitaire*), in the southern part of the city, is another of Alphand's creations, meant to mirror Buttes-Chaumont. Although it doesn't occupy as dramatic a site, it is equally romantic, with weeping willows and a lake dotted with swans. Alphand solved the problem of disguising the park by transforming their trenches into ravines lined with pine trees. It is a popular site with the students who live across the street at the Cité Universitaire.

The newest addition to the Paris park system is the Promenade Plantée, created from a former railway viaduct. It leads from Place de la Bastille as far as the Bois de Vincennes to the east; the first part used to be a raised rail track on the viaduct and is now a landscaped footpath that crosses through several parks

Jean Cocteau called the Palais-Royal gardens "the countryside in the very heart of Paris."

Interweaving paths climb to the belvedere overlooking Buttes-Chaumont.

and an overhead bridge. Bikes are allowed in the second section, from the Jardin de Reuilly in the 12th arrondissement to the Bois de Vincennes. A classy new shopping arcade called the Viaduc des Arts now occupies the former arches below the viaduct.

Not far away is the new Parc de Bercy, on the site of the former wine warehouses near the Bercy Stadium and the fortresslike Ministry of Finance. Fortunately, some of the hundred-year-old trees were saved along with some 18th-century ruins. The gardens include a canal, an orchard, vegetable garden, and gardens created around the four seasons.

A fine place to enjoy the Seine is at the Square Tino Rossi, an open-air contemporary sculpture garden created in 1977 opposite the Institut du Monde Arabe.

One of the most interesting parks in the Paris region is the Albert-Kahn Gardens (*14 rue du Port, Boulogne-Billancourt, Tel 01 46 04 52 80, closed Mon.*), on the western outskirts of the city. Recently restored, the grounds include a beautiful Japanese garden. ■

A pick of Paris's best

Formal French gardens: Tuileries (see p. 137), Luxembourg (see p. 82)

Botanical gardens: Parc Floral de Vincennes (see p. 203), Auteuil greenhouses (see p. 199), Jardin des Plantes (see pp. 70–71)

Romantic gardens: Parc Monceau (see p. 152), Buttes-Chaumont, Parc Montsouris,

Bagatelle (see p. 199), Musée Rodin (see pp. 172–73)

Contemporary gardens: Square Tino Rossi, Parc de Bercy, Parc de Belleville (see p. 207), Parc de la Villette (see pp. 208–209)

The giants: Bois de Vincennes (see p. 203), Bois de Boulogne (see p. 199) ■

Belleville/Ménilmontant

🗺 197 F3

✉ Belleville: centered
on rue de Belleville.
Ménilmontant:
centered on rue de
Ménilmontant

🚇 Métro:
Belleville: Belleville
or Pyrénées.
Ménilmontant:
Ménilmontant

WHILE BELLEVILLE ISN'T AS PICTURESQUE A BUTTE AS Montmartre, it is certainly more multicultured and dynamic—and definitely more radical. The area's population is one of the most diverse and cosmopolitan in Paris, given the successive layers of immigration. Ashkenazi Jews from Central Europe, Armenians, and Spanish republicans gravitated here beginning in the 1930s, followed by a wave of Sephardic Jews from North Africa, then North Africans and Africans, Cambodians, Thai, Vietnamese, and Chinese. The feel is definitely Asian on Rue de Belleville, with a stray couscous restaurant, kosher butcher shop, Egyptian delicatessen, or Turkish café thrown in. The Tuesday and Friday outdoor markets along Boulevard de Ménilmontant—among the cheapest and largest in Paris—reflect this cultural mix. Neighboring Ménilmontant is a curious mixture of modern housing and older residences that are becoming increasingly gentrified, making the area a thriving center of alternative Paris.

In addition to Belleville's Chinatown (above), there are several others in Paris. The Choisy Triangle, located in the 13th arrondissement, is the most famous.

THEN & NOW

Incorporated into the rapidly expanding city of Paris in 1860, the former village of Belleville was a hotbed of opposition to the Empire and the last quarter to surrender its arms during the Commune. Various attempts were made to quell working-class protests, such as splitting the Belleville area up into the 11th, 19th, and 20th arrondissements.

For a long time, the Butte—419 feet high (128 m)—maintained its 1930s look, a typically Parisian quarter with traditionally proletarian leanings. Yet it is continually changing with the influx of immigrants, and with countless rebuilding and renovation projects, which sometimes seem to be killing off the soul of old Belleville—some high-rise complexes have no ground floor markets or stores, for example. Sinuous side streets slope

down past shops, ateliers, period bistros, and villas, and hushed gardens hide behind ornate doorways.

Belleville and its neighbor, Ménilmontant, bear traces of their rural and working-class past, when craftsmen and workers exploiting the local gypsum quarries lived at the foot of the butte. Founded in the 15th century around the vineyards run by the great abbeys of Paris, Belleville was known for its *guinguettes* (refreshment stands), and Parisians would come on Sundays to drink a sourish wine called guinguet. Working-class people ousted from the city by Haussmann's 19th-century upheavals sought new residences here, and the population soared.

Until 1914, Belleville and Ménilmontant rivaled Montmartre for its *buvettes* (refreshment stands), cafés, cabarets, and *bals-musettes* (dance halls with traditional French music). The Elysée Ménilmontant (no longer standing) was one of the most famous of these; Maurice Chevalier debuted here. Edith Piaf was born at 72 Rue de Belleville; the Java nightclub features the original *bal-musette* setting. Rue des Envierges, lined with restaurants, bistros, and *cafés chantants*, comes alive each night.

One of the great panoramic views of the city can be found where Rue Piat, Rue du Transvaal, and Rue des Envierges converge, at the highest point of Belleville, with the Belleville Gardens below. Rue Piat led to two windmills in the last century; it now opens onto the **Parc de Belleville,** which has a spectacular view over Paris and a great children's play area.

Villa Castel off Rue du Transvaal is a beautiful alley with fabulous houses, where François Truffaut shot scenes for his film *Jules et Jim* in 1962. An open house organized by local painters is held once a year (usually in the spring), revealing magnificent courtyards, studios, and hidden gardens.

The intertwining side streets and passages between Rue de Belleville and Rue de Ménilmontant are mostly old paths that once linked the former vineyards. Today, Rue de Ménilmontant is becoming fashionable again as a renewed, gentrified area, particularly along the lower end near Oberkampf, where trendy bars and cafés—like Café Charbon, the intimate La Mercerie, or La Buvette (African and Caribbean music)—are burgeoning. ■

The Café Charbon, a renovated dance hall on Rue Oberkampf, has been cited by Gault Millau as the trendiest bar in Paris. Along the same strip is a slew of hip cafés, bars, and restaurants.

Parc de la Villette

Parc de la Villette
- 197 F4
- quai de la Gironde
- Métro: Porte de Pantin

ONE OF THE NEWEST REDEVELOPMENT PROJECTS IN PARIS has also been among its most successful. Just 15 years ago, the former slaughterhouses of La Villette stood in a gigantic no-man's land in the northeast corner of Paris. Today, the 62-acre (28 ha) park contains the Cité des Sciences et de l'Industrie (Science Museum), the Cité de la Musique (Music City), the Zénith (*211 avenue Jean-Jaurès, Tel 01 42 08 60 00, Métro: Porte de Pantin*), a popular venue for pop and rock concerts, and the Grande Halle, a temporary exhibition space. The two museums stand at opposite ends of the park and are therefore approached by different Métro stations.

Cité des Sciences et de l'Industrie
- 197 F5
- 30 avenue Corentin Cariou
- 01 40 05 70 00
- Closed Mon.
- $$
- Métro: Porte de la Villette

CITÉ DES SCIENCES ET DE L'INDUSTRIE

With over five million visitors per year, the Science Museum is the park's most popular attraction. As opposed to the traditional style of French museum, which tends to be heavy on text and description, the Science Museum has plenty of interactive, hands-on exhibitions in its giant, five-level glass-and-steel building. Explora, the core, permanent exhibit, lets visitors discover the galaxies, volcanoes, man and health, the environment, energy, sound, and the ocean through a multitude of innovative displays—computerized games about space, a flight simulator, and the Odorama for testing smells.

Opened in 1986, the museum also has a planetarium for trips to outer space, a greenhouse, a Géode sphere (a 100-seat IMAX theater, which has become the symbol of the futuristic park), the *Argonaute*

full-scale submarine, and the Cinaxe, a simulated film adventure. Two sections are reserved for kids: the Cité des Enfants (ages 3 to 12), and the Techno Cité (age 11 and up)—science villages where children can play with interactive exhibits. It is best to reserve one of the 90-minute sessions when you purchase your entrance ticket.

MUSÉE DE LA MUSIQUE

The Music Museum is one part of the Cité de la Musique, which, designed by Christian de Portzamparc, also houses a concert hall, a research center, the Paris Conservatory, and a complete Gamelan orchestra (traditional Indonesian gongs). Visitors explore the displays with headsets that are activated as you go around.

OTHER FEATURES

Even without the museums, the vast park, designed by Swiss Bernard Tschumi, is a great place to get away from the city. It features a magical bamboo forest; wacky 20th-century, red-metal structures known as "follies" (one of which houses an information center); a children's playground with a gigantic dragon slide; and ten different thematic gardens. Don't miss the gargantuan half-buried bicycle sculpture by Claus Oldenburg. During the summer, a giant screen is set up for open-air movies, and concerts are scheduled regularly.

The one remaining feature from its days as a slaughterhouse and cattle market is the **Grande Halle** (*avenue Jean-Jaurès, Tel 01 40 03 75 75, Métro: Porte de Pantin*), one of the most beautiful examples of glass-and-cast-iron architecture in Paris. Built in 1867, it originally was little more than a metal shelter for the cattle sold here. It has since been renovated with movable platforms that can be adapted to accommodate temporary exhibitions and concerts. ∎

A visit to the gleaming Géode housing the IMAX movie theater is just one of the many ways to while away an afternoon at the Parc de la Villette.

Musée de la Musique

- 🅰 197 F4
- ✉ 221 avenue Jean-Jaurès
- ☎ 01 44 84 44 84
- 🕐 Closed Mon.
- 💲 $$
- 🚇 Métro: Porte de Pantin

More places to visit around the Périphérique

Canal St.-Martin and the Canal de l'Ourcq link La Villette to the Seine.

GOUTTE D'OR

Just east of Pigalle and Montmartre is the Goutte d'Or (Drop of Gold) district, named for the previously highly prized wine produced on its hillsides. Since the 19th century, however, it has offered some of the cheapest (and most miserable) housing in Paris. In the last few decades it has become mostly an Arab and African neighborhood, its streets teeming with a multitude of languages, dress, spicy foods, and Kabyl (ethnic Algerian) cafés.

Browse through the crowded and ultra-cheap Tati Department Store and on to the Dejean Market (*near the Château d'Eau Métro*) or the open-air market on Boulevard de la Chapelle (*Mon. & Sat.*). Every summer, the Goutte d'Or en Fête music festival features local musicians along with big names in *rai* (North African rock 'n' roll), rap, and hip hop.

197 E4   Métro: Barbès-Rochechouart

CHINATOWN

At first sight, the stark high-rise buildings in the 13th arrondissement—known as the Choisy Triangle—form a depressing complex. Yet this is the heart of the city's thriving and colorful Chinatown, with an estimated 30,000 Asian residents and entire, transplanted cultures, complete with pagoda-fronted shops and martial arts centers. Don't miss the Tang Brothers on Avenue d'Ivry (the largest Asian supermarket in France), and the plenteous restaurants offering every type of Asian cuisine.

197 E1   Métro: Tolbiac, Porte d'Ivry

NOUVELLE ATHÈNES

Tucked into the area between Pigalle and Les Grands Boulevards is the Nouvelle Athènes, where a number of 19th-century artists, including Theodore Géricault, Eugène Delacroix, and Frédéric Chopin, congregated. The fascinating **Musée Gustave Moreau** is here (see p. 194), as is the **Musée de la Vie Romantique** (*16 Rue Chaptal, Tel 01 48 74 95 38, closed Mon.*). Installed in the studio and home of painter Ary Scheffer, this museum is a tribute to the Romantic period, with memorabilia of George Sand and others. The prettiest spot, however, is the Place St.-Georges, featuring the gorgeous facades of the neo-Renaissance Hôtel de la Païva and the Hôtel Thiers, part of which is now a museum, particularly devoted to the Napoleonic era (*Bibliothèque Thiers, 27 place St.-Georges, Tel 01 48 78 14 33, open Thurs. & Fri. 12 p.m.–6 p.m.*).

196 D4   Métro: St.-Georges, Trinité, Pigalle ■

Romantic Parisian canals

With the opening of La Villette park to the north and the refurbished Bassin de l'Arsenal, extending from Place de la Bastille to the Seine, the canals of Paris have come back in fashion. The Canal St.-Martin leading to the Bassin de la Villette and the Canal de l'Ourcq pass by a series of nine locks, two swing bridges, and some graceful footbridges. Although pleasure boats ply this 3-mile (5 km) route, the most romantic way to explore the area is on foot. The building that inspired Marcel Carné's great film *Hôtel du Nord* (1938) is at 102 Quai de Jemmapes. The building was saved from destruction in the 1980s and is now a popular café.

Boat cruises along the Canal St.-Martin to the Bassin de la Villette and the Canal de l'Ourcq provide a relaxing way to view the city and are operated by several companies (see p. 236); reservations are recommended. ■

There are abbeys, castles (real and make-believe), forests, and towns that have fed the inspiration of artists like van Gogh and Monet—all within easy reach of the capital.

Excursions

Sculpture in the Water Garden, Versailles

Excursions

A TRIP AWAY FROM HECTIC, URBAN PARIS IS A WELCOME BREAK IN ANY
season (but try to avoid traveling on weekends from mid-July to the end of August, as the
French tend to leave en masse for vacations then, so roads and public transportation services tend to be very crowded). If you're driving, note that French roads are classified as
Autoroutes (highways, with A in front of the number), *Routes Nationales* (N roads), *Routes
Départementales* (local, with D), and *Routes Communales* (C). Toll booths are called
péages; speed limits are 80 mph (130 kph) on highways, and 55 mph (90 kph) on most
Routes Nationales. If you're going by train (*Tel 08 36 35 35 35 for national lines, 01 53 90
20 20 for Île de France*), you must *composter* (punch) your ticket in the orange machines
by the platforms.

For many first-time visitors to Paris, Versailles
is a must-see—if only to view the most
flagrant example of French
royal glorification.

Outside of Paris the rest of the Île de France
region of the country is also studded with

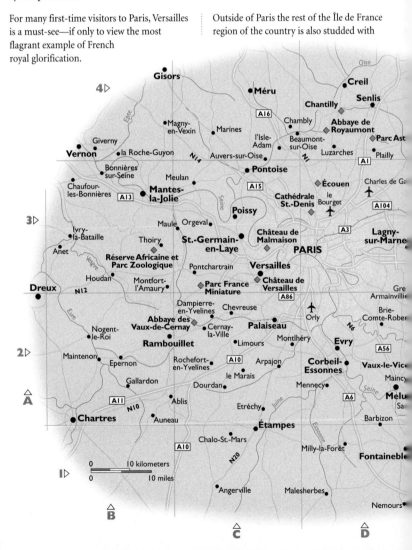

châteaus, such as the Italian-style Fontainebleau and Rambouillet, now a residence of the French president. The beautiful Vaux-le-Vicomte (see p. 222) was not a royal palace, but it was so luxurious that Louis XIV's crooked finance minister, Nicolas Fouquet, was imprisoned for embezzling state funds to build it. The Château de Chantilly's fine collection of artistic treasures includes paintings by Raphael and the stunning, medieval miniatures from the "Très Riches Heures du Duc de Berry" (see p. 232), not to mention the imposing stables built in the 18th century to house the prince of Condé's 240 horses (now a horse museum).

There are a few excursions within a reasonable distance of Paris that offer a unique glimpse into medieval French life: for example, the last remaining fortress at Blandy (see p. 222), near Vaux-le-Vicomte; and the hilltop town of Provins (see p. 223), which hosts annual fairs with costumed actors reenacting some of the more colorful aspects of medieval life. And in the suburb of St.-Denis is the 13th-century cathedral of the same name (see p. 220), the first large Gothic building in Europe.

Monet's home and gardens at Giverny (see pp. 230–31) and the town of Auvers-sur-Oise are both landmarks for art lovers. Van Gogh is the most well-known painter to have lived (and died) at Auvers, but others, including Paul Cézanne and Charles Daubigny, were attracted to this picturesque region.

The Abbaye de Vaux-de-Cernay (see p. 226), a 12th-century abbey that has been converted into a luxury hotel, is an obscure haven in the middle of the vast Rambouillet Forest. The original refectory is still standing, as is the roofless cathedral.

Lastly, Chartres Cathedral (see pp. 228–29), the jewel of medieval France, has the most brilliant collection of 13th-century stained glass anywhere. ∎

Especially for kids

Everyone knows about **Disneyland Paris** (see p. 221), but there are several other local options for kids:

The **Thoiry Wildlife Reserve** (*Réserve Africaine et Parc Zoologique, Tel 01 34 87 40 67*) west of Paris on the D11 was one of the first of its kind when it opened in 1968. Animals roam free as you drive through the park, although there is also a traditional zoo and other attractions.

The plucky cartoon-character Astérix is to French children what Mickey Mouse is to American kids. North of Paris on the A1 at Plailly is an entire theme park devoted to the comic Gaul hero, **Parc Astérix** (*Tel 08 36 68 30 10, www.parcasterix.fr, closed mid-Oct.–Easter, RER: Line B3 Aéroport Charles-de-Gaulle 1, then shuttle bus*), complete with rides, attractions, and a marine show.

Parc France Miniature (*Tel 08 36 68 53 35, Open mid-Mar.–mid-Nov.*) is a little known attraction west of Paris, beyond Versailles. More than 150 of France's famous monuments have been reconstructed at a tiny fraction of their size at a 12.3-acre (5 ha) park. ∎

Château de Versailles

212 C3

12 miles (19 km) southwest of Paris

Château de Versailles

☎ 01 30 83 78 00

🕐 Closed Mon.

$ $$

🚗 By car: A13 to exit 14, then follow signs. By train: from Paris-Montparnasse to Versailles-Chantiers; from Paris-St.-Lazare to Versailles-Rive Droite. RER line C to Versailles-Rive Gauche.

Only a few intimates of Queen Marie-Antoinette were allowed to join her at her hamlet, a farm in miniature.

FOR SHEER GLITTER, NOTHING BEATS VERSAILLES. AN extravagant palace built during Louis XIV's reign, it is not the oldest or largest of the French châteaus, but it illustrates the essence of a royal palace more than any other. Although Louis XIV (known as the Sun King) constructed the château and the famous gardens, the property had originally belonged to his father, Louis XIII. An enthusiastic hunter, Louis XIII built a lodge in 1623 in the middle of the forest; it was so modest that one of his contemporaries described it as "a miserable manor in which even a simple country squire would not take pride." Louis XIII built more spacious quarters in 1634.

When he died nine years later, his son Louis XIV was only five years old. The boy loved the small château, but his reasons for later spending so much time and money—and ultimately moving the court to Versailles—had more to do with the turbulent politics of the day than the château's bucolic attractions. As a child, Louis XIV had witnessed the uprising of the Fronde (see p. 21), and he remained distrustful of Parisians throughout his life. By forcing the nobles to follow him to the more isolated Château de Versailles, he could keep a close watch on them, curtailing their capacity for independent political action.

Throughout his 72-year reign, Louis XIV spent lavishly to build the château, hiring the best designers France had to offer: the architect Louis Le Vau (succeeded by Jules Hardouin-Mansart), the landscape designer André Le Nôtre, and the painter Charles Le Brun, all of whom had worked on the sumptuous, but ill-fated Château de Vaux-le-Vicomte (see p. 222).

The château of Versailles is inseparable from the personality of

the king. (His great-grandson Louis XV and great-great-grandson Louis XVI made only minor alterations to his grand plan.) The finished château perfectly mirrored the ambitions of the Sun King, whose reign typified the absolutism of the monarchy, guided by the principle of *la gloire* (glory). When Versailles became the seat of government in 1682, it had to be expanded to house the entire court, along with all the civil servants.

INTERIOR

The **State Apartments** give some idea of Louis XIV's practical interpretation of *la gloire*: The

Hyacinthe Rigaud's portrait of Louis XIV. Painted in 1701, it now hangs in the Louvre.

rooms were decorated throughout with gold and marble (quarried from every corner of his kingdom) and organized around the theme of the planets gravitating around the sun (the king's emblem). No sooner had these apartments been built than Louis XIV decided he needed more intimate quarters, so from 1684 on these rooms were designated for official functions and royal audiences, while the king resided in the old part of the château facing the Marble Court.

Everything at Versailles was ruled by protocol and etiquette—even in the king's private quarters. Courtiers fought jealously for the privilege of being received there, especially for the "Rising" and "Setting" ceremonies of the Royal Heavenly Body. The gilt-and-crimson **King's Bedchamber** is now restored exactly as it was on September 1, 1715, the day the king died.

The gilded splendor of the **Queen's Room** is even more lavish, though she and the other women who lived there (two queens, two dauphines, and the wife of the king's eldest son) had even less privacy. These women gave birth to a total of 19 children, always a public affair to ensure that there were no substitutes for the royal offspring.

Nowhere is Louis XIV's quest for grandeur more evident than in the gilded, slightly gaudy **Hall of Mirrors,** a 240-foot-long room constructed by Hardouin-Mansart that runs the entire length of the central part of the château and faces the huge gardens outside. The 17 tall, arched windows are matched on the opposite wall by 17 tall French mirrors, while the coffered ceiling (decorated by Charles Le Brun) immortalizes the diplomatic and military conquests of the king over such foreign powers as Spain and Holland. More recently, during

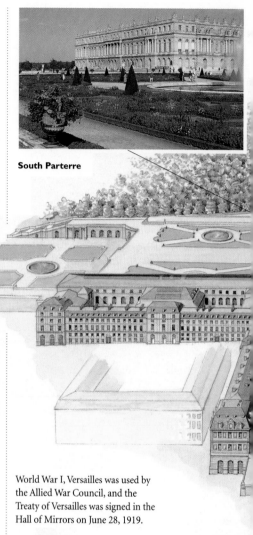

South Parterre

World War I, Versailles was used by the Allied War Council, and the Treaty of Versailles was signed in the Hall of Mirrors on June 28, 1919.

GARDENS

Making the most of the steep, marshy ground, André Le Nôtre designed what has been called the most perfect example of a formal French garden. In an era that believed that nature was to be mastered by man, Le Nôtre undertook immense drainage work, shifting masses of earth to form the terraces that begin with the **Parterre d'Eau** (two symmetrical pools)

The Royal Chapel ceiling

Salon de Mars

just below the windows of the Hall of Mirrors and lead down to the **Bassin d'Apollon** and the **Grand Canal.**

The king was so proud of his gardens that he wrote a detailed description of the best way to visit them. Although formal in design

and organized around two main axes—one running east to west, the other north to south—the gardens contain charming groves, fountains, and labyrinths with names like the "Bacchus Basin," the "Apollo Baths," and the "Room of Chestnut Trees."

The groves were equipped with a

The Hall of Mirrors, Versailles' most famous room, is still used for private banquets.

highly sophisticated system of fountains, created to accompany the festivities organized by Louis XIV. The most famous of these, held in 1664, was dedicated ostensibly to his wife Marie-Thérèse, but was actually in honor of his favorite mistress, Mademoiselle de La Vallière. The playwright Molière wrote several plays, including *Tartuffe*, for the week-long celebration, and the entire château and gardens were turned into a backdrop for ballets, fireworks, tournaments, waterworks, and ornate banquets. Today, the Grandes Eaux celebrations, held every Sunday from early May to October, re-create something of the ambience of these events.

Louis demanded that the flowers in his gardens flourish all year long. Through the ingenuity of Jean-Baptiste de La Quintinye, the king ate strawberries in March and lettuce in January. The **King's Kitchen Garden,** which has produced fruit and vegetables continuously for three centuries, is also open to the public.

GRAND & PETIT TRIANONS

Versailles was sometimes too large and too public, even for Louis XIV. With nearly 10,000 people occupying the palace, there was no way to escape the constantly jostling courtiers or the rigid rules of court protocol. The king, therefore, asked Hardouin-Mansart to build the

VISITING THE CHÂTEAU

It is impossible to see everything at the château in a single day. There are several different entrances, depending on which part you want to visit. Entrance A admits you to the star attractions—the Hall of Mirrors, the King's Apartments, and the Queen's Apartments—which can be visited either individually (with rented headsets) or as part of a guided tour. Be forewarned: There are often long lines here, so it may be worthwhile paying slightly more for one of the other entrances, which sell tickets to these rooms combined with a tour of other rooms in the château (for example, the Dauphin's Apartments, the Opéra, the Chapel, or the Petits Apartments).

A combined ticket can also be purchased for the Grand Trianon and the Petit Trianon (a small train runs between the château and the Trianons, for those who prefer not to walk). The gardens are free, except during the "Grandes Eaux" performances, when the 32 pools and fountains are turned on as part of a musical display. ■

The stunning Apollo Basin is the focal point of the park.

Grand Trianon, a pink marble mini-palace, in his gardens. Only slightly less magnificent than Versailles, the Grand Trianon became a getaway for several royal families. The building was renovated under General de Gaulle and used as the official residence for foreign heads of states.

After Louis XIV's death, Louis XV continued to live at Versailles, where he constructed the Petit Trianon in 1769 as a place where he could meet his mistress, Madame de Pompadour. When Marie-Antoinette became queen, she created an English-style garden and a miniature mock-hamlet, complete with farm animals and a mill around a small pond.

🅰 212 D3
✉ St.-Denis, 5 miles (8 km) north of Paris

Cathédrale St.-Denis
✉ 1 place de la Légion d'Honneur
☎ 01 48 09 83 54
💲 $$
🚇 Métro: Line 13 to St.-Denis-Basilique; By car: via A1

Visitor information
✉ 1 rue de la République, St.-Denis
☎ 01 55 87 08 70

Tombs of Henri II and Catherine de Médicis

Cathédrale St.-Denis

ST.-DENIS, THE CATHEDRAL THAT INSPIRED GOTHIC architecture in France, stands in an unlikely setting in the working-class suburb of St.-Denis, north of Paris. Over 800 years separate the two monuments for which St. Denis is famous: the cathedral, a landmark in the evolution of Gothic architecture begun in 1136 by Abbot Suger; and the brand-new Stade de France, the sports stadium that hosted the 1998 World Cup Soccer Tournament. Both seem too large to fit within their allotted plots of land in this northern suburb.

The official burial site for French monarchs since 1122, St.-Denis represents a turning point in the history of architecture. The popular medieval legend of the famous Christian martyr, Saint Denis (see p. 16), had inspired an earlier basilica built by Saint Geneviève (the patron saint of Paris; see p. 18) around 475. Charles Martel was

buried here, and both his son, Pépin the Short, and his grandson, Charlemagne, were crowned here. The Abbey of St.-Denis was already powerful when Abbot Suger improved the existing Merovingian basilica by adding intersecting ribbed vaults on a large scale throughout the church—an innovation for the time. The masterbuilders of the other great cathedrals that followed (including Chartres and Senlis) drew their inspiration from this prototype. Unfortunately, the church was badly damaged during the Revolution, and most of its treasures are now in the Louvre.

ROYAL MONUMENTS

The crypt represents a fascinating chronology of the French monarchy. Sometime around 1260, Saint Louis commissioned images of his predecessors, starting with the seventh century. From the 14th century on, the heart and viscera of the deposed royals were removed from their bodies and dispersed to separate monuments, while the bodies were buried at St.-Denis.

For centuries, almost every king, queen, and royal child was buried here, from Dagobert through Louis XVIII. The most interesting funerary monuments are those of Dagobert, Henri II, Catherine de Médicis, Pépin the Short, Charles Martel, Louis XII, and François I. ∎

Disneyland Paris

DESPITE A ROCKY BEGINNING, WITH SEVERAL CROSS-cultural misunderstandings between U.S. management and the French staff (who had difficulty, for example, in complying with the no-moustache dress code), the transplant of Disneyland to Paris seems to have taken root successfully. Visitors will find the same beaming "cast members," attractions similar to the U.S. versions, and the same turreted Sleeping Beauty's Castle—a somewhat hollow edifice in a country overrun with real châteaus.

Disneyland Paris

- 213 E3
- 12 miles (19 km) east of Paris in Marne-la-Vallée
- 01 60 30 60 30
- $$$$$
- By car: A4 toward Nancy-Metz, exit 14. By train: RER line A, exit Marne-la-Vallée-Chessy. Shuttles from Roissy & Orly airports.

Le Château de la Belle au Bois Dormant (Sleeping Beauty's Castle)

If you're traveling with children who balk at visiting one more museum, Disneyland can provide an entertaining break from Paris. The main entrance leads straight down Main Street U.S.A., lined with shops selling every Disney product imaginable. From here, four main sections spread out in all directions toward the attractions, whose long lines sometimes translate into more than an hour's wait.

The youngest kids love Fantasyland, where Disney habitués will recognize such rides as "It's a Small World" and the "Alice in Wonderland" maze, complete with trick fountains. Older kids and adults head straight for Discovery-land and the newest attraction, "Space Mountain," a heart-stopping roller coaster that literally shoots you off the starting line. The nearby "Star Tours" is a popular simulator ride. Frontierland offers a few other thrills, with the "Big Thunder Mountain" and "Temple of Doom" roller coasters.

Somewhere between the gentle Fanstasyland and the other wild, looping rides is the "Pirates of the Caribbean" in Adventureland, a boat trip that everyone likes. There are also small pockets of calm, such as the "Cottonwood Creek Ranch." Other Disney classics are on hand, such as the "Disney Parade," with illuminated floats and cartoon characters in costume, ready to pose for a picture. There are lots of restaurants—where, at least in some establishments, Disney has taken into account French culture by allowing wine to be served.

For an extended stay, there are six theme hotels, and outside the park itself a complex where you can hear all kinds of music—from country and western to surprisingly good jazz. ■

Vaux-le-Vicomte & Blandy

Nicolas Fouquet's Vaux-le-Vicomte, near Melun

VAUX-LE-VICOMTE IS ONE OF THE BEST EXAMPLES OF THE Louis XIV style. If you can schedule a visit on Saturday night, don't miss the special Candlelight Evenings, when 2,000 candles illuminate the castle and gardens.

Vaux-le-Vicomte
- 🗺 212 D2
- ✉ 30 miles (50 km) southeast of Paris
- ☎ 01 64 14 41 90
- 🕐 Open daily March–mid-Nov.
- 💲 $$
- 🚆 By train: Gare de Lyon to Melun, then taxi

Château Forteresse de Blandy-les-Tours
- ✉ 30 miles (50 km) southeast of Paris at Blandy-les-Tours
- ☎ 01 60 66 90 23
- 🕐 Mid-Oct.–mid-April
- 💲 $

Vaux-le-Vicomte was built for Nicolas Fouquet by the greatest 17th-century French architects and designers—Louis Le Vau, Charles le Brun, and André Le Nôtre. However, Fouquet's fatal mistake was to create a palace even more radiant than the Sun King's, and this proved his downfall, since most of the funds to build it were embezzled from the French government.

Fouquet was one of the most powerful men in the kingdom when he began work on Vaux-le-Vicomte in 1653. For six years, he spent lavishly to create his splendid château and landscaped gardens. In 1661, fearful that he had fallen from the king's favor, Fouquet invited Louis XIV to a celebration that included 6,000 guests, fireworks, and complex waterworks. A jealous

Louis had him arrested that month and thrown into prison, where he remained until his death 15 years later. The king then requisitioned the furniture, statuary, tapestries, and the same architect to build the glittering Versailles.

Highlights include the oval salon, Le Brun's painted ceilings in the Salon des Muses, the restored kitchen, and the terraced gardens.

BLANDY'S FORTRESS

Just a few miles to the east of Vaux-le-Vicomte *(Map 213 E2)* is Blandy-les-Tours, the last remaining medieval fortress in the Île de France. The ruins lie nestled in a valley, their stone towers lacking only colorful banners to make you believe you have stumbled into the Middle Ages. ■

Provins

EVERY SPRING AND SUMMER, THIS HILLTOP TOWN TRANS-
ports visitors 800 years into the past, with knights in armor astride
charging steeds, catapults assaulting ancient stone ramparts, falconry
shows, and hundreds of costumed actors roving the streets.

A 14th-century illuminated manuscript depicting activities of the centuries-old twice-annual fair held in the town of Provins

Provins was an economic capital of the Champagne region as early as the tenth century; it traded in expensive silks, exotic spices, and wool during its twice-annual fair, which brought traders from all over Europe. A good place to discover the past is at the **Grange aux Dîmes,** a wax museum on Rue St.-Jean.

The ancient upper town has been restored, and now has 58 historical monuments that form the backdrop for the colorful reenactments of medieval life. A jousting tournament re-creates a battle in 1230, when Comte Thibaud de Champagne saved Provins from the Count de Picardie, whose armies were besieging the town. Every summer nearly 80 free-flying birds of prey swoop over the crowds in a demonstration of falconry.

A self-guided walking tour of the town (brochure available from tourist office) explores the 11th-century ramparts that extend nearly a mile around the old town. The César Tower stands high above the town, offering a fine view over the Brie region.

Both the upper and lower towns are honeycombed with nearly 6 miles of ancient tunnels linking dozens of vaulted cellars. The walls bear the mysterious marks of various secret societies (including the Freemasons), who once used these underground galleries for their meetings.

A medieval feast is held during a weekend in June, and other events, including concerts and a sound-and-light show, are scheduled throughout the summer. ■

Provins
- 213 F2
- 50 miles (80 km) east of Paris
- By car: A4 toward exit 13 at Serris, follow signs to Provins (D231). By train: Paris Gare de l'Est to Troyes

Visitor information
- place Honoré de Balzac
- 01 64 60 26 26
- Medieval shows April–Oct.

Fontainebleau

The François I Gallery at Fontainebleau was initially reserved for use by the king and later became a public passageway.

FONTAINEBLEAU IS ONE OF THE MOST POPULAR WEEKEND destinations for Parisians, who flock to the forest to enjoy hiking, rock climbing, and riding. While Versailles reflects a single monarch's glory (Louis XIV), the royal abode of Fontainebleau has evolved constantly during the reigns of 30 different rulers of France, and much of its charm is due to the disparate elements and odd series of buildings they created. Like Versailles, however, it is immense; there are several different itineraries through the rooms, including the State Apartments, the Chinese Museum, the Napoleon I Museum, and the rooms of his empress, Eugénie; an additional ticket lets you see the emperor's and empress's private apartments as part of a guided tour.

THE CHÂTEAU

Drawn by the abundant game in the forest, Louis VII began building here in 1137. Subsequent kings, similarly attracted to hunting, remodeled and expanded the property. The first major work was undertaken by François I in 1530, who preferred Fontainebleau to his other royal palaces. He brought Italian artists (including Leonardo da Vinci, whose "Mona Lisa" hung on the walls at Fontainebleau before being transferred to the Louvre) and craftsmen to construct a magnificent mannerist palace to replace the existing modest hunting lodge; the frescoes and stucco work in the François I Gallery remain from this period.

Henri II continued his father's projects, including the 98-foot-long (30 m) ballroom—a dazzling display of Renaissance style, with a coffered ceiling by architect Philibert Delorme and frescoes by Italian artist Francesco Primaticcio. The exterior horseshoe staircase

was constructed by Louis XIII; it is where Napoleon I famously addressed his men in 1814 before being sent into exile.

The emblems of various rulers can be spotted in different rooms: the interlaced "H" and "C," for Henri II and Catherine de Médicis (intended to be interpreted as a "D," for his mistress, Diane de Poitiers); Napoleon's insignia of golden bees, emblazoned on red velvet in the throne room; and François I's salamander. There is also a museum of Chinese works collected by Empress Eugénie, and a Napoleon Museum.

FONTAINEBLEAU FOREST

Covering 61,750 acres (25,009 ha), the forest is crisscrossed with roads, 200 miles (320 km) of marked paths, and countless lanes. The Fontainebleau tourist office provides maps of the forest and information for excursions. Although the elevation never climbs above 482 feet (127 m), the forest is popular with rock climbers. Bicycles can also be rented. Some of the more popular sites include the Apremont Gorges, the Franchard Gorges, and the Béatrix Grotto.

OTHER PLACES NEARBY

The area around Fontainebleau is legendary in the history of painting. The village of **Barbizon** nearby *(Map 212 D2, visitor information, Tel 01 60 66 41 87)* was the mecca for a group of 19th-century landscape painters including Daubigny, Corot, and Millet. In the summer, it is often packed with tourist buses but remains a rural village. The single main street is lined with antique dealers and art galleries, and landscape painter Theodore Rousseau's studio (where he lived from 1736 to 1742) is now a museum.

Thoméry *(Map 213 E1, visitor information, Tel 01 64 70 80 14),* nestled in a loop of the Seine, has long been famous for its Chasselas Doré grapes. The fortified town of **Moret-sur-Loing** *(Map 213 E1, visitor information, Tel 01 60 70 41 66),* immortalized by painters like Camille Pissarro and Alfred Sisley, hosts a spectacular sound-and-light show on Saturday nights from mid-June through early September. And **Samois-sur-Seine** *(Map 212 D1),* in the middle of Fontainebleau Forest, hosts the annual summer Django Reinhardt Jazz Festival. ■

Fontainebleau's Gate of Honor (1809–1810) leads to the famous horseshoe staircase, which is richly decorated with Napoleonic emblems.

Visitor information

✉ 4 rue Royale, Fontainebleau

☎ 01 60 74 99 99

Rambouillet & around

Rambouillet
- 212 B2
- 30 miles (50 km) southwest of Paris
- By car: A13, then join A12 toward St. Quentin-en-Yvelines, then N10 to Rambouillet. By train: Gare Montparnasse to Rambouillet, then bus No. 72

Rambouillet's interior woodwork is rivaled only by that of Versailles.

Château de Rambouillet
- Rambouillet
- 01 34 83 00 25
- Closed Tues.
- $$

Forest & park visitor information
- place de la Libération
- 01 34 83 21 21
- Daily in summer

Rochefort-en-Yvelines
- 212 C2
- 10 miles (16 km) southeast of Rambouillet via D27

Montfort-l'Amaury visitor information
- 212 B3
- 16 miles (26 km) north of Rambouillet via N10 then D191
- 01 34 86 87 96

ALTHOUGH NOT THE MOST BEAUTIFUL CHÂTEAU IN THE Île de France region, Rambouillet (now a presidential retreat) sits in the middle of a magnificent forest, with plenty of nearby excursions.

THE CHÂTEAU

Rambouillet was renovated and modified by successive owners. Louis XVI, a frequent guest on hunting expeditions, acquired the long-coveted property in 1784, adding several rustic features for Queen Marie-Antoinette—including a dairy and sheepfold. Since 1897, the château has been used by France's heads of state.

Visitors can tour the château, apartments, queen's dairy and National Sheepfold, and magnificent French-style water gardens with their large artificial lakes. One of the château's most famous rooms is the Napoleon I bathroom decorated with mock ancient fresco in 1807. There is also a cottage adorned inside with seashells, mother of pearl, and marble.

NEARBY PLACES

Southeast of Rambouillet, **Rochefort-en-Yvelines** has hardly changed for centuries. Stone steps lead up to St.-Gilles Church, from which some of the village's old fortifications can still be seen. An 11th-century village, **Montfort-l'Amaury** is one of the prettiest in the area, its château visible atop the hillside. ∎

Abbaye de Vaux-de-Cernay

Founded in 1148, the Abbaye de Vaux-de-Cernay (*Map 212 C2, Tel 01 34 85 23 00*), 6 miles (10 km) northeast of Rambouillet, is spectacular, with vaulted ceilings, massive wooden doors, lovely antiques, and old stone walls. It functioned as a prosperous Cistercian abbey until the French Revolution and is now a luxury hotel. Enjoy a drink on the terrace overlooking the church ruins. ∎

Auvers-sur-Oise

AUVERS IS SOMETHING OF A PILGRIMAGE SITE FOR PEOPLE seeking traces of van Gogh. A series of panels representing famous paintings by van Gogh, Cézanne, and others have been placed all over town, on the exact sites where they were painted. The tourist office has suggestions for walks, taking in the Auberge Ravoux where van Gogh died after a self-inflicted bullet wound on July 29, 1890, and the church and cornfields immortalized by the painter.

Van Gogh was only here for 70 days, under the care of close friend Dr. Gachet (homeopathic doctor to the artists of Auvers-sur-Oise), but he worked frenetically, producing 70 paintings and numerous drawings. He is buried in the local cemetery next to his brother.

Before van Gogh arrived, Auvers was already a favorite destination of 19th-century landscape painters. Charles Daubigny, a member of the Barbizon school, moored a houseboat here in 1857 and was soon followed by many other artists, who used his **studio,** established in

1861 on what is now Rue Daubigny, as a meeting place. Daubigny campaigned for younger painters like Renoir, Monet, and Cézanne, who also visited him, along with Corot and Daumier. Daubigny's paintings and memorabilia are in the **Daubigny Museum.**

Two other museums are worth visiting in Auvers: The **Absinthe Museum** explores the poets' elixir known as "the green peril," outlawed in 1915; and the **Château d'Auvers** offers a 90-minute audiovisual presentation on the Impressionists. ∎

Auvers-sur-Oise
- 🅰 212 C4
- ✉ 22 miles (35 km) north of Paris
- 🚆 By train: Paris-Gare du Nord to Auvers-sur-Oise (via Pontoise)

Visitor information
- ✉ rue de la Sansonne
- ☎ 01 30 36 10 06

Auberge Ravoux
- ✉ place de la Mairie
- ☎ 01 30 36 60 63
- 💲 $

Daubigny Studio
- ✉ 61 rue Daubigny
- ☎ 01 34 48 03 03
- 🕐 Open Thurs.–Sun. Easter–Nov.
- 💲 $

Daubigny Museum
- ✉ Colombières Manor, rue de la Sansonne
- 🕐 Closed Mon., Tues., & a.m.
- ☎ 01 30 36 80 20
- 💲 $

Absinthe Museum
- ✉ 44 rue Alphonse Callé
- ☎ 01 30 36 83 26
- 🕐 Open Wed.–Sun. June–Sept., weekends Oct.–May
- 💲 $

Château d'Auvers
- ✉ 2 rue de Léry
- ☎ 01 34 48 48 48
- 🕐 Closed Mon.
- 💲 $$

Van Gogh's "Église d'Auvers-sur-Oise" (1890)

Chartres Cathedral

FOR NEARLY 800 YEARS, CHARTRES CATHEDRAL HAS STOOD like a beacon, seemingly alone amid the flat fields of the Beauce region. Little has changed since the 13th century. Despite fires, revolutions, two World Wars, and overzealous restorers, the church remains almost intact from the day it was consecrated in 1260.

Chartres Cathedral

- 212 B2
- 52 miles (83 km) southwest of Paris
- By car: Take the A6, then A10, then A11 toward Le Mans & follow signs to Chartres.
  By train: Paris-Gare Montparnasse to Chartres. Tel 08 36 35 35 35 for national lines, Tel 01 53 90 20 20 for Île de France.

Visitor information

- place de la Cathédrale
- 02 37 18 26 26

The present cathedral stands on the site of earlier churches dating from the eighth century. The most important event in its history was the gift of the "Sancta Camisia," a priceless relic presented by Charles the Bald, Charlemagne's grandson. This was the tunic supposedly worn by Mary as she gave birth to Christ, and it transformed Chartres into one of the most popular pilgrimage shrines in Europe (the relic is still stored in the Treasury). In the tenth century, the School of Chartres was one of the most prestigious centers of learning in Europe.

A series of fires destroyed the successive churches, but the most serious one was in 1194, when the entire city went up in flames, destroying everything but the Royal Portal and the western towers of the church. The local townspeople were mortified to think that the precious relic had been lost. Three days later,

as the church lay smoldering, a procession appeared holding the relic. This miracle was seen as a sign from Mary that Chartres would be an ever greater church, and the rebuilding project was begun immediately with great zeal. The result is this breathtaking Gothic cathedral. Its architectural and sculptural unity is chiefly due to the fact that it was constructed almost entirely in less than 30 years.

"CHARTRES BLUE" STAINED GLASS

The cathedral's stained-glass windows, with the unique "Chartres blue" color, are famous throughout the world. They form the most complete collection of medieval glass anywhere. The 12th-century Royal Portal survived the great fire, as did its glass and the spectacular window known as the "Blue Virgin." The 13th-century windows in the rest of the church form radiant illustrations of biblical and historical scenes, peopled with knights, peasants, kings, noble ladies in furs, and a multitude of craftsmen at work, providing a fascinating record of religion and daily life in medieval times. Each panel tells a story to be read from left to right, and bottom to top.

STATUARY & MAZE

The statuary on the three main portals completes the iconography of the church. The North Porch shows the story of Creation (on the left side), leading to the Fall of Adam and Eve (right), followed by Old Testament figures, and a nativity scene. The South Porch depicts scenes of the Last Judgment.

Unfortunately, the rows of chairs now in the nave hide the best preserved stone labyrinth in France, where pilgrims used to make their way through the 953-foot-long (291 m) maze on their knees.

WHAT TO SEE & DO

During spring and summer, take a tour (in English) by resident historian Malcolm Miller, who offers an entertaining look at the glass, sculptures, and history of the cathedral.

If you have a few extra hours, the old town is worth exploring. The tourist office provides maps of a Circuit Touristique that takes you to the former Episcopal Palace and the Fine Arts Museum and down to the river, which winds past an old mill and half-timbered Renaissance houses, and over stone bridges. A small train runs during the tourist season, and follows much the same itinerary.

Don't miss the **St.-Pierre Church** nearby at Place St.-Pierre. Usually overshadowed by the more famous cathedral, it also contains some fine 13th- and 14th-century stained glass. ■

Monet's pink-and-green shuttered house provides the perfect backdrop to the gardens.

Giverny

IN 1883, CLAUDE MONET MOVED WITH HIS FAMILY TO THIS house, where he remained until his death in 1926. The house and gardens were an unceasing source of inspiration for the painter, who devoted much time and money to his landscaping projects. Wherever he lived, Monet had always had a garden, but at Giverny it became his life's work: There he created in nature the motifs that became his obsession, transposing the water lilies, boats, and bridges of his garden onto his canvases. After Monet's death, the house was so badly neglected that by 1966, when his son Michel donated Giverny to the Académie des Beaux-Arts, the floors and ceiling beams had rotted away, and a staircase had collapsed. It took ten years to restore the house and the gardens; the museum eventually opened in 1980, and now hosts nearly 500,000 visitors every year.

Giverny

 212 B4

 49 miles (78 km) northwest of Paris

By car: Autoroute de l'Ouest (A13/ E05) from Pont de St.-Cloud, toward Rouen. Exit at Bonnières, follow the D201 to Giverny.
By train: from Paris-Gare St.-Lazare on the Rouen line, get off at Vernon, & take a local bus or a taxi, or walk the 3 miles.

GARDENS

Whatever season you arrive, the garden is as much a profusion of color as it was in Monet's lifetime. When the family first moved here, the garden was a modest orchard of about 2 acres, enclosed within high stone walls. The painter transformed it, creating patterns of symmetrical designs and perspectives by planting clumps and shapes of color that changed with every month. Monet detested the formal French garden and instead created rose-covered archways entwined with trailing nasturtiums, dividing the garden into brilliant flower beds filled with hollyhocks and annuals.

Ten years after he moved to Giverny, Monet bought the land on the other side of the railroad tracks, intending to divert the Epte River to create a pond and water garden. He met with stiff opposition from the suspicious locals, who opposed what they considered to be an extravagant project. In the end, he prevailed. Monet first had an artificial lake dug and then created an exotic garden with bamboo plants, wisteria, willows, and, of course, the famous water lilies. A local craftsman built the graceful Japanese bridge, and a wooden boat still floats at one end of the pond.

HOUSE & STUDIO

The house, with its pink, roughcast facade and green shutters, was the scene of frequent entertaining for

Monet's many friends, and he even maintained a kitchen garden across town that provided fresh produce to feed his guests. He personally oversaw menus and maintained books in which he recorded dozens of special recipes from friends such as Sacha Guitry, Stéphane Mallarmé, and Pierre-Auguste Rodin, who gathered in the blue-tiled kitchen and sunny yellow dining room.

Monet loved Japanese engravings, and his precious collection (which inspired his design of the water garden) is displayed in several of the rooms. On the walls of the modest living room hung Monet's personal collection of works he particularly admired, including a dozen Cézannes, a few Renoirs, eight Manets, a couple of Degas, and two bronzes by Rodin. Now dispersed to museums and collections around the world, these works have been reproduced to re-create the interior in Monet's day.

Visitors enter through the huge Nymphéas studio, which was constructed in 1916 to give Monet the room and light he needed to paint the giant "Waterlilies," which were commissioned by his friend Georges Clemenceau for the Musée de l'Orangerie in Paris (see p. 140). Today, the studio exhibits reproductions of his work and includes a souvenir shop.

To avoid the crowds, come on a weekday. (Wednesdays can also be a busy day.) Tour buses often leave around 4 p.m., but the gardens stay open until 6 p.m., which is a lovely time to enjoy them.

MUSEUM OF AMERICAN ART

Also worth seeing is the Museum of American Art, just a few streets from Monet's house. It exhibits works by American artists who lived and painted in France from 1865 to 1915. ■

Claude Monet Museum

- ✉ 84 rue Claude Monet
- ☎ 02 32 51 28 21
- 🕐 Open Tues.–Sun. April–Oct.
- 💲 House & garden: $$. Garden: $.

Museum of American Art

- ✉ 99 rue Claude Monet
- ☎ 02 32 51 94 65
- 🕐 Closed Nov.–March & Mon.
- 💲 $$

Monet's pond, created by diverting the nearby Epte River, looks today much as it did in the artist's time.

More places to visit around Paris

CHÂTEAU DE CHANTILLY & FOREST

Set in the middle of a romantic moat in the heart of the forest, Chantilly is one of the most beautiful châteaus around Paris. It was destroyed during the Revolution but has been re-created and is now home to the **Condé Museum,** an art collection put together by the Duc d'Aumale in the 19th century.

What sets Chantilly off from other châteaus, however, is its **Horse Museum and Great Stables** (circa 1719–1735), housed in a monumental stone building that at its height held 240 horses and 300 hounds. The public can attend dressage demonstrations daily, except Tuesdays.

Chantilly is also the site of one of France's major horse-racing tracks; you can watch thoroughbreds exercising or attend a race.

Other sites nearby include the Cistercian **Abbaye de Royaumont** (*Map 212 D4, Asnières-sur-Oise, Tel 01 30 35 59 00*) and the

ancient royal town of **Senlis** (*Map 210 D4*). 212 D4 ✉ Chantilly, 25 miles (40 km) north of Paris ☎ 03 44 62 62 60 ⊕ Closed Tues. $ \$\$ 🚗 By car: Take the A1 to the Survilliers-St.-Witz exit, then the N17 to Chantilly; By train: Gare du Nord or RER Line D to Chantilly-Gouvieux (then a short walk)

CHÂTEAU DE MALMAISON

Josephine purchased this property when Napoleon was still the First Consul. He found his official residence, the Tuileries Palace, too depressing and retreated to Malmaison whenever he could. Josephine kept the château after he divorced her, and she devoted considerable sums to the house and gardens, creating the first great collection of roses here. The house is now a museum devoted to Napoleonic history and Empire memorabilia. 212 C3 ✉ 1 avenue du Château, Rueil-Malmaison ☎ 01 41 29 05 55 ⊕ Closed Tues. $ \$\$ 🚗 By Métro or RER: Line A to the Grande Arche de la Défense, then bus 258

ÉCOUEN CHÂTEAU & MUSEUM

Many of the works in the collection of this Renaissance museum came from the Musée de Cluny in Paris. The magnificent 16th-century château was constructed by some of the most famous artists of the time, including Le Rosso and Jean Clouet; the south wing has remained nearly intact since this time. The collection includes a series of 16th-century tapestries depicting the story of David and Bathsheba. 212 D3 ✉ Écouen, 12 miles (19 km) north of Paris off N16 ☎ 01 34 38 38 50 ⊕ Closed Tues. $ \$ 🚗 By train: Gare du Nord to Écouen-Ézanville, then bus No. 269 ■

The "Quatuor Evangelia," a 12th-century Gospel from the Abbey of Werden, Germany, now displayed in the Condé Museum at Chantilly

Travelwise

Métro sign

TRAVELWISE INFORMATION

PLANNING YOUR TRIP

WHEN TO GO

When you go to Paris depends on what you are looking for. Some people find the Christmas lights on the Champs-Élysées thrillingly romantic, or come in winter to avoid other tourists.

"April in Paris" is beautiful, but may be cold and rainy. May and June usually have fine weather. During July and August, the city is fairly laid-back as many of its residents are on vacation, and the Métro is filled with tourists; many shops and restaurants are closed in August. If you can deal with that, you'll find that Paris has a special, sometimes villagelike quality in August, with less traffic and pollution, and several free entertainments, like concerts in the parks and outdoor movies at La Villette. Another advantage of the summer months is that it is low season for the hotels, and many offer reduced rates. Reservations are also easier to obtain, as there are no major conventions or events being held.

September brings la rentrée—the return of vacationing Parisians—and with it an upswing in activity. Paris is lovely in the fall, when the chestnut trees turn rust-colored and children return to school with their book-laden schoolbags strapped to their backs.

CLIMATE

Paris has moderately cold winters, with little snow; cool springs and falls; and moderately hot, humid summers.

WHAT TO TAKE

Be prepared for rain in any season, and always pack a sweater, even in the summer. Other necessities: comfortable walking shoes, a dressy outfit for evenings out, and a major credit card with an international PIN number (check with your bank) so you can withdraw cash from money machines. Don't forget the essentials: passport, driver's license, and insurance documentation.

INSURANCE

Make sure you have adequate coverage for medical treatment and expenses, including repatriation, and baggage and money loss.

PASSPORTS

For U.S. and Canadian citizens only a passport is needed to enter France for a stay of up to 90 days. No visa is required.

HOW TO GET TO PARIS

AIRLINE

Air France
Paris, Tel 08 02 80 28 02
In the U.S.
New York, Tel 212/838-7800
Los Angeles, Tel 310/271-6665

AIRPORTS

Roissy-Charles de Gaulle
(north of Paris) Tel 01 48 62 22 80
Orly (south of Paris) Tel 01 49 75 15 15

Direct flights to Paris are available from most major cities, with Air France and many other international airlines. Paris has two airports: Roissy-Charles de Gaulle and Orly. To get into town from Roissy-Charles de Gaulle, take a taxi (around 200 francs); the Air France bus (stops at Porte Maillot and Étoile); the Roissybus (stops at Opéra); or the RER, the regional mass-transport train (Line B stops at Gare du Nord, Châtelet, St.-Michel, Luxembourg, Port-Royal, and Denfert-Rochereau). From Orly, take a taxi (around 150 francs); the Orlybus (stops at Denfert-Rochereau); the Orlyval bus (connects with RER B to central Paris); or the Orlyrail (RER C to central Paris).

You can arrange for a shuttle (door-to-door)
• Airport Shuttle (75F per person/min. 2): 01 45 38 55 72; www.airportshuttle.fr
• Airport Express (85F per person/2 + people): 01 41 71 41 46; www.airportexpress.fr
• Paris Shuttle (85F per person/2 + people): 01 43 90 91 91; www.parishuttle.com
• Paris Airports Service (85F per person /2+ people): 01 49 62 78 78; www.magic.fr/pas

GETTING AROUND

BY CAR

CAR RENTALS IN FRANCE
Ada, Tel 01 55 46 19 99
Avis, Tel 08 02 05 05 05
Europcar, Tel 08 03 35 93 59
Hertz, Tel 01 39 38 38 38;
      outside Paris 08 03 86 18 61
      (local rate)

Driving in Paris is not advised—the traffic is heavy, street parking scarce, and you can get wherever you want to go using the good urban-transport system or plentiful taxis. However, if you wish to rent a car, check with your travel agent at home first before trying the agencies in France, as prices are often lower when a car is booked from the United States.

DRIVING REGULATIONS

An international driver's license is not required for short-term visitors. When driving, keep all relevant documents in the car. Remember that at unmarked intersections, the car coming from the right has priority and will not stop; always slow down and look to the right when crossing an intersection.

Seat belts are required for all passengers, even in the back seat. Children under ten are not allowed to ride in the front seat unless a special seat is provided for them.

In the absence of speed-limit signs, the limit is 30 mph/50 kph in villages, towns, and cities; 55 mph/90 kph (50 mph/80 kph in wet weather) on country roads; 70 mph/110 kph (60 mph/100 kph in wet weather) on divided roads and highways in urban areas; and 80 mph/130 kph (70 mph/110 kph in wet weather; 30 mph/50 kph in foggy conditions) on highways. If you have had more than two glasses of wine, you are over the legal limit and should not drive. If your car is towed or clamped in Paris, go to the nearest police station to find out how to retrieve it.

CAR BREAKDOWN

Europ Assistance, Tel 01 41 85 85 85
SOS Dépannage, Tel 01 47 07 99 99

For rental cars, check the package of information in the glove compartment for the emergency number. Europ Assistance offers a towing service that costs at least 1,000 francs. For 24-hour car repairs, call SOS Dépannage. Otherwise, look for a *garagiste* (garage) along the road. An "N" symbol means that it is open at night. There is one repair service open in every town on Sunday. Call the police (17) or the local *gendarmerie* (police station) if you can't find a garage. On *autoroutes* (highways), emergency phones are located alongside the road at regular intervals.

PUBLIC TRANSPORTATION

MÉTRO
Operates: 5:30 a.m.–12:30 a.m.

NOCTAMBUS (Night Bus)
Operates: 1:30 a.m.–5:30 a.m.

BALABUS
Operates: noon–9 p.m., May to Sept.

RER
Operates: 5:30 a.m.–12:45 p.m.

Métro The Parisian subway, known as the Métro, is operated by the Regie Autonome des Transports Parisiens (RATP). A map is posted in every station, or ask for a free *Plan du Métro* when you buy your ticket. Each line has a number, and is identified by the names of the station at either end: The east–west line 1, for example, is La Défense–Château de Vincennes.

Individual tickets are available, but a *carnet* (book) of ten tickets is better value if you plan to use the Métro frequently. A Carte Orange is good for unlimited trips on the Métro, RER, and buses for one month, or one week (Mon.–Sun.). You will need a passport-size photo for the Carte Orange. These tickets should not be validated on buses, just shown to the driver. A Paris Visite card, available from ticket booths in the Métro, good for one, two, three, or five days, entitles you to unlimited use of public transportation in Paris and the Île de France, and discounts at some sightseeing attractions. The Formule 1 card, also available from ticket booths in the Métro, is good for one day only, exclusively for transportation.

Do not throw away a one-use ticket until you have left the station; a green-jacketed *controlleur* (conductor) may ask to see your ticket, and will fine you if you do not have one.

RER The suburban train network, the RER, has stops in Paris, and you can use a Métro ticket to travel on it within Paris. Prices are higher for destinations outside the city.

Buses Métro tickets can also be used on city buses (validate one-use tickets in the machine behind the driver) or tickets can be purchased from the driver (exact change not required). A map of bus lines is posted at bus shelters. Most bus lines do not operate after 8:30 p.m., or on Sundays and holidays. This information is posted at bus stops. Late-night buses, called **Noctambus,** cover the main routes, and run once an hour from Rue St.-Martin and Avenue Victoria at Châtelet. Métro tickets can also be used on the **Balabus,** a sightseeing line that runs on Sundays and bank holidays only between the Gare de Lyon and La Défense.

TAXIS
Taxis can be hailed on the street or found at a *station de taxi* (taxi stand) at major intersections. When the entire light on top is glowing, the taxi is available, but if only the small bulb is lit, it is not. Extra charges are added to the fare for pickups at train stations, luggage weighing over 12 lbs/5 kg, a fourth passenger (drivers can refuse to take more than three people), and an animal (except a seeing-eye dog). Tipping is at your discretion, but about ten percent of the fare is customary.

If you call for a taxi, the meter starts running when the driver receives the call, and the fare can be expensive. It is a good idea to ask for a receipt in case you leave something behind, or have a problem with the driver. Fares go up at night and when the cab passes the city limits.

Any complaints about Paris taxis should be addressed to Service des Taxis, Préfecture de Police, 36 rue des Morillons, Paris 75015, Tel 01 55 76 20 00.

Radio-dispatched taxis:
Alpha-Taxis, Tel 01 45 85 85 85
Artaxi, Tel 01 42 03 50 50 (takes wheelchairs with prior notice)
G7 Radio, Tel 01 47 39 47 39
Les Taxis Bleus, Tel 01 49 36 10 10

Taxi-Radio Étoile, Tel 01 45 01 85 24

Motorcycle taxis (with driver, helmet supplied): SP2, Tel 01 55 65 19 99

LIMOUSINE SERVICES

Carey Limousine, Tel 01 42 65 54 20

Prestige Limousines, Tel 01 40 43 92 92

TRAINS

SNCF The national French railroad, the SNCF (Société Nationale des Chemin de Fer) links Paris and all major cities. Information and reservations, Tel 08 36 35 35 35 (7 a.m.– 10 p.m.); for suburban lines, Tel 01 53 90 20 20.

The Paris mainline SNCF train stations (each with a Métro station of the same name) are the Gare de Lyon (for traveling to/from the southeast of France and Italy); the Gare du Nord (Brussels, London, and other northern destinations); the Gare de l'Est (the east); the Gare St.-Lazare (the northwest, including Normandy); the Gare d'Austerlitz (Spain and the southwest); and the Gare Montparnasse (the west, including Brittany). Phone for times and reservations, or go directly to the station to buy your ticket (the phone service is expensive and inefficient).

TGV The high-speed *Train à Grande Vitesse* (TGV) will get you to Lyon in two hours, Brussels in one-and-a-half hours, or London in three hours (by Eurostar via the Channel Tunnel). Make reservations in advance for all TGV and Eurostar trips.

Before boarding any train, it is essential to *composter* (validate) your ticket in one of the orange machines at the start of each journey. You may be fined by the conductor if you don't.

INTERNAL FLIGHTS

For flights within France and to other European destinations. Air France Europe, Tel 08 02 80 28 02

Air Liberté, Tel 08 03 80 58 05

TOURS & ORGAN-IZED SIGHTSEEING

BUS TOURS

Tours of the city and its monuments (see also Balabus, p. 235):

Cityrama, 4 Place des Pyramides, 75001, Tel 01 44 55 61 00

Paris Vision, 214 rue de Rivoli, 75001, Tel 01 42 60 30 01

Paris L'Open Tour, Tel 01 43 46 52 06

WALKING TOURS

A variety of tours, from museums and monuments to historic districts:

Paris Contact, Tel 01 42 51 08 40

Paris Walking Tours, Tel 01 48 09 21 40

BICYCLE TOURS

Tours of different neighborhoods and parks; some night tours available:

Paris à Vélo, C'est Sympa, 37 boulevard Bourdon, 75004, Tel 01 48 87 60 01

Paris-Vélo, 2 rue du Fer-à-Moulin, 75005, Tel 01 43 37 59 22

BOAT TOURS
The Seine

Bateaux-Mouches, Pont de l'Alma, 75008, Tel 01 42 25 96 10, Métro: Alma-Marceau. Tours: 11 a.m.–9:30 p.m.

Bateaux Parisiens Notre-Dame, 17 Quai de Montebello, 75005, Tel 01 43 26 92 55, Métro: St.-Michel. Tours: 2 p.m.–10 p.m.

Bateaux Parisiens Tour Eiffel, Port de la Bourdonnais, 75007, Tel 01 44 11 33 44, Métro: Bir-Hakeim. Tours: 10 a.m.–10:30 p.m.

Bateaux Vedettes de Paris, Port de Suffren, 75007, Tel 01 47 05 71 29, Métro: Bir-Hakeim. Tours: 10 a.m.–11 p.m.

Bateaux Vedettes du Pont Neuf, square du Vert-Galant, Île de la Cité, 75001, Tel 01 46 33 98 38, Métro: Pont-Neuf. Tours: 10:30 a.m.–10:30 p.m.

Batobus: A municipal boat service with stops at the Eiffel Tower (Métro: Bir-Hakeim), Musée d'Orsay (Métro: Solferino), Louvre (Métro: Louvre), Hôtel-de-Ville (Métro: Hôtel-de-Ville), and Notre-Dame (Métro: Cité). Operates: 10 a.m.– 7 p.m., May–Sept.

The canals

Canauxrama, 13 quai de la Loire, Tel 01 42 39 15 00 (reservations required), Métro: Jaurès. Three-hour canal cruise. Departs: Bassin de la Villette, 9:45 a.m. and 2:45 p.m.; Port de l'Arsenal, 9:45 a.m. and 2:30 p.m.

Paris Canal, 19–21 quai de la Loire, Tel 01 42 40 96 97 (reservations required), Métro: Jaurès. The Canal St.-Martin and the Seine in three hours. Departs: quai Anatole France, near Musée d'Orsay, 9:30 a.m.; Parc de la Villette, 2:30 p.m.

PRACTICAL ADVICE

COMMUNICATIONS

POST OFFICES

Main branch: 52 rue du Louvre, 75001, Tel 01 40 28 20 00, Métro: Louvre or Les Halles. Open: 24 hours daily.

Local branches open: Mon.–Fri., 8 a.m.–7 p.m.; Sat., 9 a.m.– noon.

Known as "La Poste," the French postal service has branches in every neighborhood. To receive mail there, letters should be addressed with your name clearly printed, followed by "Poste Restante" and the post office's address. All Paris postal codes begin with 75, and end with the number of the arrondissement, or quarter. For example, 75010 is in the 10th arrondissement, 75002 in the 2nd arrondissement, and so on.

Mailboxes Yellow *boîtes postales*

(mailboxes) are located outside every post office. They may have separate compartments for local mail, *départemental* (mail within the départemente, and *autres départements/destinations* (elsewhere in France and foreign).

TELEPHONES

To call France from the United States, dial 011-33 (international and French country code) and the nine-digit number (leaving out the initial zero).

To make a domestic call from a telephone booth within France, buy a *télécarte* (phonecard) in a post office or *tabac* (tobacco shop). The following instructions will appear on the telephone's screen: *"décrochez"* (pick up the receiver); *"insérez votre carte"* (insert your card); *"patientez"* (wait); *"numérotez/composez"* (dial the number); and *"raccrochez"* (hang up). Cafés usually have coin-operated phones.

All French phone numbers have ten digits, with Paris-region numbers beginning with 01. The four other national prefixes are: 02 for the northwest; 03 for the northeast; 04 for the southeast; and 05 for the southwest. Numbers beginning with 08 00 are toll free. There is an extra charge for other numbers beginning with 08.

To make an international call, dial 00, followed by the country code (1 for the United States and Canada), the area code, and the number. American long-distance operators include: AT&T: 08 00 99 00 11; MCI: 08 00 99 00 19; and Sprint: 08 00 99 00 87.

To reach French directory assistance, dial 12. For international directory assistance, dial 00-33-12, followed by the country code (use 1 for the United States or Canada).

NEWSPAPERS

Most kiosks (newsstands) sell some English-language newspapers, including the *International Herald Tribune, USA Today, The Wall Street Journal, The Financial Times,* and sometimes other British or Irish dailies. The major French daily papers are the left-wing *Libération,* the left-leaning *Le Monde,* and the conservative *Le Figaro.* The only paper published on Sunday is the *Journal du Dimanche.*

TELEVISION

The national stations available on non-cable TVs are TF1, France 2, France 3, and M6. Most programs are in French. Channel 5 (la Cinquième) in the evening becomes Arte, a French-German collaboration, often showing subtitled films or documentaries. Cable stations include Canal+, a movie channel with some films in the original language, CNN, BBC Prime, MTV, MCM (music videos), Eurosport, Planète (nature and science), RAI Uno (Italian), TVE 1 (Spanish), and Euronews. Canal Jimmy shows many American programs, including *Seinfeld, Dream On,* and *Friends,* in English. Paris Première runs old movies on Mon. and Thurs. evenings in the original language. Canal J has children's programming until 8 p.m., and Téva shows *Ally McBeal* in English on Tues. evenings.

RADIO

For a mix of pop, rock, jazz, and classical with no commercials, try FIP (105.1 FM). Radio Nova (101.5 FM) offers rap, soul, and other forms of African-American, African, or Afro-Caribbean music; Radio Latina (99 FM) Latin music; France-Info (105.5 FM) 24-hour news in French; Skyrock (96 FM) pop; RFM (103.9 FM) pop and rock; Radio Classique (101.1 FM) classical music; and Radio Montmartre (102.7 FM) *chansons françaises* (French songs).

MOVIES & BOOKS SET IN PARIS

Vidéothèque de Paris, 2 Grande Galerie du Forum des Halles, Porte St.-Eustache, Tel 01 44 76 62 00, Métro: Les Halles

The romantic setting of Paris has provided the background for innumerable works of film and literature. The list is endless.

Movies

An abbreviated list of some well-known American and international movies set here includes: *An American in Paris, Love in the Afternoon, Funny Face, Desire, Paris When It Sizzles, Paris By Night, Paris Calling, National Lampoon's European Vacation, The 400 Blows, Small Change, Breathless, The Last Métro, Last Tango in Paris, Frantic, French Kiss.* If you want to see any or all of these films, visit the Vidéothèque de Paris, which has an archive of just about every film having anything to do with Paris. For a small fee, you can watch any of them on your own video screen.

Books

The following novels and memoirs are steeped in Parisian ambience: *Tropic of Cancer* and *Quiet Days in Clichy* by Henry Miller; *Quartet* by Jean Rhys; *A Moveable Feast* by Ernest Hemingway; *The Autobiography of Alice B. Toklas* and *Paris France* by Gertrude Stein; *Being Geniuses Together* by Robert McAlmon and Kay Boyle; *Shakespeare and Company* by Sylvia Beach; *The Paris Edition* by Waverly Root; *Down and Out in Paris and London* by George Orwell; *The Secret Paris of the 30s* by Brassaï; *The Diary of Anaïs Nin* by Anaïs Nin; *Force of Circumstance* by Simone de Beauvoir; *Paris Notebooks* by Mavis Gallant; *Paris Journal* and *Paris Was Yesterday* by Janet Flanner; *Paris Journal* by M.F.K. Fisher; *Paris* by Julian Green; *Paris in the '50s* by Stanley Karnow. The ultimate work set in Paris is Marcel Proust's *Remembrance of Things Past.*

ELECTRICITY

French circuits use 220 volts; a transformer and adapter plug are needed for American appliances that operate on 110 volts. Many appliances are equipped with switches that convert them from one voltage to the other, but an adapter plug is still needed. Ask at a *droguerie* (hardware store) or in the basement of the BHV store at 52 rue de Rivoli.

LOCAL CUSTOMS

Say *"bonjour"* and *"au revoir"* to the staff when entering and leaving a shop, restaurant, or café. The French tend to keep to themselves more than Americans do, but as elsewhere a friendly approach usually gets a friendly response, and certainly the natives are always more than willing to give directions. If you are invited to dinner at a French person's home, bring flowers rather than wine.

MONEY MATTERS

Banque de France, 31 rue Croix-des-Petits-Champs, 75001, Tel 01 42 92 42 92, Métro: Palais-Royal
American Express, 11 rue Scribe, 75009, Tel 01 47 77 77 07, Métro: Opéra

In December 2000, one U.S. dollar equaled approximately 7.5 French francs. One franc equals 100 centimes, which come in coins of 5, 10, 20, and 50. The franc comes in coins of 1, 2, 5, 10, and 20, and bills of 20, 50, 100, 200, and 500.

On January 1, 1999, the euro became the official currency of France, and the French franc became a denomination of the euro. Franc notes and coins continue to be legal tender during a transitional period. Euro bank notes and coins are to be introduced by January 2002. (In December 2000 one U.S. dollar equaled 1.1 euros.)

Commercial currency exchanges are located in train stations, airports, and numerous locations around the city. Bank branches that exchange currency display a sign saying *"Change."* A commission is usually charged. The Banque de France usually has the best exchange rate. Cash with-

drawals against a credit card are possible at banks and currency exchanges. The American Express office exchanges currency, offering special service to Amex cardholders.

ATMs are the easiest way to get money, but an international PIN number is required. Check with your bank before leaving. In France, credit cards now often have a chip containing the ID. Foreign cards usually have this information on a magnetic strip, which may occasionally cause problems. A fee is usually charged for credit card advances, but the exchange rate may be more advantageous than those offered by banks.

NATIONAL HOLIDAYS

January 1, Easter Monday, May 1, May 8, Ascension (40 days after Easter), Pentecost Monday (10 days after Ascension), July 14, August 15, November 1, November 11, December 25.

OPENING TIMES

Most banks are open Monday to Friday, from 9 a.m.–5 p.m. Some close at lunchtime or open on Saturday morning. Major department stores are open from about 9:30 a.m.–7 p.m., and some stay open till 10 p.m. one night of the week. Boutiques open around 10 a.m. and close at 7 p.m. or 7:30 p.m.; they may be closed on Monday and at lunchtime, usually between 1 p.m. and 2:30 p.m. More and more shops are staying open on Sunday, but check first. Cafés are open from early morning until 8 p.m., 10 p.m., or 2 a.m. Most restaurants are open from noon–3 p.m. and 7:30 p.m.–11 p.m. Many stores and restaurants close in August.

TIME DIFFERENCES

Paris is one hour ahead of Greenwich mean time. If it is

midnight in Paris, it is 6 p.m. in New York, 3 p.m. in California.

TIPPING

Most restaurant bills include a service charge. This is generally indicated at the bottom of the menu. If in doubt, ask: *"Est-ce que le service est compris?"* It is usual to leave a small additional tip for the waiter if the service has been good. It is customary to tip taxi drivers ten percent, though this is not obligatory. It is usual to give porters, doormen, tour guides, and hairdressers a tip of 5–10F, usherettes and cloakroom attendants 2F. There is no need to leave a tip for hotel maids unless you have required out of the ordinary service.

TOILETS

The self-cleaning toilets on the street (not wheelchair-accessible) cost 2F, and should not be used by children under ten unless accompanied by an adult. Some Métro stations have public toilets. Large department stores have public rest rooms. If you are desperate, go into a café and head for the *"toilette/téléphone"* sign. They are usually free, although a few may charge 2F, but don't be surprised if you are asked to buy a coffee. Your chances of not being noticed are better in a large, busy café.

While all restaurants are required to have rest rooms, they are not always up to the highest standards of cleanliness, and many still have squat toilets.

TOURIST OFFICE

Office de Tourisme de Paris
(Paris Tourist Office)
Main office: 127 avenue des Champs-Élysées, 75008, Tel 08 36 68 31 12, Métro: Étoile.
Open: daily, 9 a.m.–8 p.m.
Staff will answer questions and help with hotel reservations. There are branches at airports and train stations.

TRAVELERS WITH DISABILITIES

Information: "Paris-Île-de-France for Everyone," published by ACNRH, 236 bis rue de Tolbiac, 75013, Tel 01 53 80 66 66. Office de Tourisme de Paris (Paris Tourist Office), 127 avenue des Champs-Élysées, 75008, Tel 08 36 68 31 12, Open: daily, 9 a.m.–8 p.m.

The new Méteor metro line is wheelchair accessible. Aihrop runs adapted vehicles to and from airports, Tel 01 41 29 01 29/06 80 37 99 66, Mon.–Fri. 10a.m.–3p.m. (call in advance), or request Renault-Espace taxi when calling any taxi service.

Access to the Métro is nearly impossible for anyone in a wheelchair, and only a few RER stations are easily accessible. Cité Universitaire, Auber, and Charles-de-Gaulle-Étoile have public elevators. At the following stations, you must ask a station employee to accompany you as the elevators require a key: Châtelet-Les Halles, Gare de Lyon, Grande Arche de La Défense, Denfert-Rochereau, St.-Michel-Notre-Dame, Porte de Clichy, Porte Maillot, Avenue Foch, Avenue Henri-Martin, Boulainvilliers, Avenue du Président-Kennedy, and Invalides. Other stations are not accessible. Of the bus lines, only Line 20 (Gare St.-Lazare-Gare de Lyon) is wheelchair-accessible. Spaces are reserved for wheelchairs in the high-speed TGV trains, and there are accessible toilets.

Taxis are obliged to accept passengers with disabilities even if they require assistance, and to accept seeing-eye dogs. Persons with disabilities do not have to wait in line for a taxi at an airport or train station. When calling for a taxi, ask for a Renault Espace van (see Taxis, p. 235). Hertz and Avis (see Car Rentals, p. 234) have adapted cars; reserve 48 hours in advance.

Most hotel elevators are usually too small for a wheelchair, and bathrooms can be tiny. Large, modern hotels are the most likely to be accessible. There is a ramp at the curb on every street corner. Street toilets are not accessible.

For the visually impaired, there is a strip of bumps on the edge of Métro *quays* (platforms) and tactile numbers on elevator buttons.

It is strongly recommended that travelers with disabilities order the English-language book "Paris-Île-de-France for Everyone," which contains thorough information on the accessibility of transportation, hotels, and museums in the Paris area. It's available by mail from ACNRH. The Paris Tourist Office also has information on the accessibility of transportation, museums, and monuments. Pamphlets on train and Métro accessibility are available at all stations. Always clearly describe your needs when booking any travel service.

ESCORT SERVICES FOR TRAVELERS WITH DISABILITIES

Auxiliaires des Aveugles, 71 avenue de Breteuil, 75015, Tel 01 43 06 39 68. Free escorts for the visually impaired.

Les Compagnons de Voyage, 17 quai de l'Austerlitz, 75013, Tel 01 45 83 67 77. Payment by the hour; reserve 24 hours in advance.

EMERGENCIES

EMBASSIES & CONSULATES

United States Embassy, 2 avenue Gabriel, 75008, Tel 01 43 12 22 22; Consulate, 2 rue St.-Florentin, 75001, Tel 01 43 12 22 22, Métro: Concorde.
Canadian Embassy & Consulate, 35 ave. Montaigne, 75008, Tel 01 44 43 29 00, Métro:

Franklin D. Roosevelt. For legal assistance in an emergency, contact your embassy or consulate for a list of English-speaking lawyers.

EMERGENCY PHONE NUMBERS/ ADDRESSES

Police, Tel 17
Fire or **emergency medical assistance,** Tel 18
Ambulance, Tel 15 or 01 45 67 50 50
Poisoning, Tel 01 40 05 48 48
SOS Médecin, Tel 01 47 07 77 77. Medical emergency house calls.
SOS Dentiste, 87 boulevard de Port-Royal, 75013, Tel 01 43 37 51 00. Métro: Gobelins. Emergency dental service from 8:30p.m.–midnight and on weekends and holidays.
American Hospital, 63 blvd. de Victor-Hugo, Neuilly, Tel 01 46 41 25 25. Métro: Pont de Levallois or Pont de Neuilly. Bus: 82. For 24-hour bilingual emergency medical and dental services.
24-hour pharmacy, Pharmacie les Champs-Élysées, 84 avenue des Champs-Élysées, 75008, Tel 01 45 62 02 41. Métro: George-V. (Closed pharmacies post a sign in the window with the address of the nearest one open.)
SOS Help, Tel 01 47 23 80 80. English-language crisis hotline, 3 p.m.–11 p.m.

LOST PROPERTY

Bureau des Objets Trouvés (Lost & Found Bureau), 36 rue des Morillons, 75015, Tel 01 55 76 20 20. Métro: Convention. Open: Mon., Wed.: 8:30–5 p.m., Tues., Thurs.: 8:30 a.m.–8 p.m. (except July & Aug. till 5 p.m.), Fri.: 8:30–5:30 p.m.
RATP lost and found: 01 40 30 52 00

LOST CREDIT CARDS

American Express, Tel 01 47 77 72 00
Diners Club, Tel 01 49 06 17 50
MasterCard, Tel 01 45 67 53 53
Visa, Tel 08 36 69 08 80

HOTELS & RESTAURANTS

Parisian hotels (listed here by price then in alphabetical order) are officially rated from no stars to four stars. Only the larger hotels have in-house restaurants, noted in the listings. Unless otherwise mentioned, all these hotels have private bathrooms with shower and/or bathtub. Value-added tax and service are included in the prices, but a hotel tax of between 1 and 7 francs per person per night will be added to the bill.

Most hotels now charge extra for breakfast, usually continental style (bread, croissant, jam, and tea or coffee), but sometimes buffet style. Where two prices are given, the first is for continental breakfast, the second is for a buffet breakfast. (F = French francs)

Street parking is extremely difficult to find in Paris, and most hotels do not have parking lots or garages. Reservations are recommended for all restaurants: The greats are often booked well in advance, and the small ones fill up quickly. All the following restaurants serve French cuisine unless otherwise noted.

Little has been done to make the city's hotels and restaurants accessible to the disabled. "Accessible room" means that a wheelchair would be able to get into a room and move around, and "adapted" means that the bathroom is up to standards. However, there are no specific facilities for the disabled, and buildings may have one or more steps to navigate before entering. Travelers with disabilities should check when booking to make sure the hotel or restaurant meets their needs.

If your hotel is on a main street, ask for a room at the back where you will not be disturbed by traffic noise.

Grading system
✪✪✪✪ Four stars indicate a hotel with a restaurant and all rooms with private bath/shower rooms.
✪✪✪ Three-star hotels have at least 80 percent of the rooms with bath/shower, and offer breakfast in the room.
✪✪ Two-star establishments must have 40 percent of the rooms with bath/shower and a telephone in each room.
✪ One-star hotels offer plain but adequate accommodation. Room price categories are given only for guidance and do not take into account seasonal variations.

In high season, always try to book in advance, if possible confirming by fax. You may be asked for a deposit or credit card number.

RESTAURANTS
One of the great pleasures of visiting France is its glorious food, and Paris is no exception. Many hotels have their own restaurants, and some restaurants also have rooms to rent. Restaurants in this directory are listed by price then in alphabetical order.
L = lunch
D = dinner
See also the menu reader on pp. 263–64.

Credit & debit cards
Many hotels and restaurants accept all major cards. Smaller ones may only accept some, as shown in their entry. Abbreviations used are: AE American Express, DC Diners Club, MC MasterCard, V Visa.

Dining hours
Lunch usually starts around midday, and continues until 2 p.m. Dinner is usually eaten around 8 p.m., but may start about 7 p.m. At the height of the season, or if you have a particular place in mind, do make a reservation.

Menus must by law be displayed outside any establishment serving food, and studying and comparing these before making your choice is part of the pleasure. Most restaurants offer one or more prix-fixe menus, set menus at a fixed price, sometimes including wine. Otherwise (and usually more expensively), you order individual items à la carte—from the menu. The French usually eat a salad after the main course and sometimes with the cheese course, which always comes before dessert. Bread and water are supplied free. (French tap water is safe to drink.)

Although smoking is now forbidden in all public places in France, it is in fact still widely accepted, and you should specify if you prefer a non-smoking (non-fumeurs) section.

Cafés
Although their numbers have declined in recent years, cafés remain a French institution, good for morning coffee, leisurely drinks, modest meals, or just people-watching. They are usually busy all day, opening early to serve the traditional grand crème (large cup of white coffee) with croissants to people on their way to work.

Tipping
A service charge is usually

included in the bill. Only add more if the service has been particularly good.

THE ISLANDS

The Île de la Cité and the Île St.-Louis, while major sightseeing attractions, are home to mostly minor restaurants. There are, however, a few cozy and charming hotels, especially on the Île St.-Louis.

HOTELS

🏨 DES DEUX ÎLES
$$$ ✪✪✪
59 RUE ST.-LOUIS-EN-L'ÎLE, 75004
TEL 01 43 26 13 35
FAX 01 43 29 60 25
Located on the chic Île St.-Louis. Small, attractive rooms with exposed wooden beams. Breakfast: 55F.
🛈 17 🚇 Pont Marie 🔁 🅢 🅢 AE, MC, V

🏨 DU JEU DE PAUME
$$$ ✪✪✪✪
54 RUE ST.-LOUIS-EN-L'ÎLE, 75004
TEL 01 43 26 14 18
FAX 01 40 46 02 76
A 17th-century tennis court creatively converted into a hotel with striking mezzanines. Rooms are comfortable and attractive, but small. Garden. Breakfast: 80F.
🛈 32 + suites 🚇 Pont Marie 🔁 🅢 🐦 🅢 All major cards

🏨 DE LUTÈCE
$$$ ✪✪✪
65 RUE ST.-LOUIS-EN-L'ÎLE, 75004
TEL 01 43 26 23 52
FAX 01 43 29 60 25
A fire burns in the lobby's fireplace, and each modest room has an interesting detail, like exposed beams or a pretty mirror. Breakfast: 47F.
🛈 23 🚇 Pont Marie 🅢 AE, MC, V

🏨 HENRI IV
$ ✪
25 PLACE DAUPHINE, 75001
TEL 01 43 54 44 53
For those on a tight budget. Clean and basic. Shared bathroom on each floor.
🛈 22 🚇 Pont-Neuf or Cité 🅢 No credit cards

QUARTIER LATIN

Small hotels are the rule in the famous student quarter, which has hundreds of cheap restaurants (often of dubious quality), as well as one of the most expensive, La Tour d'Argent.

HOTELS

🏨 LE CLOS MÉDICIS
$$$$ ✪✪✪
56 RUE MONSIEUR-LE-PRINCE, 75006
TEL 01 43 29 10 80
FAX 01 43 54 26 90
Designer furnishings amid stone walls and exposed beams in this mid-19th-century hotel. Small, comfortable rooms, charming staff, fireplace, and garden. Breakfast: 60F.
🛈 38 🚇 Odéon or RER: Luxembourg 🔁 🅢 🅢 All major cards

🏨 DES GRANDS HOMMES
$$$ ✪✪✪
17 PLACE DU PANTHÉON, 75005
TEL 01 46 34 19 60
FAX 01 43 26 67 32
Ask for a room with a view of the Panthéon across the street in this pretty, comfortable hotel. Some rooms have canopy beds and exposed beams. Breakfast: 50F.
🛈 32 + suites 🚇 Maubert Mutualité or RER: Luxembourg 🔁 🅢 🅢 All major cards

🏨 LIBERTEL MAXIM
$$ ✪✪
28 RUE CENSIER, 75005
TEL 01 43 31 16 15

FAX 01 43 31 93 87
Adorable little rooms decorated in Toile-de-Jouy fabric, near the Jardin des Plantes. Breakfast: 50F.
🛈 36 🚇 Censier Daubenton 🔁 🅢 🅢 All major cards

🏨 PARC SAINT-SÉVERIN
$$ ✪✪✪
22 RUE DE LA PARCHEMINERIE, 75005
TEL 01 43 54 32 17
FAX 01 43 54 70 71
An attractively decorated hotel with a mix of modern and antique furnishings on a quiet street. Bright, spacious rooms, some with rooftop terraces. Breakfast: 55F.
🛈 27 🚇 St.-Michel or Cluny La Sorbonne 🔁 🅢 🅢 All major cards

🏨 GAY-LUSSAC
$ ✪
29 RUE GAY-LUSSAC, 75005
TEL 01 43 54 23 96
FAX 01 40 51 79 49
Cheap, clean, comfortable, and located near the Luxembourg Garden. Breakfast included in price of room.
🛈 35 (many do not have private bathrooms) 🚇 RER: Luxembourg 🔁 🅢 No credit cards

RESTAURANTS

🍴 LA TOUR D'ARGENT
$$$$$
15 QUAI TOURNELLE, 75005
TEL 01 40 46 71 11
Its reputation may have slipped a little, and it now has only two Michelin stars instead of three, but it's still a great favorite with visitors for its duckling, and its spectacular views of the Seine and Notre-Dame. Fixed-price L menu.
🚇 Maubert Mutualité ⊕ Closed Mon. 🔁 🅢 🅢 All major cards

🍴 BALZAR
$$
49 RUE DES ÉCOLES, 75005
TEL 01 43 54 13 67

An old-fashioned brasserie as we like them: simple, handsome, mirrored decor and good, solid food.
🚇 Cluny La Sorbonne 💲
💳 AE, MC, V

🍴 LE BISTRO D'À CÔTÉ
$$
16 BOULEVARD ST.-GERMAIN, 75005
TEL 01 43 54 59 10
One of famed chef Michel Rostang's lower-priced bistros. Reliably good food, lively ambience, and attractive decor. Fixed-price menus.
🚇 Maubert Mutualité 💲
💳 AE, MC, V

🍴 BOUILLON RACINE
$$
3 RUE RACINE, 75006
TEL 01 44 32 15 60
Amazing art nouveau decor, and good Belgian cooking (and beer). Typical dishes include a fish *waterzoi* (a type of stew) and veal sweetbreads braised in beer. Fixed-price menus.
🚇 Cluny La Sorbonne 💲
💳 AE, MC, V

🍴 LA TABLE D'AUDE
$$
8 RUE DE VAUGIRARD, 75006
TEL 01 43 26 36 36
Rich dishes like cassoulet from the south of France in a small, friendly, family-run restaurant. Fixed-price menus.
🚇 Cluny La Sorbonne
🕐 Closed Sun., & three weeks in Aug. Reservations for Mon. D and Sat. L 💲
💳 All major cards

ST.-GERMAIN & MONTPARNASSE

The chic and beautiful St.-Germain-des-Prés neighborhood has many wonderfully charming hotels, some of them quite reasonably priced, as well as a plethora of interesting little restaurants. While lively Montparnasse is more downmarket, it has its own points of interest, with plenty of artistic and literary associations.

HOTELS

🏨 LE MÉRIDIEN
🍴 MONTPARNASSE
$$$$$ ◗◗◗◗
19 RUE DE COMMANDANT MOUCHOTTE, 75014
TEL 01 44 36 44 36
FAX 01 44 36 49 00
A modern, high-rise hotel with business facilities and good views from the upper floors. Choice of two restaurants. Breakfast: 129F (buffet) 99F (continental).
🛏 953 + suites
🚇 Montparnasse-Bienvenue
🛗 💲 💳 💳 All major cards

🏨 RELAIS CHRISTINE
$$$$$ ◗◗◗◗
3 RUE CHRISTINE, 75006
TEL 01 40 51 60 80
FAX 01 40 51 60 81
Discreet, Left Bank luxury in a former convent, in whose vaulted, 13th-century kitchens breakfast is served. Garden and courtyard. Breakfast: 145F (buffet) 115F (continental).
🛏 51 + suites 🚇 Odéon
🅿 🛗 💲 💳 💳 All major cards

🏨 DE L'ABBAYE
$$$$ ◗◗◗
10 RUE CASSETTE, 75006
TEL 01 45 44 38 11
FAX 01 45 48 07 86
Charming 18th-century building with a courtyard garden on a quiet street. Four duplex suites with terraces. Some rooms are small. Breakfast: 34F.
🛏 46 + suites 🚇 St.-Sulpice
🛗 💲 💳 AE, MC, V

🏨 L'HÔTEL
$$$$ ◗◗◗◗
13 RUE DES BEAUX-ARTS, 75006
TEL 01 44 41 99 00
FAX 01 43 25 64 81
Has a marvelous, round stairway and extravagantly decorated rooms. Oscar Wilde died in room 16; recent guests have included Robert de Niro and Mick Jagger. Breakfast: 110F.

🛏 20 + suites 🚇 St.-Germain-des-Prés 🛗 💲
💳 All major cards

🏨 LUTÉTIA
🍴 $$$$ ◗◗◗
45 BOULEVARD RASPAIL, 75006
TEL 01 49 54 46 46
FAX 01 49 54 46 00
A stunning, art deco pile whose past residents include James Joyce, Pablo Picasso, and Henri Matisse. Respected restaurant and brasserie. Breakfast: 75F/135F.
🛏 250 + suites 🚇 Sèvres-Babylone 🛗 💲 💳
💳 All major cards

🏨 DES SAINTS-PÈRES
$$$$/$$$ ◗◗◗
65 RUE DES STS.-PÈRES, 75006
TEL 01 45 44 50 00
FAX 01 45 44 90 83
Beloved of the fashion crowd, most of its antique-furnished rooms have views of the garden. Breakfast: 65F.
🛏 39 + suites 🚇 St.-Germain-des-Prés 🛗 💲
💳 💳 AE, MC, V

🏨 D'ANGLETERRE SAINT-GERMAIN-DES-PRÉS
$$$ ◗◗◗
44 RUE JACOB, 75006
TEL 01 42 60 34 72
FAX 01 42 60 16 93
A friendly staff, historical associations (Washington Irving and Ernest Hemingway stayed here), and loads of charm in individually decorated rooms keep regulars coming back. Breakfast: 60F.
🛏 27 + suites 🚇 St.-Germain-des-Prés 🛗
💳 All major cards

🏨 LENOX ST.-GERMAIN
$$$ ◗◗◗
9 RUE DE L'UNIVERSITÉ, 75007
TEL 01 42 96 10 95
FAX 01 42 61 52 83
A fashionable, intimate, Left Bank hotel with smallish rooms. Bar. Breakfast: 50F (continental) 75F (buffet).
🛏 34 + suites 🚇 St.-Germain-des-Prés or Rue

du Bac 🔲 ⬛ All major cards

🏨 **LEFT BANK
ST.-GERMAIN
BEST WESTERN**
$$$ ◐◐◐
9 RUE DE L'ANCIENNE
COMÉDIE, 75006
TEL 01 43 54 01 70
FAX 01 43 26 17 14
In the heart of the Left Bank, this small hotel has an antique-furnished lobby, wooden beams, and marble bathrooms. Breakfast included in price of room.
🚪 31 + 1 suite 🚇 Odéon
🔲 🔆 ⬛ All major cards

🏨 **DE L'ODÉON**
$$$ ◐◐◐
13 RUE ST.-SULPICE, 75006
TEL 01 43 25 70 11
FAX 01 43 29 97 34
Antiques and tapestries in this 16th-century manor house create a romantic setting. Most rooms overlook garden. Breakfast: 65F.
🚪 29 🚇 Odéon 🔲 🔆
⬛ All major cards

🏨 **ODÉON-HÔTEL**
$$$ ◐◐◐
3 RUE DE L'ODÉON, 75006
TEL 01 43 25 90 67
FAX 01 43 25 55 98
A quiet location between the Boulevard St.-Germain and the Luxembourg Garden, with individually decorated rooms. Breakfast: 70F.
🚪 33 🚇 Odéon 🔲 🔆
⬛ All major cards

🏨 **ISTRIA**
$$ ◐◐
29 RUE CAMPAGNE-PREMIÈRE,
75014
TEL 01 43 20 91 82
FAX 01 43 22 48 45
A well-kept, comfortable hotel on a quiet street near Montparnasse, its past guests have included such greats as Rainer Maria Rilke, Marcel Duchamp, and Man Ray. Breakfast: 45F.
🚪 26 🚇 Raspail 🔆 ⬛ All major cards

🏨 **RIVE GAUCHE**
$ ◐◐
25 RUE DES STS.-PÈRES, 75006
TEL 01 42 60 34 68
FAX 01 42 61 29 78
Clean, comfortable rooms, and a cheap price for this classy location. Breakfast: 40F.
🚪 21 🚇 St.-Germain-des-
Prés 🔲 ⬛ All major cards

RESTAURANTS

🍴 **CLOSERIE DES LILAS**
$$$$
171 BOULEVARD
MONTPARNASSE, 75006
TEL 01 40 51 34 50
A new chef has improved the quality of the food at this famous Montparnasse bar/brasserie/restaurant, a former hangout of Hemingway, Picasso, Apollinaire, Lenin, and more. A good place to drink amid the literary crowd. Fixed-price menus available.
🚇 Vavin ⬛ All major cards

🍴 **LE DUC**
$$$$
243 BOULEVARD RASPAIL,
75014
TEL 01 43 20 96 30
The freshest fish, prepared simply and served in a yacht-like setting. Fixed-price menus available.
🚇 Raspail ⏰ Closed Sat. L, Sun., Mon., & public hols. 🔆
⬛ All major cards

🍴 **JACQUES CAGNA**
$$$$
14 RUE DES GRANDS-
AUGUSTINS, 75006
TEL 01 43 26 49 39
Once the darling of the food critics, this famous chef's reputation has slipped recently. Specialties include *tarte aux chipirons* (small squid), and beef fillet with truffles. Fixed-price menus available.
🚇 St.-Michel ⏰ Closed Sat. L, Mon. L, Sun., first 3 weeks of Aug. & Christmas 🔆
⬛ All major cards

🍴 **LES BOOKINISTES**
$$$
53 QUAI DES GRANDS-
AUGUSTINS, 75006
TEL 01 43 25 45 94
A fashionable bistro on the quays of the Seine, owned by top chef Guy Savoy. Try the lamb with rosemary and celeriac, or the artichoke and mushroom crêpe with fennel-flavored sauce. Fixed-price lunch menus available.
🚇 St.-Michel ⏰ Closed Sat. L & Sun. 🔆 ⬛ AE, MC, V

🍴 **LES BOUCHONS DE
FRANÇOIS CLERC**
$$$
12 RUE DE L'HÔTEL COLBERT,
75005
TEL 01 43 54 15 34
Bourgeois ambience and decor, fine food, friendly service, and wonderful wines at cost-price. Fixed-price menus available.
🚇 St.-Michel ⏰ Closed Sat. L & Sun. 🔆 ⬛ AE, MC, V

🍴 **LE DÔME**
$$$
108 BOULEVARD
MONTPARNASSE, 75014
TEL 01 43 35 25 81
Fine fish in the lively ambience of this famous Montparnasse brasserie. À la carte menu.
🚇 Montparnasse 🔆 ⬛ All major cards

🍴 **LA ROTISSERIE D'EN
FACE**
$$$
2 RUE CHRISTINE, 75006
TEL 01 43 26 40 98
A lower-priced annex of chef Jacques Cagna's restaurant, with creative bistro food and a cozy atmosphere. Fixed-price menus available.
🚇 St.-Michel ⏰ Closed Sat. L & Sun. 🔆 ⬛ All major cards

🍴 **LA BASTIDE ODÉON**
$$
7 RUE CORNEILLE, 75006
TEL 01 43 26 03 65
Provençal cooking with a modern twist in a pretty

setting. Fixed-price lunch menus available.

🚇 Odéon   🕐 Closed Sun., Mon., & Aug.   💳 MC, V

🍴 BRASSERIE LIPP
$$
151 BOULEVARD ST.-GERMAIN, 75006
TEL 01 45 48 53 91
A place to go for its historical and literary connections (patrons have included Ernest Hemingway and F. Scott Fitzgerald), and its wonderful, intact, turn-of-the-20th-century decor, but not for the indifferent food and service. Fixed-price menu available.

🚇 St.-Germain-des-Prés   🈳
💳 AE, MC, V

🍴 CAFÉ DE FLORE
$$
172 BOULEVARD ST.-GERMAIN, 75006
TEL 01 45 48 55 26
The prices are astronomical, but it's worth a visit for the art deco interior, classy service, and (French) celebrity-spotting opportunities.

🚇 St.-Germain-des-Prés   🈳
💳 AE, MC, V

🍴 LA CAGOUILLE
$$
10 PLACE CONSTANTIN BRANCUSI, 75014
TEL 01 43 22 09 01
Exquisite seafood, yummy desserts, and friendly service in a stark setting. Outdoor terrace in summer. Fixed-price menus available.

🚇 Gaîté   💳 AE, MC, V

🍴 LA COUPOLE
$$
102 BOULEVARD MONTPARNASSE, 75014
TEL 01 43 20 14 20
A lively, art deco brasserie with great service, good food, and impeccable historical credentials—everyone who was anyone came here in the 1920s. Fixed-price menu available.

🚇 Montparnasse   🛗   🈳
💳 All major cards

🍴 L'OS À MOELLE
$$
3 RUE VASCO DE GAMA, 75015
TEL 01 45 57 27 27
Trained by Christian Constant, the young chef makes a serious effort to provide refined cuisine at low prices. Fixed-price menus available.

🚇 Lourmel   🕐 Closed Sun., Mon., & Aug.   💳 AE, MC, V

🍴 LE PETIT SAINT BENOÎT
$
4 RUE ST.-BENOÎT, 75006
TEL 01 42 60 27 92
Cheap, funky, old-time bistro with decent foods.

🚇 St.-Germain-des-Prés
🕐 Closed Sun. & Aug.
💳 No credit cards

🍴 POLIDOR
$
41 RUE MONSIEUR-LE-PRINCE, 75006
TEL 01 43 26 95 34
A 19th-century bistro that serves classics like boeuf bourguignon at basic prices. Fixed-price menus available.

🚇 Odéon   💳 No credit cards

The heart of the city is noisy and congested, but the hotels listed below are on relatively quiet streets. Many of the area's restaurants are throwbacks to the days when Les Halles was the major food market; they serve hearty, copious meals that are heavy on meat.

HOTEL

🏨 BRITANNIQUE
$$$ 🅿🅿🅿
20 AVENUE VICTORIA, 75001
TEL 01 42 33 74 59
FAX 01 42 33 82 65
Cozy, British-style comfort on a quiet street in the busy city center. Breakfast: 55F.

🛏 40   🚇 Châtelet   🛗
💳 All major cards

🏨 SAINT-MERRY
This used to be a presbytery of the St.-Merri Church, whose flying buttresses enter some of the rooms. Expensive rooms have authentic, carved-wood Gothic furnishings; cheaper ones might not have private bathrooms, but do have showers, and are charmingly decorated with matching wallpaper, bedspreads, and curtains. Breakfast: 55F.

$$$/$$ 🅿🅿🅿
78 RUE DE LA VERRERIE, 75004
TEL 01 42 78 14 15
FAX 01 40 29 06 82
🛏 12 + 1 suite
🚇 Hôtel-de-Ville
💳 MC, V

RESTAURANTS

🍴 GÉRARD BESSON
$$$$
5 RUE DU COQ-HÉRON, 75001
TEL 01 42 33 14 74
The chef serves the freshest produce in his creatively prepared, classic dishes. Fixed-price menus available.

🚇 Les Halles   🕐 Closed Sat. L, Sun. and July–Aug.   🈳
💳 All major cards

🍴 PHARAMOND
$$$$
24 RUE DE LA GRANDE-TRUANDERIE, 75001
Norman specialties in an authentic, turn-of-the-century, art deco bistro. Fixed-price menus available.

🚇 Les Halles   🕐 Closed Sun. & Mon. L   💳 All major cards

🍴 LE BÉARN
$$
2 PLACE STE.-OPPORTUNE, 75001
TEL 01 42 36 93 35
Classic French dishes at modest prices in a small bistro with 1950s decor.

 Châtelet Closed Sun.
 MC, V

▮ CAFÉ BEAUBOURG
$$
100 RUE ST.-MARTIN, 75004
TEL 01 48 87 63 96
A good place for a snack or a
drink in a fashionable, designer
atmosphere, right next to the
Pompidou Center.
 Rambuteau All
major cards

▮ AU PIED DE COCHON
$$
6 RUE COQUILLIÈRE, 75001
TEL 01 40 13 77 00
Lively, all-night restaurant
specializing in pig's feet and
shellfish platters, among other
brasserie dishes. Fixed-price
menus available.
 Louvre or Les Halles
 Open 24 hours a day,
 All major cards

▮ LA POULE AU POT
$$
9 RUE VAUVILLIERS, 75001
TEL 01 42 36 32 96
A popular, all-night restaurant
serving traditional food that
attracts a variety of night-owls
and theater people. Fixed-
price menu available.
 Les Halles Open
every day until 5 a.m.
 MC, V

▮ BISTROT BEAUBOURG
$
25 RUE QUINCAMPOIX, 75004
TEL 01 42 77 48 02
Lively, bohemian atmosphere,
with decent, inexpensive food,
near the Pompidou Center.
 Rambuteau MC, V

MARAIS/BASTILLE

The historic Marais does not
have many hotels, but there are
a few interesting options, as
well as lots of good, small
restaurants. The bustling Bastille
area is slowing moving upscale,
thanks to the opera house, but
is still not the most desirable
area to stay.

HOTELS

▦ HOLIDAY INN PARIS RÉPUBLIQUE
$$$$$ ○○○○
10 PLACE DE LA RÉPUBLIQUE,
75011
TEL 01 43 55 44 34
FAX 01 47 00 32 34
Typical, international-style
rooms in a turn-of-the-
century building. Courtyard
garden, bar. Breakfast: 125F.
 318 + suites
 République
 All major cards

▦ PAVILLON DE LA REINE
$$$$$ ○○○○
28 PLACE DES VOSGES, 75003
TEL 01 40 29 19 19
FAX 01 40 29 19 20
Antique-furnished rooms,
some with four-poster beds.
Garden. Breakfast: 115F/145F.
 55 + suites St.-Paul
     All major
cards

▦ CARON DE BEAUMARCHAIS
$$$ ○○○
12 RUE VIEILLE-DU-TEMPLE,
75004
TEL 01 42 72 34 12
FAX 01 42 72 34 63
The 18th century brought
back to life in this pretty hotel.
Breakfast: 54F/78F.
 19 St.-Paul or Hôtel-
de-Ville   All
major cards

▦ LE PAVILLON BASTILLE
$$$ ○○○
65 RUE DE LYON, 75012
TEL 01 43 43 65 65
FAX 01 43 43 96 52
Just across from the Opéra-
Bastille, a small, pleasant hotel
with modern, designer decor.
Breakfast: 75F.
 25 + 1 suite Bastille
     All major
cards

▦ DE NICE
$$ ○○
42 BIS RUE DE RIVOLI, 75004

TEL 01 42 78 55 29
FAX 01 42 78 36 07
Lovely antique furnishings
and a central location at
very reasonable prices.
Breakfast: 35F.
 23 Hôtel de Ville
 MC, V

▦ GRAND HÔTEL JEANNE D'ARC
$ ○○
3 RUE DE JARENTE, 75004
TEL 01 48 87 62 11
FAX 01 48 87 37 31
A fine little hotel, much in
demand because of its
location and low prices.
Breakfast: 38F.
 36 St.-Paul
 V

▦ GRAND HÔTEL DU LOIRET
$ ○○
8 RUE DES MAUVAIS-GARÇONS,
75004
TEL 01 48 87 77 00
FAX 01 48 04 96 56
Clean, cheap, modest hotel on
the evocatively named street
of "bad boys."
 30 Hôtel-de-Ville
 AE, MC, V

RESTAURANTS

🍴 L'AMBROISIE
$$$$$
9 PLACE DES VOSGES, 75004
TEL 01 42 78 51 45
Classic French food (too classic for some) by chef Bernard Pacaud in a highly refined setting.
🚇 St.-Paul 🕐 Closed Sun., Mon., first 3 weeks of Aug., & school vacation in Feb. 🔌
💳 AE, MC, V

🍴 AU BASCOU
$$$
38 RUE RÉAUMUR, 75003
TEL 01 42 72 69 25
Basque regional specialties lovingly prepared in a lively little restaurant run by a Basque native. Fixed-price L menu available.
🚇 Arts et Métiers 🕐 Closed Mon. L, Sat. L, Sun., Aug., & Christmas week 💳 AE, MC, V

🍴 BISTRO DU DÔME
$$$
2 RUE DE LA BASTILLE, 75004
TEL 01 48 04 88 44
Good seafood at lower prices than in the original Dôme on the Left Bank.
🚇 Bastille 🔌 💳 AE, MC, V

🍴 LE 404
$$$
69 RUE DES GRAVILLIERS, 75003
TEL 01 42 74 57 81
Fashionable Moroccan restaurant with extra-fine couscous, tagines, and *pastillas*. Fixed-price L menu available.
🚇 Arts et Métiers 🕐 Closed Mon. & L in Aug. 🔌 💳 All major cards

🍴 LE TRAIN BLEU
$$$
GARE DE LYON,
20 BOULEVARD DIDEROT,
75012
TEL 01 43 43 09 06
Go for a drink to see the breathtaking belle epoque decoration in this train-station restaurant; rather than for its typical brasserie

food. Fixed-price menu available.
🚇 Gare de Lyon 🛗 💳 All major cards

🍴 BOFINGER
$$
5 & 7 RUE DE LA BASTILLE, 75004
TEL 01 42 72 87 82
Huge brass mirrors and decor announce a classic brasserie, beloved by tourists and residents alike. Fixed-price menu available.
🚇 Bastille 🔌 💳 All major cards

🍴 CHEZ OMAR
$$
47 RUE DE BRETAGNE, 75003
TEL 01 42 72 36 26
Excellent couscous, old-fashioned bistro decor, and extra-friendly service.
🚇 Filles-de-Calvaire 🕐 Closed Sun. L 💳 No credit cards

SOMETHING SPECIAL

🍴 CLOWN BAR
This unusual restaurant/wine bar next to the Cirque d'Hiver (Winter Circus), with 1920s art nouveau decor and colorful, original, clown-motif tiles, guarantees a lively evening. Creative, quality French cooking, warm ambience, and a good selection of reasonably priced wines. Reservations recommended.
$$
114 RUE AMELOT, 75011
TEL 01 43 55 87 35
🚇 Filles-de-Calvaire 🕐 Closed Sun. L 💳 MC, V

🍴 JULIEN
$$
16 RUE DU FAUBOURG-ST.-DENIS, 75010
TEL 01 47 70 12 06
A brasserie with an opulent, art nouveau decor, lively service, and tasty food. Fixed-

price menu available.
🚇 Strasbourg-St.-Denis 🔌 💳 All major cards

🍴 LE PETIT BOFINGER
$$
6 RUE DE LA BASTILLE, 75004
TEL 01 42 72 05 23
Friendly service, 1950s decor, and good bistro food at reasonable prices in the annex of the famous Bofinger (see entry this page). Fixed-price menu available.
🚇 Bastille 🛗 🔌 💳 All major cards

🍴 AU SOLEIL EN COIN
$$
21 RUE RAMBUTEAU, 75004
TEL 01 42 72 26 25
Homey little restaurant with Provençal decor, a friendly owner, and carefully prepared dishes.
🚇 Rambuteau 🕐 Closed Sat. L & Sun. 💳 MC, V

SOMETHING SPECIAL

🍴 LA TARTINE
The red banquettes have sprung, and the owner must be at least 90, but this shows what an authentic Parisian wine bar of 50 years ago was like. Stop for a glass of wine and a *tartine* (open-faced sandwich) before this relic, once frequented by Trotsky, is gone.
$
24 RUE DE RIVOLI, 75004
TEL 01 42 72 76 85
🚇 Hôtel-de-Ville or St.-Paul 🕐 Closed after 10 p.m.; Tues., Wed. a.m., & first 2 weeks of Aug.
💳 No credit cards

🍴 LE PETIT FER À CHEVAL
$
30 RUE VIEILLE-DU-TEMPLE, 75004
TEL 01 42 72 47 47
Fashionable little bar/restaurant; one of the few places in the Marais where

you can eat till 1 a.m.
🚇 St.-Paul or Hôtel-de-Ville
🅂 MC, V

🍴 LE TRUMILOU
$
84 QUAI DE L'HÔTEL-DE-VILLE,
75004
TEL 01 42 77 63 98
An old-time bistro on the
quays of the Seine. Fixed-price
menus available.
🚇 Hôtel-de-Ville or Pont
Marie 🅂 MC, V

THE LOUVRE &
PALAIS-ROYAL

A few grand hotels and some
chic restaurants can be found in
this palatial neighborhood.

HOTELS

🏨 INTER-CONTINENTAL
🍴 PARIS
$$$$$ 😀😀😀😀
3 RUE CASTIGLIONE, 75001
TEL 01 44 77 11 11
FAX 01 44 77 14 60
The century-old splendor of
this hotel has been recently
refurbished. Courtyard
garden, restaurant. Breakfast:
115F/165F.
🛏 450 + suites
🚇 Concorde 🔄 ❄ ✦
🅂 All major cards

🏨 DU LOUVRE
🍴 $$$$$ 😀😀😀😀😀
1 PLACE ANDRÉ MALRAUX,
75001
TEL 01 44 58 38 38
FAX 01 44 58 38 01
Camille Pissarro, the 19th-
century Impressionist artist,
painted the view from his
window in this luxury hotel.
Café. Breakfast: 125F
🛏 199 + suites 🚇 Palais-
Royal 🔄 ✦ 🅂 All major
cards

🏨 MEURICE
$$$$$ 😀😀😀😀
228 RUE DE RIVOLI, 75001
TEL 01 44 58 10 10
FAX 01 44 58 10 15
This lavish hotel was once

Salvador Dalí's favorite in
Paris. Business facilities.
Breakfast: 175F/250F.
🛏 180 + suites
🚇 Concorde 🔄 ❄ ✦
🅂 All major cards

🏨 DE LA PLACE
DU LOUVRE
$$$ 😀😀😀
21 RUE DES PRÊTRES-ST.-
GERMAIN-L'AUXERROIS, 75001
TEL 01 42 33 78 68
FAX 01 42 33 09 95
Facing the Louvre. Rooms
decorated in beige and white.
Breakfast (55F) served in an
ancient, vaulted basement.
🛏 20 🚇 Louvre or Pont
Neuf 🔄 ✦ 🅂 All major
cards

🏨 AU RELAIS DU
LOUVRE
$$$ 😀😀😀
19 RUE DES PRÊTRES-ST.-
GERMAIN-L'AUXERROIS, 75001
TEL 01 40 41 96 42
FAX 01 40 41 96 44
A cozy little hotel between
the Louvre and St.-Germain-
l'Auxerrois. Breakfast: 60F.
🛏 21 + suites 🚇 Louvre or
Pont-Neuf 🅿 🔄 🅂 All
major cards

RESTAURANTS

🍴 CARRÉ DES
FEUILLANTS
$$$$$
14 RUE CASTIGLIONE, 75001
TEL 01 42 86 82 82
Excellent traditional,
southwestern French cuisine:
variations on foie gras and
truffles. Fixed-price menus
available.
🚇 Concorde or Tuileries
🕐 Closed Sat. L, Sun., & Aug.
✦ 🅂 All major cards

🍴 MACÉO
$$$
15 RUE DES PETITS-CHAMPS,
75001
TEL 01 42 97 53 85
A new, à la mode restaurant.
Second Empire decor and
creative cuisine with an

international flavor. Fixed-price
menus available.
🚇 Pyramides 🕐 Closed
Sun. 🅂 MC, V

🍴 LE GRAND VÉFOUR
The most romantic
restaurant in Paris has a
jewel-box decor (unchanged
since the mid-19th century),
a fine Savoyard chef,
charming staff, and an
amazing list of historical
customers (Napoleon,
Cocteau, Colette, Garbo).
This 3-Michelin-star
restaurant is the place for
those who want to splurge.
Recommended dish: the
incredibly rich and complex
lièvre à la royale (hare cooked
in red wine and stuffed with
foie gras and truffles). Fixed-
price menus available.
$$$$$
17 RUE DE BEAUJOLAIS,
75001
TEL 01 42 96 56 27
🚇 Palais-Royal or Bourse
🕐 Closed Sat., Sun., &
Aug. ✦ 🅂 All major
cards

🍴 RESTAURANT DU
PALAIS ROYAL
$$$
110 GALERIE DE VALOIS,
JARDINS DU PALAIS-ROYAL,
75001
TEL 01 40 20 00 27
The main reason to go to this
stylish restaurant with fine, but
not outstanding, food is for its
terrace in the peaceful Palais-
Royal garden.
🚇 Palais-Royal 🕐 Closed
Sun. May–Oct; Sun.& Sat. L
Nov.–April & Christmas
week 🅂 All major cards

🍴 AUX BONS CRUS
$$
7 RUE DES PETITS-CHAMPS,
75001
TEL 01 42 60 06 45
A wine bar that's been around
for nearly a century, with a

HOTELS & RESTAURANTS

corresponding ambience and traditional dishes. 🚇 Bourse or Palais-Royal 🕐 Closed Sun. & Mon. D 🔇 💳 MC, V

🍴 CAFÉ MARLY
$$
COUR NAPOLÉON, 93 RUE DE RIVOLI, 75001
TEL 01 49 26 06 60
Incredible setting in the Louvre for a chic, designer café-restaurant with fine international food.
🚇 Palais-Royal 🔇 💳 All major cards

🍴 LE GRAND COLBERT
$$
2 RUE VIVIENNE, 75002
TEL 01 42 86 87 88
Attractively restored brasserie decor, friendly service, and respectable food. Fixed-price menu available.
🚇 Bourse 💳 All major cards

🍴 JUVENILES
$$
47 RUE DE RICHELIEU, 75001
TEL 01 42 97 46 49
Small, laid-back, wine bar with tasty food and excellent international wines. Fixed-price menus available.
🚇 Palais-Royal 🕐 Closed Sun. 💳 MC, V

🍴 TOUPARY
$$
LA SAMARITAINE, MAGASIN 1, 2 QUAI DU LOUVRE, 75001
TEL 01 40 41 29 29
Forget the food (acceptable) and the decor (orange and turquoise), and enjoy the fabulous view over the Seine from this department-store restaurant. Fixed-price menus available.
🚇 Louvre 🕐 Closed Sun. 🔇 💳 All major cards

🍴 WILLI'S WINE BAR
$$
13 RUE DES PETITS-CHAMPS, 75001
TEL 01 42 61 05 09
Even the French like it,

although it's owned by an Englishman. Top-notch wines, fine cooking, debatable service. Fixed-price menu available.
🚇 Bourse 🕐 Closed Sun. 💳 MC, V

CHAMPS-ÉLYSÉES

The Champs-Élysées isn't what it used to be, but most of the palace hotels are located in its environs, along with some top restaurants.

HOTELS

🏨 ASTOR WESTIN
🍴 DEMEURE
$$$$$ ◆◆◆◆
11 RUE D'ASTORG, 75008
TEL 01 53 05 05 05
FAX 01 53 05 05 30
Elegant Regency-revival decor on a quiet street in a tiny neighborhood. Some rooms have balconies or terraces. Gourmet restaurant (see L'Astor, p. 250). Breakfast: 150F.
🛏 134 + suites 🚇 Champs-Élysées–Clemenceau 🛗 🔇 🔇 📺 💳 All major cards

🏨 BALZAC
🍴 $$$$$ ◆◆◆◆
6 RUE BALZAC, 75008
TEL 01 44 35 18 00
FAX 01 44 35 18 05
Luxurious, elegant, belle epoque building with huge rooms. The restaurant is the home of the great chef, Pierre Gagnaire (see Pierre Gagnaire, p. 250). Breakfast: 120F.
🛏 70 + suites 🚇 George-V 🛗 🔇 💳 All major cards

🏨 DE CRILLON
🍴 $$$$$ ◆◆◆◆
10 PLACE DE LA CONCORDE, 75008
TEL 01 44 71 15 00
FAX 01 44 71 15 02
One of the great palace hotels, with views over the Place de la Concorde toward

the Eiffel Tower. There are two restaurants: the gourmet Les Ambassadeurs (see p. 249) and L'Obelisque, more modest and less expensive. Winter garden, tea room, and English bar. Breakfast 185F (continental) 275F (buffet).
🛏 163 🚇 Concorde 🛗 🔇 🔇 📺 💳 All major cards

🏨 FOUR SEASONS
🍴 HOTEL GEORGE V
$$$$$ ◆◆◆◆
31 AVENUE GEORGE V, 75008
TEL 01 49 52 70 00
FAX 01 49 52 70 04
This venerable palace hotel with its fine antiques and tapestries reopened in 1999 after renovation. Courtyard garden and in-house restaurants. Breakfast: 170F.
🛏 260 🚇 George-V 🛗 🔇 🔇 📺

🏨 MARIGNAN-ÉLYSÉES
🍴 WESTIN DEMEURE
$$$$$ ◆◆◆◆
12 RUE MARIGNAN, 75008
TEL 01 40 76 34 56
FAX 01 40 76 34 34
Antique furnishings, a Beauvais tapestry in the salon, and comfortable, simply decorated rooms. Tea room. Breakfast: 150F.
🛏 57 + 16 duplex suites 🚇 Franklin D. Roosevelt 🛗 🔇 💳 All major cards

🏨 MÉRIDIEN ÉTOILE
🍴 $$$$$ ◆◆◆◆
81 BOULEVARD GOUVION ST.-CYR, 75017
TEL 01 40 68 34 34
FAX 01 40 55 67 88
Modern high-rise with standard comforts and little charm. The Lionel Hampton Jazz Club in the lobby presents live concerts every night. Two restaurants. Breakfast: 99F/129F.
🛏 1,025 + suites 🚇 Porte Maillot 🛗 🔇 🔇 💳 All major cards

PRICES

HOTELS

An indication of the cost of a double room without breakfast is given by **$** signs.

$$$$$	over $280
$$$$	$200–$280
$$$	$120–$200
$$	$80–$120
$	under $80

RESTAURANTS

An indication of the cost of a three-course dinner without drinks is given by **$** signs.

$$$$$	over $80
$$$$	$50–$80
$$$	$35–$50
$$	$20–$35
$	under $20

LE PLAZA ATHÉNÉE
$$$$$ ✪✪✪✪

25 AVENUE MONTAIGNE, 75008
TEL 01 53 67 66 65
FAX 01 53 67 66 66

The Parisian palace has rooms in Louis XV, Louis XVI, and Regency styles, chandeliers, and potted palms in the lobby. Two restaurants (see Le Régence, p. 250), bar, business facilities. Breakfast: 177F/263F.

🛈 255 + suites 🚇 Franklin D. Roosevelt 🔄 ❄ 🕘
🄫 All major cards

PRINCE DE GALLES
$$$$$ ✪✪✪✪

33 AVENUE GEORGE V, 75008
TEL 01 53 23 77 77
FAX 01 53 23 78 78

An art deco palace now owned by Sheraton; nicely spruced-up rooms with Toile-de-Jouy fabric and modern amenities. Business facilities. Breakfast: 155F/195F.

🛈 168 + suites
🚇 George-V 🔄 ❄ 🕘
🏋 🄫 All major cards

RAPHAËL
$$$$$ ✪✪✪✪

17 AVENUE KLÉBER, 75116
TEL 01 53 64 32 00
FAX 01 53 64 32 01

Truly classy, luxury hotel with a painting by Turner in the lobby. Spacious rooms amid elegant furnishings. Wonderful, wood-paneled bar. Business facilities. Breakfast: 140F/180F.

🛈 90 + suites 🚇 Charles-de-Gaulle–Étoile 🔄 ❄
❄ 🄫 All major cards

ROYAL MONCEAU
$$$$$ ✪✪✪✪

37 AVENUE HOCHE, 75008
TEL 01 42 99 88 00
FAX 01 42 99 89 90

A special, muted luxury distinguishes this establishment from the flash and glitter of the other palaces. Two restaurants, garden, spa, business facilities. Breakfast: 145F/200F.

🛈 219 + suites 🚇 Charles-de-Gaulle–Étoile 🅿 🔄
❄ ❄ 🎱 🏋 🄫 All major cards

VERNET
$$$$$ ✪✪✪✪

25 RUE VERNET, 75008
TEL 01 44 31 98 00
FAX 01 44 31 85 69

A highly intimate, luxurious gem. Fireplace and piano in the lobby, and Jacuzzis in all the bathrooms. Belle epoque gourmet restaurant; access to the Royal Monceau's spa (see entry above) and pool. Breakfast: 140F/180F.

🛈 57 + suites 🚇 George-V 🅿 🔄 ❄ 🏋 🄫 All major cards

WESTIN DEMEURE HÔTEL CASTILLE
$$$$$ ✪✪✪✪

33–37 RUE CAMBON, 75001
TEL 01 44 58 44 58
FAX 01 44 58 44 00

Venetian-style luxury near the Place Vendôme in a former annex of the Ritz. Italian restaurant with terrace. Breakfast: 150F.

🛈 107 + suites
🚇 Madeleine 🅿 🔄 ❄
❄ 🄫 All major cards

CAMBON
$$$$ ✪✪✪✪

3 RUE CAMBON, 75001
TEL 01 44 58 93 93
FAX 01 42 60 30 59

Stylish, modern comfort near the Place de la Concorde. Breakfast: 80F.

🛈 40 + suites 🚇 Concorde
🔄 ❄ 🄫 All major cards

MAJESTIC
$$$$ ✪✪✪✪

29 RUE DUMONT D'URVILLE, 75116
TEL 01 45 00 83 70
FAX 01 45 00 29 48

Bourgeois comfort, with period furnishings and spacious rooms, near the Arc de Triomphe. Breakfast: 80F.

🛈 27 + suites 🚇 Kléber
🔄 ❄ ❄ 🄫 All major cards

DE L'ÉLYSÉE
$$$ ✪✪✪

12 RUE DES SAUSSAIES, 75008
TEL 01 42 65 29 25
FAX 01 42 65 64 28

Antique furnishings and individually decorated rooms, some with views of the Eiffel Tower. Breakfast: 65F.

🛈 32 + suites
🚇 Miromesnil 🔄 ❄
🄫 All major cards

GALILÉO
$$$ ✪✪✪

54 RUE GALILÉE, 75008
TEL 01 47 20 66 06
FAX 01 47 20 67 17

An Aubusson tapestry hangs in the lounge, and the rooms are comfortable in this wonderfully refined small hotel. Breakfast: 50F.

🛈 27 🚇 George-V 🔄
❄ 🄫 AE, MC, V

RESTAURANTS

LES AMBASSADEURS
$$$$$

HÔTEL DE CRILLON
(see p. 248), 10 PLACE DE LA CONCORDE, 75008
TEL 01 44 71 16 16

Opulent marble decor, formal service, and new chef,

Dominique Bouchet, who is upholding the standards of this fine restaurant. Fixed-price menus available.
🚇 Concorde 💲 💳 All major cards

🍴 L'ASTOR
$$$$$
HÔTEL ASTOR WESTIN DEMEURE (see p. 248), 11 RUE D'ASTORG, 75008
TEL 01 53 05 05 20
Joël Robuchon, considered by some the greatest (retired) chef in France, "supervises" titular chef Eric Lecerf, with excellent results. Fixed-price menus available.
🚇 Champs-Élysées–Clemenceau 🕐 Closed Sat. & Sun. 💲 💳 All major cards

🍴 GUY SAVOY
$$$$$
18 RUE TROYON, 75017
TEL 01 43 80 40 61
An elegant, modern setting for this beloved chef's refined, creative haute cuisine. Fixed-price menu available.
🚇 Charles-de-Gaulle–Étoile 🕐 Closed Sat. L, Sun., & one week in July 💲 💳 MC, V

🍴 LEDOYEN
$$$$$
CARRÉ DES CHAMPS-ÉLYSÉES, 75008
TEL 01 53 05 10 01
One of the few female chefs to make her mark in the world of haute cuisine, Ghislaine Arabian holds her own in a parklike setting on the Champs-Élysées. Fixed-price menus available.
🚇 Champs-Élysées–Clemenceau 🅿 🕐 Closed Sat.-Sun., & Aug. 💲 💳 All major cards

🍴 LA MAISON BLANCHE
$$$$$
15 AVENUE MONTAIGNE, 75008
TEL 01 47 23 55 99
A rooftop terrace with views over the Seine, modern decor, and uneven cooking.
🚇 Alma-Marceau 🕐 Closed

Sat. L, Sun., & Aug. 💲
💳 AE, MC, V

🍴 MICHEL ROSTANG
$$$$$
20 RUE RENNEQUIN, 75017
TEL 01 47 63 40 77
Elegance and tradition dominate in this Savoyard chef's restaurant. Truffles are a specialty in season (Dec.–Mar.). Fixed-price menus available.
🚇 Ternes 🕐 Closed Sat. L, Sun., Mon. L. & first two weeks of Aug. 💲 💳 All major cards

🍴 PIERRE GAGNAIRE
$$$$$
HÔTEL BALZAC (see p. 248) 6 RUE BALZAC, 75008
TEL 01 44 35 18 25
One of France's greatest chefs recently opened this 3-Michelin-star restaurant and is wowing the city with his artistic haute cuisine. Specialties include *encornets* (small squid) with walnuts. Fixed-price menus available.
🚇 George-V 🕐 Closed Sat. & Sun. in Feb., & mid-July–mid-Aug. 💲 💳 All major cards

🍴 LE RÉGENCE
$$$$$
HÔTEL LE PLAZA ATHÉNÉE (see p. 249), 25 AVENUE MONTAIGNE, 75008
TEL 01 53 67 65 00
A new chef, Eric Briffard, is successfully running the kitchens at this classy hotel restaurant. Fixed-price menus available.
🚇 Franklin D. Roosevelt 💲 💳 All major cards

🍴 TAILLEVENT
$$$$$
15 RUE LAMENNAIS, 75008
TEL 01 44 95 15 01
A longstanding leader in haute cuisine, this restaurant, with 3 Michelin stars, has lovely dining rooms, refined cuisine, perfect service, and a renowned wine cellar.
🚇 George-V 🕐 Closed

Sat., Sun., public hols., & late July–late Aug. 💳 All major cards

🍴 CAP VERNET
$$$
82 AVENUE MARCEAU, 75008
TEL 01 47 20 20 40
Seafood in a Guy Savoy (see entry this page) annex with a pretty, blue-and-white decor. Fixed-price menu available.
🚇 Charles-de-Gaulle–Étoile 💲 💳 MC, V

SOMETHING SPECIAL

🍴 ANGÉLINA
Join the ladies-who-shop and the fashion crowd for a cup of sinfully rich, "African" hot chocolate in this elegant, turn-of-the-20th-century Viennese tea room. Busy weekends.
$$
226 RUE DE RIVOLI, 75001
TEL 01 42 60 82 00
🚇 Tuileries 🕐 Closed D & Tues. in Aug. 💲
💳 AE, MC, V

LES GRANDS BOULEVARDS

Pockets of tranquility, like the ritzy Place Vendôme, along with a few fine restaurants and brasseries, can be found here.

HOTELS

🏨 BRISTOL
🍴 $$$$$ ✪✪✪✪
112 RUE DU FAUBOURG ST.-HONORÉ, 75008
TEL 01 53 43 43 00
FAX 01 53 43 43 01
Top luxury and discretion for the rich and/or famous, with fine works of art and antiques, Gobelin tapestries, Persian carpets. Garden, bar, tea room. Breakfast: 185F/270F.
ℹ 192 + suites
🚇 Miromesnil 💲 💳
🏧 💳 All major cards

PRICES

HOTELS

An indication of the cost of a double room without breakfast is given by $ signs.

$$$$$	over $280
$$$$	$200–$280
$$$	$120–$200
$$	$80–$120
$	under $80

RESTAURANTS

An indication of the cost of a three-course dinner without drinks is given by $ signs.

$$$$$	over $80
$$$$	$50–$80
$$$	$35–$50
$$	$20–$35
$	under $20

🏨 COSTES
🍽 $$$$$ ✪✪✪✪
239 RUE ST.-HONORÉ, 75001
TEL 01 42 44 50 00
FAX 01 42 44 50 01
In Paris, the name "Costes" guarantees good design and the ultimate in fashionableness. Lavish, neoclassic decor. Bar, business facilities. Breakfast: 170F.
🛈 85 + suites 🚇 Tuileries
🚭 🎾 🍸 🞏 All major cards

🏨 LE GRAND HÔTEL
🍽 INTER-CONTINENTAL
$$$$$ ✪✪✪✪
2 RUE SCRIBE, 75009
TEL 01 40 07 32 32
FAX 01 42 66 12 51
The public rooms are truly grand, but some rooms are small. Home of the famous Café de la Paix; two other restaurants. Breakfast: 115F/165F.
🛈 514 + suites 🚇 Opéra
🚭 🚭 🚭 🞏 All major cards

🏨 RITZ
🍽 $$$$$ ✪✪✪✪
15 PLACE VENDÔME, 75001
TEL 01 43 16 30 30
FAX 01 43 16 31 78
All the gilt, crystal chandeliers,

and hushed luxury you would expect from the legendary Ritz. Gourmet restaurant (see L'Espadon this page), bar, health spa. Breakfast: 200F.
🛈 187 + suites
🚇 Concorde 🚭 🚭 🎾
🞏 🞏 All major cards

🏨 BEAU MANOIR
BEST WESTERN
$$$$ ✪✪✪✪
6 RUE DE L'ARCADE, 75008
TEL 01 42 66 03 07
FAX 01 42 68 03 00
An Aubusson tapestry, antique furnishings, marble bathrooms, and a quiet location. Breakfast 100F (continental) 80F (Buffet).
🛈 32 + suites 🚇 Madeleine
🅿 🚭 🚭 🞏 All major cards

🏨 LIDO BEST WESTERN
$$$$ ✪✪✪
4 PASSAGE DE LA MADELEINE, 75008
TEL 01 42 66 27 37
FAX 01 42 66 61 23
The rooms are recently renovated, with exposed beams, and the lobby is tastefully furnished with antiques. Breakfast: 80F.
🛈 32 🚇 Madeleine 🚭
🚭 🞏 All major cards

🏨 LE STENDHAL HÔTEL
$$$$ ✪✪✪✪
22 RUE D. CASANOVA, 75002
TEL 01 44 58 52 52
FAX 01 44 58 52 00
Stendhal once lived in this little hotel with charming, individually decorated rooms. Breakfast: 100F.
🛈 20 + suites 🚇 Opéra
🚭 🚭 🞏 All major cards

🏨 LIBERTEL LAFAYETTE
$$$ ✪✪✪
49 RUE LAFAYETTE, 75009
TEL 01 42 85 05 44
FAX 01 49 95 06 60
Recently redecorated hotel near the Opéra Garnier and the major department stores. Breakfast: 82F.
🛈 103 + suites 🚇 Le

Pelletier 🚭 🚭 🞏 All major cards

🏨 MANSART
$$$ ✪✪✪
5 RUE DES CAPUCINES, 75001
TEL 01 42 61 50 28
FAX 01 49 27 97 44
Next door to the Ritz, with spacious, individually decorated rooms and striking decoration in the lobby—an homage to Mansart, Louis XIV's architect. Breakfast: 60F.
🛈 57 + suites 🚇 Opéra
🚭 🞏 All major cards

🏨 GAILLON OPÉRA
BEST WESTERN
$$ ✪✪✪
9 RUE GAILLON, 75002
TEL 01 47 42 47 74
FAX 01 47 42 01 23
A helpful staff runs this tastefully decorated little hotel near the Opéra Garnier. Breakfast: 45F.
🛈 26 + 1 suite 🚇 Opéra
🚭 🚭 🞏 All major cards

RESTAURANTS

🍽 L'ESPADON
$$$$$
RITZ HÔTEL (see this page), 15 PLACE VENDÔME, 75001
TEL 01 43 16 30 80
It's the Ritz, and the setting and service are as they should be, though the food is not quite up to standards of late. Fixed-price menus available.
🚇 Concorde 🚭 🞏 All major cards

🍽 LUCAS-CARTON
$$$$$
9 PLACE DE LA MADELEINE, 75008
TEL 01 42 65 22 90
One of the most reliable haute cuisines, an art nouveau setting, and impeccable service, with 3 Michelin stars. Fixed-price menus available,
🚇 Madeleine 🕒 Closed Sat. L, Sun., & 3 weeks in Aug.
🚭 🞏 All major cards

HOTELS & RESTAURANTS

🍴 TERMINUS NORD
$$
23 RUE DE DUNKERQUE, 75010
TEL 01 42 85 05 15
Bustling brasserie with good food, perfect for a late dinner. Fixed-price menus available.
🚇 Gare du Nord 🕒
🅢 All major cards

🍴 LE VAUDEVILLE
$$
29 RUE VIVIENNE, 75002
TEL 01 40 20 04 62
Art deco decor, amiable, efficient service, lively ambience, and reasonable brasserie fare. Fixed-price menus available.
🚇 Bourse 🅢 All major cards

🍴 CHARTIER
$
7 RUE DU FAUBOURG-MONTMARTRE, 75009
TEL 01 47 70 86 29
Beloved by tourists for its cheap prices, it's worth going to for the setting of the 19th-century workingman's restaurant, but don't expect much from the food. Fixed-price menus.
🚇 Grands Boulevards
🅢 MC, V

TOUR EIFFEL & LES INVALIDES

A quiet, upper-class, residential area with some lovely hotels and fine eateries.

HOTELS

🏨 HILTON
🍴 **$$$$$ ✪✪✪✪**
18 AVENUE SUFFREN, 75015
TEL 01 44 38 56 00
FAX 01 44 38 56 10
Everything you would expect from a modern Hilton, but this one has the Eiffel Tower next door. Courtyard garden, business facilities. Breakfast: 105F/140F.
🛏 462 + suites 🚇 Bir-Hakeim 🅿 🕒 🅢 🛗
🅢 All major cards

🏨 MONTALEMBERT
🍴 **$$$$$ ✪✪✪✪**
3 RUE MONTALEMBERT, 75007
TEL 01 45 49 68 68
FAX 01 45 49 69 49
Fashionable hotel with designer lobby and attractive, contemporary- or traditional-style rooms. Business facilities, Le Montalembert restaurant (see p. 253). Breakfast: 100F.
🛏 56 + suites 🚇 Rue du Bac 🕒 🅢 🅢 All major cards

🏨 DUC DE SAINT-SIMON
$$$$ ✪✪✪
14 RUE ST.-SIMON, 75007
TEL 01 44 39 20 20
FAX 01 45 48 68 25
A luxurious haven on the Left Bank, with exquisite antique furnishings. Courtyard garden, charming basement breakfast room. Breakfast: 75F.
🛏 34 + suites 🚇 Rue du Bac 🕒 🅢 AE, MC, V

🏨 DE L'ACADÉMIE
$$$ ✪✪✪
32 RUE DES STS.-PÈRES, 75007
TEL 01 45 49 80 00
FAX 01 45 49 80 10
A 17th-century building with exposed beams in rooms and 18th-century furnishings. Breakfast: 75F.
🛏 34 + suites 🚇 St.-Germain-des-Prés 🅿 🕒 🅢 🅢 All major cards

🏨 BERSOLY'S
$$$ ✪✪✪
28 RUE DE LILLE, 75007
TEL 01 42 60 73 79
FAX 01 49 27 05 55
A quiet hotel with small but attractive rooms. The breakfast room is in a vaulted cellar. Breakfast: 50F.
🛏 16 🚇 Rue du Bac 🅿 🕒 Closed Aug. 🕒 🅢 🅢 AE, MC, V

🏨 LIBERTEL BELLECHASSE
$$$ ✪✪✪
8 RUE BELLECHASSE, 75007
TEL 01 45 50 22 31
FAX 01 45 51 52 36
A short walk from the Musée

d'Orsay, with bright, cozy rooms. Breakfast: 80F.
🛏 41 🚇 Solferino 🕒 🅢
🅢 All major cards

🏨 DE L'UNIVERSITÉ
$$$ ✪✪✪
22 RUE DE L'UNIVERSITÉ, 75007
TEL 01 42 61 09 39
FAX 01 42 60 40 84
Antique-furnished hotel distinguished by attention to detail. Two rooms have private terraces. Breakfast: 50F.
🛏 27 🚇 St.-Germain-des-Prés 🕒 🅢 🅢 All major cards

RESTAURANTS

🍴 L' ARPÈGE
$$$$$
84 RUE DE VARENNE, 75007
TEL 01 45 51 47 33
Alain Passard, one of Paris's top chefs, runs this highly rated restaurant with a clean, modern decor. Try the sole with ginger and lime, or the baby onion fondue with herbs and broad beans. Fixed-price menus available.
🚇 Varenne 🕒 Closed Sat., Sun. 🅢 🅢 All major cards

🍴 LE DIVELLEC
$$$$$
107 RUE DE L'UNIVERSITÉ, 75007
TEL 01 45 51 91 96
The "big fish" among Parisian seafood restaurants, with a big bill at the end of the meal. Fixed-price menus available.
🚇 Invalides 🕒 Closed Sun. (and Mon. in July & Aug.) 🅢 🅢 All major cards

🍴 LE JULES VERNE
$$$$$
EIFFEL TOWER, 2ND FLOOR 75007
TEL 01 45 55 61 44
A gourmet restaurant with sleek, modern decor in one of the world's most famous monuments. Dinner with a view, and chef Alain Reix. Fixed-price menus available.
🚇 Trocadéro 🅢 🅢 All major cards

VIOLON D'INGRES
$$$$
135 RUE ST.-DOMINIQUE, 75007
TEL 01 45 55 15 05
Christian Constant, the former chef at Les Ambassadeurs (see p. 249), provides the same high-quality cuisine at lower prices in this restaurant. Fixed-price menus available.
Pont de l'Alma
Closed Sun., Mon., & Aug.
AE, MC, V

LE BELLECOUR
$$$
22 RUE SURCOUF, 75007
TEL 01 45 51 46 93
Traditional cuisine from the Lyon region, along with a few innovative touches like oyster tartare. Impressive wine list.
Invalides Closed Sat. L, Sun., & Aug. All major cards

LE MONTALEMBERT
$$$
HÔTEL MONTALEMBERT (see p. 252), 3 RUE MONTALEMBERT, 75007
TEL 01 45 49 68 68
Designer hotel-restaurant with an eclectic menu that includes some interesting vegetarian dishes.
Rue du Bac All major cards

LE BAMBOCHE
$$
15 RUE DE BABYLONE, 75007
TEL 01 45 49 14 40
Chef Claude Colliot shows his creative cooking skills in this unpretentious restaurant. Fixed-price menus available.
Sèvres-Babylone
Closed Sat., Sun., & first 2 weeks of Aug. AE, MC, V

L'OEILLADE
$$
10 RUE ST.-SIMON
TEL 01 42 22 01 60.
A cozy little restaurant where you can count on creative cooking. Fixed-price menu available.
Rue du Bac Closed

Sat. L, Sun., Mon L, & last 2 weeks of Aug. MC, V

AU PIED DE FOUET
$
45 RUE DE BABYLONE, 75007
TEL 01 47 05 12 27
Small family restaurant with 19th-century decor, homey atmosphere, and low-priced selection of French classics.
Sèvres-Babylone
Closed Sat. D, Sun., public hols., Aug., & Christmas
No credit cards

THE 16TH ARRONDISSEMENT

A stylish residential area with some equally stylish hotels and restaurants.

HOTELS

BALTIMORE WESTIN DEMEURE
$$$$$ ◊◊◊◊
88 BIS AVENUE KLÉBER, 75116
TEL 01 44 34 54 54
FAX 01 44 34 54 44
Wood paneling, tapestries, and plush period furnishings for a homey feel. Bertie's restaurant serves English haute cuisine. Breakfast: 150F.
105 + 1 suite
Boissière
All major cards

LE PARC WESTIN DEMEURE
$$$$$ ◊◊◊◊
55 AVENUE RAYMOND-POINCARÉ, 75116
TEL 01 44 05 66 66
FAX 01 44 05 66 00
Chintz fabrics, canopied beds, and antique paintings in this luxury hotel in five buildings, with a garden. Chef is top-rated Alain Ducasse (see Alain Ducasse and Le Relais du Parc, this page). Business facilities. Breakfast: 150F.
116 + suites
Trocadéro
All major cards

PERGOLÈSE
$$$$ ◊◊◊◊
3 RUE PERGOLÈSE, 75016
TEL 01 53 64 04 04
FAX 01 53 64 04 40
Warm, modern, designer decor with marble bathrooms. Near the Bois de Boulogne and Arc de Triomphe. Bar. Breakfast: 70F/95F.
40s Argentine
All major cards

RESTAURANTS

ALAIN DUCASSE
$$$$$
57 AVENUE RAYMOND-POINCARÉ, 75116
TEL 01 47 27 12 27
Ducasse swiftly won over Parisian gourmets after taking over Joël Robuchon's former domain—a hard act to follow, but he's succeeded as the new star of haute cuisine. Specialties at this 3-Michelin-star restaurant include spit-roasted milk-fed lamb with vegetables and fried fruits. Fixed-price menus available.
Victor-Hugo Closed Sat., Sun., public hols., mid-July–mid-Aug., & Christmas week All major cards

JAMIN
$$$
32 RUE DE LONGCHAMPS 75116
TEL 01 45 53 00 07
Joël Robuchon created this restaurant, which has a plush, intimate atmosphere. Now run by Robuchon's right-hand man Benoît Guichard but little has changed.
Trocadero Closed Sat., Sun. first 3 weeks of Aug. All major cards

LE RELAIS DU PARC
$$$
55 AVENUE RAYMOND-POINCARÉ, 75016
TEL 01 44 05 66 10
For those who can't afford Alain Ducasse, this lower-priced bistro is supervised by the master.

Non-smoking Air-conditioning Indoor/ Outdoor swimming pool Health club Credit cards

HOTELS & RESTAURANTS

🏨 Victor-Hugo 🔁 🅿 All major cards

MONTMARTRE

Montmartre still has a bohemian feel, and Pigalle is becoming less sleazy as more fashionable nightspots open.

RESTAURANTS

🍴 BEAUVILLIERS
$$$$
52 RUE LAMARCK, 75018
TEL 01 42 54 54 42
As idiosyncratic as its Montmartre setting, with a romantic, somewhat kitschy decor, friendly service, and fine food. Fixed-price menus available.
🚇 Lamarck Caulaincourt 🕐 Closed Sun., & Mon. L 🔁 🅿 All major cards

🍴 LA TABLE D'ANVERS
$$$$
2 PLACE D'ANVERS, 75009
TEL 01 48 78 35 21
The two brothers (one a pastry chef) in the kitchen have a faithful following for their inventive cuisine. Fixed-price menus available.
🚇 Anvers 🕐 Closed Sat. L & Sun. 🔁 🅿 AE, MC, V

🍴 LA CLOCHE D'OR
$$$
3 RUE MANSART, 75009
TEL 01 48 74 48 88
A lively actors' hangout that serves decent, basic meals till 5 a.m.
🚇 Blanche 🕐 Closed Sat L, Sun. L, & Aug. 🅿 AE, MC, V

🍴 LE MOULIN À VIN
$$
6 RUE BURQ, 75018
TEL 01 42 52 81 27
A little piece of Old Montmartre: traditional food, good wines, and group singing to the strains of an accordion.
🚇 Abbesses 🕐 Closed Sun., Mon. & Aug. 🅿 MC, V

🍴 LE TAROUDANT II
$$
8 RUE ARISTIDE-BRUANT, 75018
TEL 01 42 64 95 81
Moroccan restaurant that makes some of the best couscous in Paris. Also serves *tajines* and *pastillas*.
🚇 Abbesses or Blanche 🕐 Closed Wed. & Aug. 🅿 MC, V

IN & AROUND THE PÉRIPHÉRIQUE

These are areas not often visited by tourists, but the restaurants listed below provide good reasons to make an excursion.

RESTAURANTS

🍴 LA GRANDE CASCADE
$$$$
BOIS DE BOULOGNE,
ALLÉE DE LONGCHAMP, 75016
TEL 01 45 27 33 51
Second Empire restaurant in a beautiful setting in the Bois de Boulogne with Provençal-influenced dishes. Fixed-price menus available.
🚇 Porte Maillot, then Bus 144 (till 8 p.m.) 🅿 🕐 Closed Jan. 20–Feb. 20 🅿 All major cards

🍴 LE PRÉ CATALAN
$$$$
ROUTE DE SURESNES, 75016
TEL 01 44 14 41 14
A talented new chef, Eric Anton, is livening up the cuisine of this lovely restaurant with a garden terrace in the Bois. Fixed-price menus available.
🚇 Porte Maillot, then Bus 144 (till 8 p.m.) 🕐 Closed Sun. D, Mon., & Feb. school vacation 🅿 All major cards

🍴 LA CAVE GOURMANDE
$$$
10 RUE DU GÉNÉRAL-BRUNET, 75019
TEL 01 40 40 03 30
Menu by Eric Frenchon; the restaurant is run by his wife. Uninspired decor and out-of-

the-way location (northeastern Paris), but worth the trip. Fixed-price menu available.
🚇 Danube 🕐 Closed Sat., Sun. & Aug. 🅿 MC, V

🍴 BRASSERIE FLO
$$
7 COUR DES PETITES-ÉCURIES, 75010
TEL 01 47 70 13 59
A sparkling, 19th-century Alsatian brasserie near the Gare de l'Est with typical dishes and warm, friendly service. Fixed-price menus available.
🚇 Château d'Eau 🔁 🅿 All major cards

🍴 LA RÉGALADE
$$
49 AVENUE JEAN-MOULIN, 75014
TEL 01 45 45 68 58
Chef Yves Camdeborde packs them in with haute cuisine at *petits prix* (small prices) in this restaurant in southern Paris. Fixed-price menu available.
🚇 Alésia 🅿 🕐 Closed Sat. L, Sun., Mon., & Aug. 🔁 🅿 All major cards

SHOPPING IN PARIS

Spending money is easy in this shopper's paradise, where tempting window displays abound. Shop owners are required to price each item displayed, so you'll know what you're in for, but bring a little extra cash if you don't want to go home frustrated. Items purchased include a 13 percent sales tax that is refundable to visitors from outside the European Union on purchases over 1,200F made from the same shop on the same day (ask the assistant for a *détaxe* form).

Department stores For those who prefer large department stores where they can find everything in one place, next-door neighbors Galeries Lafayette and Printemps (Closed Sun., Métro: Havre-Caumartin or Chaussée-d'Antin) have it all. The smaller Bon Marché (Closed Sun., Métro: Sèvres-Babylone) is less crowded and more exclusive. Mid-market department stores are BHV (Closed Sun., Métro: Hôtel-de-Ville) and Samaritaine (Closed Sun., Métro: Louvre). The low-priced chains Monoprix and Prisunic (Closed Sun.) have branches all over town, and are interesting for children's clothes, cosmetics, and accessories. The cheapest chain of all is Tati (Closed Sun., Métro: Barbès, République), which has become popular with trendy types of late. Attractive, youthful women's fashion at reasonable prices can be found at specialist chain stores like Kookaï, Naf Naf, Promod, Zara, and H&M.

Shopping centers Paris has few American-style shopping centers. The notable exception is the Forum des Halles (Métro: Les Halles), a rather unsavory underground mall full of chain-store branches. The beautiful, 19th-century Galerie Vivienne (Métro: Bourse) and the 18th-century arcades of the Palais-Royal (Métro: Palais-Royal) might be called forerunners of the mall, but they are worlds apart from the modern U.S. version.

Antique shops Antique shops can be found on the Quai Voltaire, Rue de Beaune (Métro: Rue du Bac), and neighboring streets, where exclusive dealers sell museum-quality pieces; the Louvre des Antiquaires (Closed Mon., Métro: Palais-Royal) has 250 boutiques; and the Village St.-Paul (Closed Tues. & Wed., Métro: St.-Paul), where the '50s seem to be the most popular era.

Boutiques The real joy of shopping in Paris, however, is boutiquing. Wander through the Marais, Montmartre, St.-Germain-des-Prés, Sèvres-Babylone, or the Place des Victoires to discover your own favorite boutique.

Flea markets There are also several permanent flea markets on the edges of Paris: the enormous Puces de St.-Ouen (Closed Tues.–Fri., Métro: Porte de Clignancourt), specializing in antiques; the more junk-oriented Puces de Montreuil (Open Sat.–Mon., Métro: Porte-de-Montreuil); and the Puces de Vanves (Open Sat. & Sun., Métro: Porte-de-Vanves), with some antiques and lots of miscellaneous stuff. As with most flea markets, the rules are: Go as early in the a.m. as possible, and don't hesitate to bargain. Prices are generally high, especially for antiques, but there are a lot of finds.

PERFUME

This is a city where any man can name the scent being worn by a woman. Your preferred Poison (Christian Dior) may not be Opium (Yves St. Laurent), but you will surely find a fragrance to your liking.

Parfumeries Bernard Marionnaud 23 boulevard de la Madeleine, 75001. Tel 01 40 20 08 80. Closed Sun. Métro: Madeleine.
A wide selection of brand-name perfumes offered by this chain. Call for other locations.
Séphora 70 avenue Champs-Élysées, 75008. Tel 01 53 93 22 50. Closed Sun. a.m. Métro: Franklin D. Roosevelt.
The ultimate perfume and cosmetics store, with testers of nearly every brand in existence. Added touches: free Internet access, relaxation recliners, bookstore. Open till midnight.
Shiseido Palais-Royal, 142 Galerie de Valois, 75001. Tel 01 49 27 09 09. Closed Sun. Métro: Palais-Royal.
Luxurious boutique where you can pamper yourself with a custom-designed perfume.

CLOTHING

The boutiques of the top designers are concentrated on Rue du Faubourg St.-Honoré, Avenue Montaigne, and in St.-Germain-des-Prés. Along with these, the other boutiques listed here have something a little different, with many offering bargain prices on designer labels.

Act 2 2 rue des Trois-Frères, 75018. Tel 01 42 54 01 56. Closed Sun. L. Métro: Abbesses.
For the fasionable man who wants to look just a little bit out of the ordinary.
Alternatives 18 rue du Roi-de-Sicile, 75004. Tel 01 42 78 31 50. Closed Sun., Mon., & L. Métro: St.-Paul.
Carefully selected used clothing (mostly for women), much of it with trendy designer labels.
Amatchi 13 rue du Roi-de-Sicile, 75004. Tel 01 40 29 97 14. Closed Sun. a.m. and Mon. a.m. Métro: St.-Paul.
The latest in men's and women's underwear and swimwear by popular designers like Nikos and Dolce & Gabbana.
Azzedine Alaïa 7 rue de Moussy, 75004. Tel 01 42 72 19 19. Closed Sun. Métro: Hôtel-de-Ville.

The lovely Marais boutique of a unique designer whose clothes make women look sexy.

Bonnie Cox 38 rue des Abbesses, 75018. Tel 01 42 54 95 68. Métro: Abbesses.
Trendy teen togs in a Montmartre boutique.

Chanel 31 rue Cambon, 75001. Tel 01 42 86 28 00. Closed Sun. Métro: Concorde.
The sacred, snooty precincts of Chanel fashion, now designed by Karl Lagerfeld.

Christian Dior 30 ave. Montaigne, 75008. Tel 01 40 73 54 00. Closed Sun. Métro: Franklin D. Roosevelt.
Designer John Galliano's extravagant creations in the plush setting of the refurbished Dior salons off the Champs-Élysées.

Colette 213 rue St.-Honoré, 75001. Tel 01 55 35 33 90. Closed Sun. Métro: Tuileries.
Cool designer clothing to sophisticated electronic gadgets, in a terribly minimalist shop with a popular basement café. Prices range from very reasonable to ridiculously high.

L'Eclaireur 3 ter rue de Rosiers, 75004. Tel 01 48 87 10 22. Closed Sun., & Mon. a.m. Métro: St.-Paul.
24 rue de l'Echaudé, 75006. Tel 01 44 27 08 03. Closed Sun., & Mon. a.m. Métro: Mabillon.
26 avenue des Champs-Élysées, 75008. Tel 01 45 62 12 32. Closed Sun. Métro: Franklin D. Roosevelt.
A judicious selection of men's and women's clothing and accessories by designers including Dries Van Noten, Clements-Ribeiro, and Helmut Lang.

Emporio Armani 149 boulevard St.-Germain, 75006. Tel 01 53 63 33 50. Closed Sun. Métro: St.-Germain-des-Prés.
The Italian designer's huge new store in the heart of St.-Germain-des-Prés, all stark-white, clean lines.

Galerie Gaultier 30 rue du Faubourg St.-Antoine, 75012. Tel 01 44 68 84 84. Closed Sun. Métro: Bastille.

Jean-Paul Gaultier's men's and women's ready-to-wear, lower-priced Gaultier jeans, accessories, and perfumes.

L'Habilleur 44 rue de Poitou, 75003. Tel 01 48 87 77 12. Closed Sun. Métro: Filles-de-Calvaires.
A fine selection of hip men's and women's designer clothing at reduced prices.

Hermès 24 rue du Faubourg-St.-Honoré, 75008. Tel 01 40 17 47 17. Closed Sun and Mon. L. Métro: Madeleine.
Famous for its silk *foulards* (scarves), this venerable house is trying to liven up its classic image with Martin Margiela designing its women's collection.

Maré Saint-Pierre 2 rue Charles-Nodier, 75018. Tel 01 46 06 92 25. Closed Sun. & Mon. a.m. Métro: Anvers.
This five-floor Montmartre store sells all kinds of fabric amid dozens of other nearby fabric shops.

La Marelle 21–25 Galerie Vivienne, 75002. Tel 01 42 60 08 19. Closed Sat. a.m. & Sun. Métro: Bourse.
Upscale, used clothing in perfect condition, by the likes of Dior and Chanel.

Maria Luisa 2 rue Cambon, 75001. Tel 01 47 03 96 15. Closed Sun. Métro: Concorde.
Clothing by designers Helmut Lang, Eric Bergère, Lainey Keogh, Ann Demeulemeester, and others. Men's and accessories boutiques are across the street.

Mouton à Cinq Pattes 8 rue St.-Placide, 75006. Tel 01 45 48 86 26. Closed Sun. Métro: St.-Placide.
19 rue Grégoire de Tours, 75006. Tel 01 43 29 73 56. Closed Sun. Métro: Odéon.
15 rue Vieille-du-Temple, 75004. Tel 01 42 71 86 30. Closed Sun. & Mon. a.m. Métro: Hôtel-de-Ville.
Paw through the masses of men's and women's clothing to find the designer seconds you're looking for.

Nina Jacob 23 rue des Francs-Bourgeois, 75004. Tel 01 42 77 41 20. Closed Sun. a.m. & Mon.

a.m. Métro: St.-Paul.
Hip yet feminine, flowing, colorful women's clothing in a pretty Marais boutique.

Passé Devant 62 rue d'Orsel, 75018. Tel 01 42 54 75 15. Closed Sun. a.m. & Mon. a.m. Métro: Abbesses.
Carefully selected women's used clothing, some of it by famous designers.

Plein Sud 14 place des Victoires, 75002. Tel 01 42 36 75 02. Closed Sun. Métro: Bourse.
21 rue des Francs-Bourgeois. Tel 01 42 72 10 60. Closed Sun. Métro: St.-Paul.
Designer Fayçal Amor's fashions are fairly affordable and fashionable.

Suzette Idier 9 rue de Birague. Tel 01 42 77 72 52. Closed Mon. & Sun. Métro: St.-Paul.
Colorful original women's clothing with a good selection of accessories and lots of Kenzo. Run by Suzette who has good taste and great fashion tips.

Vicxite A 47 rue des Abbesses, 75018. Tel 01 42 55 31 68. Closed Sun. Métro: Abbesses.
A place to see young designers' work before they become famous and expensive.

Yves St. Laurent 38 rue du Faubourg-St.-Honoré, 75008. Tel 01 42 65 74 59. Closed Sun. Métro: Madeleine.
One of the last remaining, great French designer's women's clothing boutique.

ACCESSORIES

Frenchwomen seem to be born with a knack for accessorizing. Ask the salesperson for tips on tying that *foulard*.

Axes et Soirs 97 rue Vieille-du-Temple, 75003. Tel 01 42 74 43 06. Closed Sun. Métro: Hôtel-de-Ville or Filles-de-Calvaire.
Flamboyant handmade hats and other accessories.

Bains Plus 51 rue des Francs-Bourgeois/corner of rue Vieille du Temple, 75004. Tel 01 48 87 83 07. Closed Mon. & Sun. a.m. Métro: St.-Paul.

A Marais boutique with luxurious bathing and lounging accessories.

Catherine Martineau 42 rue Vieille-du-Temple, 75004. Tel 01 42 72 42 32. Métro: Hôtel-de-Ville.
Lively, inexpensive accessories and silver-plated jewelry inspired by medieval designs.

Droguerie 9–11 rue du Jour, 75001. Tel 01 45 08 93 27.
Closed Mon. a.m. & Sun. a.m. Métro: Les Halles.
Colorful yarns, feathers, unusual buttons and beads, and other trimmings.

L'Heure du Bijou 3 rue du Perronet, 75007. Tel 01 45 44 16 42. Closed Mon. a.m. & Sun. Métro: St.-Germain-des-Prés.
An Ali Baba's cave filled with fabulous vintage costume jewelry originally made for film and theater.

Jean-Claude Monderer 22 rue des Francs-Bourgeois, 75003. Tel 01 48 04 51 41. Closed Sun. a.m. Métro: St.-Paul.
Men's and women's accessories that are trendy but not ridiculously expensive.

Kabuki 13 rue de Turbigo, 75002. Tel 01 42 36 44 34. Closed Sun.& Mon. Métro: Etienne Marcel.
Wild shoes for wild women, by designers like Dries Van Noten, Dirk Bikkembergs, and Vivienne Westwood.

Madeleine Gély 218 boulevard St.-Germain, 75007. Tel 01 42 22 63 35. Closed Sun. & Mon. Métro: Rue du Bac.
A truly Parisian shop more than 150 years old, stuffed with every type and shape of umbrella and cane imaginable.

Michel Georges 26 rue de Richelieu, 75001. Tel 01 42 61 32 57. Closed weekday a.m. & weekends. Métro: Palais-Royal.
A tiny shop near the Palais-Royal, specializing in antique fans.

Michel Perry 42 rue de Grenelle, 75007. Tel 01 42 84 12 45. Closed Sun. & L. Métro: Sèvres-Babylone.
4 rue des Petits-Pères, 75002. Tel 01 42 44 10 07. Closed Sun. Métro: Bourse.

High-style, high-priced, and very high-heeled women's shoes.

Sentimentale 14 rue du Roi-de-Sicile, 75004. Tel 01 42 78 84 04. Closed Sun., Mon., & weekday a.m. Métro: St.-Paul.
Off-the-beaten-track men's and women's shoes, custom-made to fit your feet; not too expensive.

Tati Or 19 rue de la Paix, 75008. Tel 01 40 07 06 76. Métro: Opéra. Closed Sun.
Bargain prices on gold jewelry, near Cartier and other fine jewelers on Place Vendôme.

CHILDREN

Even W.C. Fields went all gooey at the sight of the unbelievably cute children's clothing in Paris. Prices are just as unbelievably high.

C'est Ma Chambre 45 rue des Archives, 75003. Tel 01 48 87 26 67. Closed Sun. & Mon. Métro: Hôtel-de-Ville.
Parents and children alike will fall in love with the children's furnishings and bedroom accessories in this Marais shop.

Chat Perché 54 rue du Roi de Sicile, 75004. Tel 01 42 77 20 48. Closed Sun. & Mon. Métro: Hôtel de Ville.
A variety of music boxes, animal lamps, puzzles, puppets, and toys, plus a collection of old games and toys for show only.

Jacadi 17 rue Tronchet, 75008. Tel 01 42 65 84 98. Closed Sun. Métro: Madeleine.
Flagship chainstore selling traditional French children's clothing.

Du Pareil au Même 128 boulevard Courcelles, 75017. Tel 01 47 66 03 31. Closed Sun. Métro: Ternes.
The main store of a chain with great prices on colorful, quality children's clothes.

Petits Petons 23 rue Tronchet, 75008. Tel 01 47 42 75 69. Closed L on Mon., Tues., & Sun. Métro: Madeleine.
135 rue du Faubourg St.-Antoine, 75011. Tel 01 40 19 07 19. Closed Sun. Métro: Ledru-Rollin.

The cutest, most colorful kiddie shoes imaginable.

BOOKS & MUSIC

Paris has many English-language bookshops, and even the French stores listed below carry some foreign-language books.

Abbey Bookshop 29 rue de la Parcheminerie, 75005. Tel 01 46 33 16 24. Closed Sun. Métro: St.-Michel.
New and used English-language books.

La Chaumière à Musique 5 rue de Vaugirard, 75006. Tel 01 43 54 07 25. Closed Sun. a.m. RER: Luxembourg.
A huge collection of used CDs at low prices, great for classical music fanatics.

FNAC 74 avenue des Champs-Élysées, 75008. Tel 01 53 53 64 64. Open till midnight. Closed Sun. a.m. Métro: Franklin D. Roosevelt.
Every record and (French) book imaginable is sold in the newest branch of this chain. All CDs can be tested on headphones.

Galignani 224 rue de Rivoli, 75001. Tel 01 42 60 76 07. Closed Sun. Métro: Tuileries.
English and French books in an Old World-style shop with wooden shelves.

Shakespeare & Company 37 rue de la Bûcherie, 75005. Tel 01 43 26 96 50. Métro: St.-Michel.
An American bookstore that has nothing to do with Sylvia Beach's famous establishment, whose name it has borrowed. Its stacks are dusty and the owner cranky, but it still attracts plenty of tourists.

Virgin Megastore 52 avenue des Champs-Élysées, 75008. Tel 01 49 53 50 00. Open till midnight. Closed Sun. a.m. Métro: Franklin D. Roosevelt.
Huge selection of CDs, cassettes, books, and videos, plus a restaurant and bar.

The Village Voice 6 rue Princesse, 75006. Tel 01 46 33 36 47. Closed Mon. a.m. & Sun. a.m.

Métro: St.-Germain-des Prés. The finest selection of English-language books in Paris.

TASTE TREATS

Barthélemy 51 rue de Grenelle, 75007. Tel 01 45 48 56 75. Métro: Sèvres-Babylone. Closed L and Sun. & Mon. Some of the best cheeses in Paris, in a charming, old-fashioned shop.
Berthillon's 31 rue St.-Louis-en-Île, 75004. Tel 01 43 54 31 61. Métro: Pont Marie. Closed Mon., Tues., last two weeks of July, Aug., & during school vacations, except Christmas. Makers of the famous Parisian ice cream, also sold in other outlets on the Île St.-Louis.
Couderc 6 boulevard Voltaire, 75011. Tel 01 47 00 58 20. Closed Sun. L & Mon. Métro: République.
This pastry shop makes mouth-watering almond croissants and incredible chocolate tarts.
Fauchon 26, 28, 30, place de la Madeleine, 75008. Tel 01 47 42 60 11. Closed Sun. Métro: Madeleine.
The finest of foodstuffs.
Izraël 30 rue François-Miron, 75004. Tel 01 42 72 66 23. Closed Sun., Mon., & L on weekdays. Métro: St.-Paul.
Don't miss this imported-food shop, redolent of spices and filled with good food.
Legrand 1 rue de la Banque, 75002. Tel 01 42 60 07 12. Closed Sun., Mon., & Sat. L. Métro: Bourse.
One of the best wine merchants in Paris; also sells carafes, other wine accessories, and French regional food specialties.
Nicolas Main store: 31 place de la Madeleine, 75008. Tel 01 42 68 00 16. Closed Sun. Métro: Madeleine.
A chain of franchised wine shops with a reliable selection and knowledgable (often English-speaking) owners. Branches in all Parisian neighborhoods.

Les Papilles 30 rue Gay-Lussac, 75005. Tel 01 43 25 20 79. Closed Sun. RER: Luxembourg. The name means "taste buds," and there is plenty to tickle them here, from fine wines to gourmet delicacies packaged to travel.
Poujauran 20 rue Jean Nicot, 75007. Tel 01 47 05 80 88. Closed Sun. & Mon. Métro: Latour Maubourg.
Top bakery known throughout the city for its baguettes, as well as its chocolate cake.

HOUSEWARES & INTERIOR DESIGN

The French claim to know the most about about *l'art de vivre* (the art of living). The following stores sell some of the elements that go into this fine art.

Boutiques Paris-Musées
Forum des Halles, 1 rue Pierre-Lescot, 75001. Tel 01 40 26 56 65. Closed Sun., & Mon. a.m. Métro: Les Halles.
29 bis rue des Francs-Bourgeois, 75004. Tel 01 42 74 13 02. Closed Mon. a.m. Métro: St.-Paul.
Reproductions of objects from Paris museums, including dishes, glassware, and other arty items.
La Chaise Longue
30 rue Croix-des-Petits-Champs, 75001. Tel 01 42 96 32 14. Closed Sun. Métro: Palais-Royal.
8 rue Princesse, 75006. Tel 01 43 29 62 39. Closed Sun. Métro: St.-Germain-des-Prés.
20 rue des Francs-Bourgeois, 75003. Tel 01 48 04 36 37. Closed Sun. a.m. Métro: St.-Paul.
Cheap, chic accessories for the kitchen and the bathroom.
The Conran Shop 117 rue du Bac, 75007. Tel 01 42 84 10 01. Closed Sun. Métro: Sèvres-Babylone.
Terence Conran's design domain, with attractive, amusing furniture and home accessories.
Cuisinophile 28 rue du Bourg-Tibourg, 75004. Tel 01 40 29 07 32. Closed Sun., Mon., & a.m. Métro: Hôtel-de-Ville.

Antique kitchen utensils (wooden coffee grinders, egg beaters, jelly jars, on so on).
Diners en Ville 27 rue de Varenne, 75007. Tel 01 42 22 78 33. Closed Sun., & Mon. a.m. Métro: Varenne.
Cheerful, colorful, elegant tableware.
Galerie VIA 29–37 avenue Daumesnil, 75012. Tel 01 46 28 11 11. Open everyday. Métro: Gare de Lyon.
A gallery promoting avant-garde French furniture designers in a row of art- and crafts-related shops.
Maison de Famille 29 rue St.-Sulpice, 75006. Tel 01 40 46 97 47. Closed Sun. Métro: St.-Sulpice.
Kitchen gadgets to bedding and decorative objects, plus selected men's and women's clothing.
Matins Bleus 92 rue de Rennes, 75006. Tel 01 42 22 94 40. Closed Sun. Métro: St.-Germain-des-Prés.
Fine bed linens, as only the French know how to make.
Muriel Grateau 37 rue de Beaune, 75007. Tel 01 40 20 42 82. Closed Sun. Métro: Rue du Bac.
Luxurious, 100-percent linen bedsheets in a palette of colors and tableware with pure, modern, elegant lines.
Villa Marais 40 rue des Francs-Bourgeois, 75003. Tel 01 42 78 42 40. Métro: Hôtel-du-Ville.
Exotic furniture and fun, decorative items for your home.

STATIONERY

Art du Bureau 47 rue des Francs-Bourgeois, 75004. Tel 01 48 87 57 97. Closed Sun. a.m. Métro: St.-Paul.
Elegant, unusual supplies for the well-dressed office.
Charta 16 rue Elzevir, 75003. Tel 01 42 77 25 37. Closed Sun. Métro: St.-Paul.
Beautiful writing paper and greeting cards handmade by a Florentine artist, plus original jewelry and books.

ENTERTAINMENT

As a major world capital, Paris has more than its share of entertainment possibilities. Parisians love to go out, so many performances are sold out in advance—try to book tickets ahead of time for the theater, concerts, dance performances, and the opera.

For details on concert times and complete movie listings, buy a copy of the weekly *Pariscope* or *l'Officiel des Spectacles* at any newsstand. Both come out on Wednesday, and *Pariscope* has a section in English. They include up-to-date admission charges and a list of restaurants open after midnight. *Le Figaro* has a section on entertainment in its Wednesday issue. The monthly *Nova* is aimed at a hip young readership, with listings that would interest them (rock, jazz, pop). *Lylo*, a pocket-size monthly, is available free in most music venues, and has good listings of pop, rock, jazz, and world music performances. The bi-monthly English-language *What's On* highlights the latest events in Paris and the provinces. You can also find out what's happening in the city on the Internet via Rendez-vous à Paris: www.parisvisit.com.

THEATER

Going to the theater in Paris provides an opportunity to soak up the ambience, but otherwise there is not much point unless your command of French is excellent—most of the plays are in French. However, a few theaters occasionally stage plays in English (listed below; otherwise, in French). Booking usually starts two weeks in advance.

Café-théâtres are small theaters (without cafés), the equivalent of Off-off-Broadway plays and stand-up comedy of varying quality, but don't go unless your French is really good.

Bouffes du Nord 37 bis boulevard de la Chapelle, 75010. Tel 01 46 07 34 50. Métro: La Chapelle.
Director Peter Brook stages plays of excellent quality—many in English—in a handsome old theater.
Café de la Gare 41 rue du Temple, 75004. Tel 01 42 78 52 51. Métro: Hôtel-de-Ville.
A café-théâtre presenting plays and comedy sketches.
Cartoucherie-Théâtre du Soleil route du Champ-de-Manoeuvre, 75012. Tel 01 43 74 24 08. Métro: Château-de-Vincennes, then shuttle service or bus.
Acclaimed director Ariane

Mnouchkine's troupe performs plays in an old warehouse near the Bois de Vincennes.
Comédie Française 2 rue de Richelieu. Tel 01 44 58 15 15. Métro: Palais-Royal.
Molière's company was the founding troupe of this venerable theater next to the Palais-Royal; his works are performed, along with pieces by Chekhov, Corneille, Racine, Shakespeare, Anouilh, and others. The acting is usually superb. French only.
Odéon-Théâtre de l'Europe place de l'Odéon, 75006. Tel 01 44 41 36 36. Métro: Odéon.
This national theater, in a handsome, neoclassic building, stages a variety of French and foreign productions, some in English.
Point Virgule 7 rue St.-Croix-de-la-Bretonnerie, 75004. Tel 01 42 78 67 03. Métro: Hôtel-de-Ville.
A small, popular café-théâtre with mostly comic sketches.
Théâtre de Bobigny La Maison de la Culture, 1 boulevard Lénine, Bobigny. Tel 01 41 60 72 72. Métro: Bobigny-Pablo Picasso.
Avant-garde pieces (Robert Wilson, Peter Sellars) are the mainstay of this modern theater in one of Paris's "red" suburbs. Some plays (notably, from the annual visit of London's Royal Shakespeare Company) are in English.

Théâtre de Nesle 8 rue de Nesle, 75006. Tel 01 46 34 61 04. Métro: Odéon.
Tiny Left Bank theater with occasional English-language plays by Pinter and others.
Théâtre du Rond Point 2 bis avenue Franklin D. Roosevelt, 75008. Tel 01 44 95 98 10. Métro: Franklin D. Roosevelt.
Marcel Maréchal's company presents classic plays, as well as works by Samuel Beckett and Harold Pinter to name but two, in this skating-rink-turned-theater. French only.
Théâtre du Vieux-Colombier 21 rue du Vieux-Colombier, 75006. Tel 01 44 39 87 00. Métro: St.-Sulpice.
A smaller, Left Bank outpost of the Comédie Française, with a selection of both classic and modern pieces.
Théâtre National de Chaillot 1 place du Trocadéro, 75016. Tel 01 53 65 30 00. Métro: Trocadéro.
Enormous theater directed by Jérôme Savary, who presents lavish spectacles. Free mini-concerts are sometimes held in the Grand Foyer at the cocktail hour or on Sunday afternoon.

OPERA/DANCE/CLASSICAL MUSIC

All the international greats in the worlds of classical music, opera, and dance eventually perform in Paris. Many churches regularly hold concerts of classical music. Check *Pariscope* for details, or call 01 44 62 00 55, Les Grands Concerts Sacrés (Tel 01 40 82 75 15), or Musique Sacré à Notre-Dame de Paris (Tel 01 44 41 49 99). Also for concerts:
www.paris-touroffice.com

Châtelet place du Châtelet. Tel 01 40 28 28 40. Métro: Châtelet.
High-quality opera, classical concerts, and dance productions are held in this attractive theater.
Cité de la Musique 211 avenue Jean-Jaurès, 75019. Tel 01

44 84 44 84. Métro: Porte de Pantin.
The lovely new building designed by Christian Portzamparc is home to avant-garde composer Pierre Boulez's Ensemble InterContemporain; it holds mostly modern and classical concerts, and regularly sets trends with special commissions.

Maison de Radio France
116 avenue du Président-Kennedy, 75016. Tel 01 56 40 10 45. Métro: Ranelagh or Passy.
The home base of the Orchestre National de France and the Orchestre Philharmonique, which present a selection of classical and modern concerts (some free).

Opéra Comique 5 rue Favart, 75002. Tel 01 42 44 45 46. Métro: Richelieu Drouot.
Operas, operettas, and classical concerts are staged in this beautiful, sumptuously decorated 100-year-old theater, built by Louis Bernier.

Opéra National de Paris-Bastille 2 bis place de la Bastille, 75012. Tel 08 36 69 78 68. Métro: Bastille.
Major opera and dance productions in the new opera house that Parisians love to hate, but flock to anyway.

Opéra National de Paris Palais-Garnier place de l'Opéra, 75009. Tel 08 36 69 78 68. Métro: Opéra.
Opera and dance performances (by the Ballet de l'Opéra National de Paris and visiting companies) in this wonderfully overdecorated, 19th-century opera house with ceiling frescoes by Marc Chagall.

Salle Pleyel 252 rue du Faubourg-St.-Honoré, 75008. Tel 01 45 61 53 00. Métro: Ternes.
Many of the great names of the classical world have staged recitals and concerts in this prestigious venue.

Théâtre des Champs-Élysées 15 avenue Montaigne, 75008. Tel 01 49 52 50 50. Métro: Alma-Marceau.
Hosts the Orchestre National de France, plus visiting

orchestras and opera companies.

Théâtre de la Ville 2 place du Châtelet, 75004. Tel 01 42 74 22 77. Métro: Châtelet.
The major venue for an adventurous program of dance performances by all the best international companies.

POP/ROCK/JAZZ

The French have adopted American jazz and made it their own, with many Parisian smoky-basement jazz clubs. They can get very crowded; arrive early but don't expect things to get going before 11 p.m.

Bilboquet 13 rue St.-Benoît, 75006. Tel 01 45 48 81 84. Métro: St.-Germain-des-Prés
This Left Bank, belle epoque-style club in the heart of St.-Germain-des-Prés has been around for half a century and is very popular with tourists. It offers dinner and New Orleans-style jazz.

Caveau de la Huchette 5 rue de la Huchette, 75005. Tel 01 43 26 65 05. Métro: St.-Michel.
A smoky, Latin Quarter basement club with '50s-style rock, boogie, and swing. Still going strong.

La Cigale 120 boulevard Rochechouart, 75018. Tel 01 49 25 89 99. Métro: Pigalle.
Rock concerts by international and local groups in a former theater.

Le Divan du Monde 75 rue des Martyrs, 75018. Tel 01 44 92 77 66. Métro: Pigalle.
All types of music—rock, chansons française (French songs), gospel, and Central European.

Duc des Lombards 42 rue des Lombards. Tel 01 42 33 22 88. Métro: Châtelet.
The club heats up with lively jazz concerts beginning around 10 p.m.

Élysée-Montmartre 72 boulevard Rochechouart, 75018. Tel 01 55 07 06 00. Métro: Anvers.

A former Pigalle music hall with good rock and rap concerts.

Instants Chavirés 7 rue Richard Lenoir, 93100 Montreuil. Tel 01 42 87 25 91. Métro: Robespierre.
Just outside of Paris, this friendly club is the best for avant-garde jazz.

Jazz Club Lionel Hampton Hôtel Meridien, 81 boulevard Gouvion St.-Cyr. Tel 01 40 68 30 42. Métro: Porte Maillot.
Good, live jazz and blues in the lobby of the otherwise unexciting Méridien hotel.

New Morning 7 rue des Petites-Écuries, 75010. Tel 01 45 23 51 41. Métro: Château d'Eau.
Top jazz, blues, African, and South American musicians perform in this smoky club.

Olympia 28 boulevard des Capucines, 75009. Tel 01 47 42 25 49. Métro: Opéra.
Recently renovated concert hall with a variety of music acts, including many French chanteurs and chanteuses (singers).

Petit Journal Montparnasse 13 rue du Commandant-Mouchotte, 75014. Tel 01 43 21 56 70. Métro: Montparnasse.
Classic, live jazz, and Latin groups in this popular club.

Petit Journal Saint-Michel 71 boulevard St.-Michel, 75005. Tel 01 43 26 28 59. RER: Luxembourg.
Basement club featuring New Orleans-style jazz.

Sunset 60 rue des Lombards, 75001. Tel 01 40 26 46 60. Métro: Châtelet.
Central, basement jazz club with good French and international groups.

La Villa 29 rue Jacob, 75006. Tel 01 43 26 60 00. Métro: St.-Germain-des-Prés.
Top-level jazz concerts in the cozy basement of a Left Bank hotel.

Zénith 211 avenue de Jean-Jaurès, 75019. Tel 01 42 08 60 00. Métro: Porte de Pantin.
Cavernous rock venue where international superstars perform.

BARS/NIGHTCLUBS

Salsa dancing is all the rage in Paris, with new, inexpensive bars opening frequently (especially on Rue Oberkampf, the current happening area). These provide a good alternative to pricey discos.

Les Bains 7 rue du Bourg-l'Abbé, 75003. Tel 01 48 87 01 80. Métro: Étienne Marcel.
This popular, long-running disco in a former bathhouse attracts stars like Brad Pitt and Jack Nicholson.
Banana Café 13 rue de la Ferronnerie, 75001. Tel 01 42 33 35 31. Métro: Châtelet.
Bored male go-go dancers entertain crowds in this mostly gay bar.
Barrio Latino 46–48 rue du Fbg. St.-Antoine, 75012. Tel 01 55 78 84 75. Open daily. Métro: Bastille.
A three-floor 900-seater bar and restaurant with a neo-Cuban decor. Owned by the same people who run the Buddha Bar. It's worth a trip just for an eyeful.
Le Blue Note 38 rue Mouffetard, 75005. Tel 01 45 87 36 09. Métro: Mouffetard.
A tiny, Left Bank bar with live Brazilian and jazz music.
Buddha Bar 8 rue Boissy-d'Anglas, 75008. Tel 01 53 05 90 00. Métro: Concorde.
Huge basement restaurant/bar for beautiful people, with an enormous Buddha statue.
Le Bus Palladium 6 rue Fontaine, 75009. Tel 01 53 21 07 33. Closed Sun. & Mon. Métro: Blanche.
Free entry for women on Tues., which is Motown night at this lively, unpretentious club.
Le Cabaret 68 rue Pierre-Charron, 75008. Tel 01 42 89 44 14. Métro: Franklin D. Roosevelt.
This cabaret-turned-hip-bar has cabaret acts and an exclusive door policy (entry if you look fashionable). Popular with the fashion and showbiz crowds.
La Casbah 20 rue de la Forge-Royale, 75011.

Métro: Ledru-Rollin.
The lavish Moroccan decor is the main interest of this restaurant/club. Acid house and jazz alternate on different days with dance and disco music.
La Chapelle des Lombards 19 rue de Lappe, 75011. Tel 01 43 57 24 24. Closed Sun.–Wed. Métro: Bastille.
Latin rhythms and live concerts on Thurs. nights in a warm and friendly atmosphere. Women get in free before midnight on Thursdays.
Le Charbon 109 rue Oberkampf, 75011. Tel 01 43 57 55 13. Métro: Parmentier.
A former music hall, this was the first hip café to open on this street, now lined with funky, inexpensive bars. Its decor must be seen (high ceiling, turn-of-the-century mural of cabaret dancers), but avoid the crowds on weekend nights.
Chez Georges 11 rue des Canettes, 75006. Tel 01 43 26 79 15. Closed Sun. & Mon. Métro: St.-Germain-des-Prés.
Friendly, unpretentious, cheap bar in a classy neighborhood.
Chez Richard 37 rue Vieille-du-Temple, 75004. Tel 01 42 74 31 65. Métro: Hôtel-de-Ville.
Three-level bar/restaurant in the Marais that attracts a coolish, yuppie-type crowd.
China Club 50 rue de Charenton, 75012. Tel 01 43 43 82 02. Métro: Ledru-Rollin.
The place to go for a quiet drink and conversation in a comfortable, colonial-style setting.
Cithéa 114 rue Oberkampf, 75011. Tel 01 40 21 70 95. Métro: St.-Maur.
Live music—everything from jazz to Latin and Jungle—from Wed. to Sat. evenings in a small club with a dance floor.
Le Comptoir 14 rue Vauvilliers, 75001. Tel 01 40 26 26 66. Métro: Les Halles.
A good place to enjoy a drink and tapas amid a designer decor.
La Coupole 102 boulevard de Montparnasse, 75014. Tel 01 43 20 14 20. Métro: Montparnasse.
Tea dancing on Sat. & Sun.

afternoons, Salsa on Tues. night (live), disco/R&B/Rock on Fri. night (live), and retro disco on Sat. night in the basement of this famous art deco café/restaurant.
Les Étoiles 61 rue Château-d'Eau, 75010. Tel 01 47 70 60 56. Closed Sun.–Wed. Métro: Château d'Eau.
Salsa reigns in this former movie theater. Dinner with salsa Thurs., Fri., Sat. 9pm. Dancing only 11pm (no lessons).
La Flèche d'Or 102 bis rue de Bagnolet, 75020. Tel 01 43 72 04 23. Métro: Alexandre Dumas or Gambetta.
A barnlike former train station, now one of the coolest spots in town. Live music on Fri. and Sat. nights, and a salsa party on the third Sun. of the month at 5 p.m. Packed on weekends.
Les Folies Pigalle 11 place Pigalle, 75009. Tel 01 48 78 25 26. Closed Mon. Métro: Pigalle.
Once a strip joint, this place attracts its share of drag queens and an otherwise mixed crowd. Gay tea dance on Sun.
Harry's Bar 5 rue Danou, 75002. Tel 01 42 61 71 14. Métro: Opéra.
The venerable American bar in Paris, where the Bloody Mary was first concocted.
La Java 105 rue du Faubourg-du-Temple, 75010. Tel 01 42 02 20 52. Closed Mon.–Wed. Métro: Belleville.
Unchanged since 1938, this old music hall offers salsa on Thurs. and Fri. nights, mambo on Sat. night, and a tea dance on Sun. afternoons.
La Locomotive 90 boulevard de Clichy, 75018. Tel 08 36 69 69 28. Métro: Blanche.
A young crowd frequents this huge, three-level disco.
Lou Pascalou 14 rue des Panoyaux, 75020. Tel 01 46 36 78 10. Métro: Ménilmontant.
One of the original trendy/funky bars in the Ménilmontant area, just to the north of Rue Oberkampf.
Niel's 27 avenue des Ternes, 75017. Tel 01 47 66 45 00. Métro: Étoile or Ternes.
A moneyed, artsy crowd

frequents this upscale club/restaurant with a highly selective door policy. Popular with the press and showbiz people.

Le Piano Zinc 49 rue des Blancs-Manteaux, 75004. Tel 01 40 27 97 42. Métro: Hôtel-de-Ville.

Multilevel bar where gay and straight customers can belt out a tune on the open mike.

Queen 102 avenue des Champs-Élysées, 75008. Tel 01 53 89 08 90. Métro: George-V. Still the hottest gay disco in town, with mostly house music and theme nights that attract straights also (women are generally frowned upon).

Sanz Sans 49 rue du Faubourg St.-Antoine, 75011. Tel 01 44 75 78 78. Métro: Bastille. A bar/restaurant with a found-object decor and DJ, packed with trendy youngsters.

Satellit' Café 44 rue de la Folie-Méricourt. Tel 01 47 00 48 87. Closed Sun. & Mon. Métro: Oberkampf. All-night bar (weekends) with a huge and varied record collection.

Les Scandaleuses 8 rue des Écouffes, 75004. Tel 01 48 87 39 26. Métro: St.-Paul. A new Marais lesbian bar; men welcome when accompanied by a woman.

Le Sous Bock 49 rue St.-Honoré, 75001. Tel 01 40 26 46 61. Métro: Pont-Neuf or Les Halles. A large, all-night pub serving food 24 hours a day.

CINEMA

Parisians are movie-mad; they love everything from the latest American blockbuster to the most intellectual East European offering. Many cinemas regularly show the classics as well, from the Marx Brothers to Frank Capra. Cinema snobs go only to films in "VO" *(version originale)*, so you will find many screenings in English. "VF" means *version française*, and the film will be dubbed into French. Make sure you check before you buy your ticket. On Friday and Saturday nights there are long lines outside cinemas on the Champs-Élysées and les Grands Boulevards. Don't be surprised if you have to sit through up to 20 minutes of advertising before the film starts; this is standard practice. It is customary to tip usherettes. The following are a few of the more interesting cinemas.

Accatone 20 rue Cujas, 75005. Tel 01 46 33 86 86. Métro: Luxembourg or Cluny La Sorbonne. Artsy offerings like *Hiroshima Mon Amour* and erotic classics like *The Empire of the Senses.* Classics only.

Le Champo 51 rue des Écoles, 75005. Tel 01 43 54 51 60. Métro: St.-Michel or Odéon. Woody Allen and Monty Python classics, recent films you may have missed, and new releases.

UGC Cité-Ciné Les Halles 7 place de la Rotonde, Forum des Halles, Niveau-3, (entry: Porte du Jour), 75001. Tel 08 36 68 68 58. Métro: Les Halles. Multiplex with 22 screens, the latest technology, a café, and American-style refreshment stands. New releases.

Grand Action 5 rue des Écoles, 75005. Tel 01 43 29 44 40. Métro: Cardinal Lemoine or Jussieu. Art-house movies, with festivals of everything from Tennessee Williams to the Marx Brothers.

Max Linder Panorama 24 boulevard Poissonnière, 75009. Tel 01 48 24 00 47. Métro: Grands Boulevards. New releases in a serious cinema with good seating, digital THX sound, and a balcony.

La Pagode 57 bis rue de Babylone, 75007. Tel 08 36 68 75 07. Métro: St.-François-Xavier. Cinema in an imitation pagoda with a tea room in the lovely garden.

Studio Galande 42 rue Galande, 75005. Tel 01 43 26 94 08. Métro: St.-Michel.

The *Rocky Horror Picture Show* is shown every Fri. and Sat. at 10:30 p.m. plus other recent and not-so-recent films, including the restored Fritz Lang classic, *Metropolis.*

CABARET

These famous, Vegas-type shows with topless dancing girls are expensive, and attended mostly by busloads of tourists. If going, skip the overpriced, mediocre meals and just have a pricey drink at the bar.

Crazy Horse Saloon 12 avenue George-V, 75008. Tel 01 47 23 93 92. Métro: Alma Marceau. Considered the most erotic of the cabarets. The dancers have names like "Kismy Patchwork," with shows like "Teasing."

Folies-Bergère 32 rue Richer, 75009. Tel 01 44 79 98 98. Métro: Grands Boulevards. Musical comedies and variety shows in a beautiful old theater.

Lido 116 bis avenue des Champs-Élysées, 75008. Tel 01 40 76 56 10. Métro: George-V. The Bluebell Girls sing, dance, and ice skate in fabulous costumes.

Moulin Rouge 82 boulevard de Clichy, 75009. Tel 01 53 09 82 82. Métro: Blanche. The Doriss Girls still do the can-can in thousands of varied costumes. Dance numbers are interspersed with circus acts.

LANGUAGE GUIDE

USEFUL WORDS & PHRASES

General

Yes *Oui*
No *Non*
Excuse me *Excusez-moi*
Hello *Bonjour*
Hi *Salut*
Please *S'il vous plaît*
Thank you (very much) *Merci (beaucoup)*
You're welcome *De rien*
Have a good day! *Bonne journée!*
OK *D'accord*
Goodbye *Au revoir*
Good night *Bonsoir*
Sorry *Pardon*
here *ici*
there *là*
today *aujourd'hui*
yesterday *hier*
tomorrow *demain*
now *maintenant*
later *plus tard*
right away *tout de suite*
this morning *ce matin*
this afternoon *cet après-midi*
this evening *ce soir*
Do you have...? *Avez-vous...?*
Do you speak English? *Parlez-vous anglais?*
I am American *Je suis Américain* (man); *je suis Américaine* (woman)
I don't understand *Je ne comprends pas*
Please speak more slowly *Parlez plus lentement, s'il vous plaît*
Where is...? *Où est...?*
I don't know *Je ne sais pas*
No problem *Ce n'est pas grave*
That's it *C'est ça*
Here it is *Voici*
There it is *Voilà*
What is your name? *Comment vous-appelez-vous?*
My name is... *Je m'appelle...*
Let's go *On y va*
At what time? *À quelle heure?*
When? *Quand?*
What time is it? *Quelle heure est-il?*

In the hotel

Do you have...? *Avez-vous...?*
a single room *une chambre simple*
a double room *une chambre double*
with/without bathroom/shower *avec/sans salle de bain/douche*

Help

I need a doctor/dentist *J'ai besoin d'un médecin/dentiste*
Can you help me? *Pouvez-vous m'aider?*
Where is the hospital? *Où est l'hôpital?*
Where is the police station? *Où est le commissariat?*

Shopping

I'd like... *Je voudrais...*
How much is it? *C'est combien?*
Do you take credit cards? *Est-ce que vous acceptez les cartes de crédit?*
size (clothes) *la taille*
size (shoes) *la pointure*
cheap *bon marché*
expensive *cher*
Have you got...? *Avez vous...?*
I'll take it *Je le prends*
Anything else? *Avec ça?*
enough *assez*
too much *trop*
bill *la note*

Shops

bakery *la boulangerie*
bookshop *la librairie*
chemist *la pharmacie*
delicatessen *la charcuterie/le traiteur*
department store *le grand magasin*
fishmonger *la poissonnerie*
grocery *l'alimentation/l'épicerie*
junk shop *la brocante*
library *la bibliothèque*
supermarket *le supermarché*
tobacconist *le tabac*

Sightseeing

visitor information office *l'office de tourisme/le syndicat d'initiative*
open *ouvert*
closed *fermé*
every day *tous les jours*
all year round *toute l'année*
all day long *toute la journée*
free *gratuit/libre*
abbey *l'abbaye* (f)
castle, country house *le château*
church *l'église* (f)
museum *le musée*
staircase *l'escalier* (m)
tower *la tour* (La Tour Eiffel)
tour (walk or drive) *le tour*
town *la ville*
old town *la vieille ville*
Town hall *Hôtel de ville/la mairie*

MENU READER

breakfast *le petit déjeuner*
lunch *le déjeuner*
dinner *le dîner*
I am on a diet *Je suis au régime*
I'd like to order *Je voudrais commander*
Is service included? *Est-ce que le service est compris?*

Le menu

menu à prix fixe meal at set price
à la carte dishes from the menu, charged separately
entrée/hors d'oeuvre first course
le plat principal main course
le plat du jour dish of the day
le dessert dessert
boisson compris drink included
carte des vins wine list
l'addition the bill

Les boissons drinks
café coffee
    au lait ou crème with milk or cream
    deca/decaffeine decaffeinated coffee
    express/noir black espresso
    filtre American filtered coffee
thé tea
tisane infusion of herbs or flowers, e.g., camomile, verveine, limeflower
le lait milk
eau minérale mineral water
    gazeux fizzy
    non-gazeux non-fizzy
limonade ginger ale
citron pressé fresh lemon juice served with sugar
orange pressée fresh squeezed orange juice
frais, fraîche fresh or cold
bière beer
    en bouteille bottled
    à la pression on tap
panaché mixed
le panaché shandy
la carafe/le pichet pitcher of tap water or wine
la demi-carafe half liter
un quart quarter of a liter
vin de maison house wine
vin de pays local wine
digestif after-dinner drink
Santé! Cheers!

Le repas the meal
le pain bread
le poivre pepper

le *potage* soup
le *sel* salt
le *sucre* sugar
Meat dishes
l'*agneau* lamb
l'*andouille* tripe sausage
le *bifteck* steak
  à point just cooked
  bien cuit well done
  bleu very rare
  contre-filet cut of sirloin steak
  entrecôte rib steak
  faux-filet sirloin steak
  grillé grilled
  hachis chopped
  saignant rare
blanquette stew of veal, lamb, or
  chicken with creamy egg
  sauce
boeuf à la mode beef in
  red wine with carrots,
  mushrooms, and onions
bordelaise with red wine and
  shallots
bourguignonne cooked in red
  wine, onions, and mushrooms
le *canard* duck
la *carbonnade* stew of beef in beer
la *cargolade* grill of snails
le *carré d'agneau* rack of lamb
le *cassoulet* stew of beans,
  sausages, pork, and duck
la *choucroute* sauerkraut
le *confit* duck or goose preserved
  in its own fat
le *coq au vin* chicken in red wine
le *côte d'agneau* lamb chop
les *cuisses de grenouille* frog's legs
la *daube* beef stew with red
  wine, tomatoes, and onions
le *dinde* turkey
l'*escargot* snail
le *faisan* pheasant
farci stuffed
le *foie de veau* calf's liver
le *foie gras* liver of force-fed
  duck or goose
le *jambon* ham
le *lapin* rabbit
le *magret de canard* breast of duck
le *médaillon* round piece of meat
l'*oie* goose
la *perdrix* partridge
le *petit-gris* small snail
la *pintade* guinea fowl
le *porc* pork
le *pot-au-feu* casserole of beef
  and vegetables
le *poulet* chicken
le *poussin* young chicken
les *rognons* kidneys

rôti roast
le *sanglier* wild boar
la *saucisse* fresh sausage
le *saucisson* salami
le *veau* veal
Fish dishes
l'*anchois* anchovy
l'*anguille* eel
le *bar (or loup)* similar to sea bass
la *barbue* brill
le *belon* Brittany oyster
le *brochet* pike
le *bigorneau* sea snail
la *bouillabaisse* fish soup
le *cabillaud* cod
le *colin* hake
le *coquillage* shellfish
la *coquille Saint-Jacques* scallop
la *crevette* shrimp
la *daurade* sea bream
l'*encornet* squid
le *flétan* halibut
les *fruits de mer* seafood
l'*homard* lobster
l'*huître* oyster
la *langoustine* large prawn
la *limande* lemon sole
la *lotte* monkfish
la *moule* mussel
moules marinières mussels in
  white wine and onions
la *poulpe* octopus
la *raie* skate
le *saumon* salmon
le *thon* tuna
la *truite* trout
Some sauces
aïoli garlic mayonnaise
américaine sauce of white wine,
  tomatoes, butter, and Cognac
bearnaise egg, butter, wine, and
  herbs
forestière mushrooms and bacon
hollandaise egg, butter, and lemon
meunière butter, lemon, and
  parsley
meurette red wine sauce
Mornay cream, egg, and cheese
paysan rustic style with local
  ingredients
pistou Provençal sauce with
  basil, garlic, and olive oil
Provençal usually tomatoes,
  garlic, and olive oil
Légumes vegetables
l'*ail* garlic
l'*artichaut* artichoke
les *asperges* asparagus
l'*aubergine* eggplant
l'*avocat* avocado
le *cèpe* cep, boletus mushroom

le *champignon* mushroom
les *chips* potato chips
le *chou* cabbage
le *chou-fleur* cauliflower
le *concombre* cucumber
le *cornichon* gherkin
la *courgette* zucchini
cru raw
les *crudités* raw vegetables
les *épinards* spinach
le *haricot* dried bean
les *haricots rouges* kidney beans
les *haricots verts* green beans
les *lentilles* lentils
le *maïs* corn
le *mange-tout* snow pea
le *mesclun* mixed leaf salad
le *navet* turnip
la *noisette* hazelnut
la *noix* nut, walnut
l'*oignon* onion
le *poireau* leek
le *pois* pea
le *poivron* bell pepper
les *pommes de terre* potatoes
les *pommes frites* french fries
le *radis* radish
le *riz* rice
la *roquette (arugula)* rocket
  (arugula)
la *salade verte* green salad
la *truffe* truffle
Fruits
l'*ananas* pineapple
la *cerise* cherry
le *citron* lemon
le *citron vert* lime
la *figue* fig
la *fraise* strawberry
la *framboise* raspberry
la *groseille* redcurrant
la *mangue* mango
la *mirabelle* yellow plum
le *pamplemousse* grapefruit
la *pêche* peach
la *poire* pear
la *pomme* apple
le *raisin* grape
la *prune* plum
le *pruneau* prune
Snacks
le *croque-monsieur* toasted ham
  and cheese sandwich
l'*oeuf à la coque* boiled egg
oeufs au jambon ham and eggs
oeufs brouillés scrambled eggs
oeufs sur le plat fried eggs
le *yaourt* yogurt

INDEX

Bold page numbers
indicate illustrations.

ILLUSTRATIONS CREDITS

Abbreviations for terms appearing below: (t) top; (b) bottom; (l) left; (r) right; (c) center.

Cover: (tl/bl), Tony Stone Images. (tr), Powerstock. (br), Eye Ubiquitous. 1, Spectrum. 2/3, Image Bank. 4, Images. 9, Pix. 10/11, James L. Stanfield. 12/13, James L. Stanfield. 14/15, Pix. 16, AKG. 17, Giraudon. 18, AKG. 19, AKG. 20, Giraudon. 23, Pix. 24, Pix. 26/27, Giraudon. 28, AKG. 29, AKG. 30/31, Pix. 33, James L. Stanfield. 34 (l), AKG. 34 (r), Giraudon. 35, Roger Viollet. 36/37, Giraudon. 38, AKG. 39, Roger-Viollet. 40 (l), Hulton Getty. 40/41, CFCL/Image Select. 42/43, James L. Stanfield. 45, Pix. 47, Pix. 48, Pix. 50(t), Pix. 50(b), Telegraph Colour Library. 50/51, A/W Maltings. 51(t), Pix. 51(b), Pix. 52, CFCL. 53, Pix. 54, Pix. 56/57, James L. Stanfield and Victor R. Boswell, Jr. 58, AA Picture Library K.Paterson. 58/59, National Geographic Society. 60, Pix. 61, AA Picture Library/K. Paterson. 63, Pix. 65(t), AA Picture Library/K.Paterson. 65(b), AA Picture Library/J.Tims. 67, Giraudon. 68, Pix. 69, Pix. 70, Pix. 71, Pix. 73(t), Giraudon. 73(bl), Pix. 73(br), Bavaria. 74, AA Picture Library/ B.Rieger. 75, AA Picture Library/ K.Paterson. 76, Pix. 77, AA Picture Library/K.Paterson. 80, Pix. 81, AA Picture Library. 82, Pix. 83, Pix. 85(tl), AA Picture Library/ A.Souter. 85(tr), J. Allan Cash. 85(b), AA Picture Library/P.Kenwood. 86, Pix. 87, Pix. 88, AA Picture Library/K.Paterson. 89, AA Picture Library/B.Rieger. 90, Pix. 91, AA Picture Library/W.Voysey. 94, AA Picture Library/P.Kenwood. 95, AA Picture :Library/ J.Tims. 97(t), J.Allan Cash. 97(b), AA Picture Library/J.Tims. 98, Giraudon. 99, AA Picture Library/ K.Paterson. 100, AA Picture Library/ K.Paterson. 101, AA Picture Library/ K.Paterson. 102, AA Picture Library/ K.Paterson. 103, Pix. 104, AA Picture Library/ K.Paterson. 106(t), J.Allan Cash. 106(b), AA Picture Library/B.Rieger. 107, Pix. 109 (t), AA Picture Library/ B.Rieger. 109(c), AA Picture Library/ P.Kenwood. 109(b), AA Picture Library/ P.Enticknap. 110, J. Allan Cash. 111, AA Picture Library/A.Souter. 112, Pix. 113, AA Picture Library/ K.Paterson. 115(t), Giraudon. 115(b) Giraudon. 116, AA Photo Library. 118, AA Picture Library/K.Paterson. 119, Pix. 120, AA Picture Library/ K.Paterson. 121, Pix. 124/5, James L. Stanfield. 126(l), Giraudon. 126(r), Giraudon. 126, A/W Maltings. 127, Giraudon. 128, Giraudon.129, Giraudon. 130, Giraudon. 131, Giraudon. 132, Giraudon. 133, Bridgeman Art Library. 134, RMN. 135, RMN. 136, AKG. 137, CFCL/Image Select. 139(t), Giraudon. 139 (bl), AA Picture Library/A.Souter. 139(br), AA Picture Library/T.Souter. 140, Giraudon. 141, Pix. 142, Pix. 143, AA Picture Library/ K.Paterson. 146, AA Picture Library/B.Rieger. 147, Tony Stone. 148, Rex Features. 149(t), Rex. 149(b), AA Picture Library/A.Souter. 150, Pix. 151, AA Picture Library/A.Souter. 152, AA Picture Library. 153, AA Picture Library/B.Rieger. 156, Pix. 157, AA Picture Library/K.Paterson. 158, Pix. 160, Giraudon. 161, Pix. 162, AA Picture Library/ K.Paterson. 163, AA Picture Library/J.Tims. 166(all images), Giraudon. 167, AA Picture Library/T.Souter. 168, Giraudon. 169, Pix. 170, AA Picture Library/B.Rieger. 171, AA Picture Library/ K.Paterson. 172, Giraudon. 173, Pix. 174(l), Roger Viollet. 174/5, Giraudon. 177, Pix. 178, AA Picture Library/ A.Souter. 179, Pix. 182, AA Picture Library/B.Rieger. 183, Giraudon. 184, AA Picture Library/J.Tims. 185, AA Picture Library/T.Souter. 186, AA Picture Library. 188, CFCL/Image Select. 189, J. Allan Cash. 190, Pix. 192, Guardian. 193(t), AA Picture Library/ A.souter. 193(b), Bavaria/ Telegraph Colour Library. 194(t), RMN. 194(b), AA Picture Library/A.Souter. 195, J.Allan Cash. 198, Pix. 199, Pix. 200, AA Picture Library/T.Souter. 201(t), Pix. 201(b), Pix. 202, Pix. 203, AA Picture Library/J.Tims. 204, Pix. 205, Pix. 206, Pix. 207, Pix. 208/9, AA Picture Library/J.Tims. 210, AA Picture Library/B.Rieger. 211, AA Picture Library/D.Noble. 214, Pix. 215, Giraudon. 216, AA Picture Library/D.Noble. 216/7, A/W Maltings. 217(t), J Allan Cash. 217(b), J Allan Cash. 218/9, James L. Stanfield. 219, AA Picture Library/D.Noble. 220, Pix. 221, J Allan Cash. 222, AA Picture Library/B.Rieger. 223, Giraudon. 224, AA Picture Library/D.Noble. 225, Pix. 226, AA Picture Library/D.Noble. 227, AA Picture Library/ T.Souter. 228, Pix. 229, Giraudon. 230, Pix. 231, J Allan Cash. 232, Giraudon.

The world's largest nonprofit scientific and educational organization, the National Geographic Society was founded in 1888 "for the increase and diffusion of geographic knowledge." Since then it has supported scientific exploration and spread information to its more than nine million members worldwide.

The National Geographic Society educates and inspires millions every day through magazines, books, television programs, videos, maps and atlases, research grants, the National Geography Bee, teacher workshops, and innovative classroom materials.

The Society is supported through membership dues, charitable gifts, and income from the sale of its educational products. Members receive NATIONAL GEOGRAPHIC magazine—the Society's official journal—discounts on Society products, and other benefits.

For more information about the National Geographic Society, its educational programs, publications, or how to support its work, call 1-800-NGS-LINE (647-5463), or write to: National Geographic Society, 1145 17th Street, N.W., Washington, D.C. 20036 U.S.A.

Printed in the U.S.A.

Published by the National Geographic Society
John M. Fahey, Jr., *President and Chief Executive Officer*
Gilbert M. Grosvenor, *Chairman of the Board*
Nina D. Hoffman, *Executive Vice President,*
                        President, Books and School Publishing
William R. Gray, *Vice President and Director, Book Division*
David Griffin, *Design Director*
Elizabeth L. Newhouse, *Director of Travel Publishing*
Barbara A. Noe, *Senior Editor*
Caroline Hickey, *Senior Researcher*
Carl Mehler, *Director of Maps*
K. M. Kostyal, *Editorial Consultant*
R. Gary Colbert, *Production Director*
Richard S. Wain, *Production Project Manager*
DeShelle Downey, *Staff Assistant*

Edited and designed by AA Publishing (a trading name of Automobile
Association Developments Limited, whose registered office is Norfolk
House, Priestley Road, Basingstoke, Hampshire, England RG24 9NY.
Registered number: 1878835).
Betty Sheldrick, *Project Manager*
David Austin, *Senior Art Editor*
Allen Stidwill, Karen Kemp, *Editors*
Mike Preedy, Keith Russell, *Designers*
Simon Mumford, *Senior Cartographic Editor*
Nicky Barker-Dix, Helen Beever, *Cartographers*
Richard Firth, *Production Director*
Picture Research by Poppy Owen at I. S. I.
Area maps drawn by Chris Orr Associates, Southampton, England
Cutaway illustrations drawn by Maltings Partnership, Derby, England

Updated 2001.

Library of Congress Cataloging-in-Publication Data
   The National Geographic traveler. Paris.
         p. cm.
     Includes index.
     ISBN 0-7922-7429-6 (alk. paper)
     1. Paris (France)—Guidebooks.
   DC708.N35 1999
   914.4'36—dc21   99-11168
                               CIP

Printed and bound by R.R. Donnelley & Sons, Willard, Ohio. Color separations by
Leo Reprographic Ltd., Hong Kong. Cover separations by L.C. Repro, Aldermaston,
U.K. Cover printed by Miken Inc., Cheektowaga, New York.

Visit the Society's Web site at http://www.nationalgeographic.com

THE NATIONAL
GEOGRAPHIC TRAVELER

A Century of Travel Expertise in Every Guide

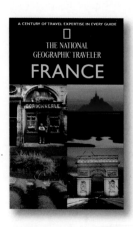
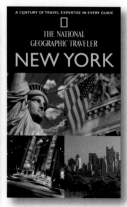